# DAY TRIPS
## FROM CALGARY

# DAY TRIPS
## FROM CALGARY
### REVISED & UPDATED

**Bill Corbett**

whitecap

Copyright © 1995, 2006, 2010 by Bill Corbett

Whitecap Books

First edition published 1995

Second edition 2006

Third edition 2010

Edited by Elaine Jones

Cover design by Mauve Pagé

Interior design by Mauve Pagé

and Warren Clark

Typesetting & "Hot Picks" icon by Janos Sitar

All photographs by Bill Corbett (cover and interior) except pages 239 (Travel Alberta) and 292 (by Susanne Swibold)

Maps by Leslie Bell

Printed in Canada

**Library and Archives Canada Cataloguing in Publication**

Corbett, Bill

    Day trips from Calgary / Bill Corbett.

— Rev. and updated

Includes index.

ISBN 978-1-77050-011-2

    1. Calgary Region (Alta.)—Guidebooks.
I. Title.

FC3697.18.C67 2010    917.123'38044

C2009-906421-9

The publisher acknowledges the financial support of the Government of Canada through the Canada Book Fund (CBF) and the Province of British Columbia through the Book Publishing Tax Credit.

13 14    5 4 3

For Teresa

# CONTENTS

# PREFACE

The advice passed down for generations has been this: go west. Thus armed, countless Calgary residents and visitors have made a beeline for the mecca that is Banff. This mountain resort town is a marvellous destination for Calgarians and first-time visitors to the Rocky Mountains. So, too, is the mountain splendour of nearby Kananaskis Country. But there are other places that beckon, albeit more subtly than the seductive peaks on the skyline.

I wrote this book to entice Calgary residents and visitors to consider all directions of the compass when embarking on a day trip from the city. Those who do will be wonderfully surprised.

Calgarians have at their doorstep some of the most spectacular and varied landscapes in the world. These include the fantastically shaped badlands of Drumheller, the sublime ranchlands of Millarville, the rolling hills of Rumsey, the cottonwood forests of Lethbridge, the prairies and pelicans of Brooks, and the foothills of Pincher Creek, to name a few. Where else can one hop in the car and within an hour travel from prairies to foothills to mountains—or find all three ecosystems merged in one location?

The southern half of Alberta is also rich in human history. It dates from prehistoric hunters of 10,000 years ago and extends through the millennia during which buffalo and Aboriginal people of the plains ruled the landscape. More recently, it covers the eras of white explorers and fur traders, whisky traders and Mounties, ranchers and settlers. These and other stories are well told in many small-town museums and the multi-million-dollar interpretive facilities that attract visitors from around the world.

The premise of this book is simple: what can you see and do within a two-hour drive in any direction from Calgary? Some destinations can be reached in 20 minutes, others in a full two hours or a bit longer.

Trips to many of the farthest destinations have much to offer along the way. In such cases, I've described the journey as much as the destination. If you think Lethbridge or the Crowsnest Pass is too distant for a day trip, consider the tourists willing to make a day's pilgrimage to Lake Louise, which is almost two hours from the city.

This isn't a wilderness guide, though you might well find solitude on many of these trips, especially if you chart your own course on back roads. The prairies have been ploughed, the foothills claimed by ranches and acreages, and the mountains marked by tourist developments. But there are still tracts of native prairie, patches of aspen parkland, and numerous other unspoiled areas protected within parks or natural reserves. Even the altered landscape still possesses the power to inspire with varied topography and distant vistas.

This latest edition of *Day Trips from Calgary* has been extensively revised and includes three additional entries: a superb new $25-million Aboriginal facility—Blackfoot Crossing Historical Park—a new provincial park west of Calgary, and a National Historic Site that commemorates a fascinating Mormon agricultural village.

This edition also has an updated and expanded list of recommended places to get coffee and tea, breakfast, lunch, and snacks for many of the day trips. In recent years, the number of good cafés, restaurants, and diners has grown considerably in the cities, towns, and countryside of central and southern Alberta. They range from some of the best dining spots in Alberta to decent, independently owned alternatives to the highway-side franchises. The list of suggested places is by no means comprehensive, just spots I've enjoyed or had recommended to me.

I've again included, at the back of the book, lists of my favourite things on day trips from Calgary, such as short drives, best small towns, finest museums, and so on. These can be especially useful to those with limited opportunities to tour southern and central Alberta or to those wanting to hit just the highlights. The restaurant list no longer appears in this section, as there are simply too many now to fit on a manageable list.

The trips described in this book can be enjoyed by families, seniors, avid naturalists, and anyone interested in places and people. Many are loop trips or offer alternative return routes to the city. While the automobile is the primary means of touring this country, there are lots of opportunities to stretch your legs. Wherever possible, I've included a short, often interpretive, walk of usually no more than a kilometre or two.

These trips require no expertise and no special equipment other than a tank of gas, a road map, perhaps a picnic lunch, and a plentiful supply of curiosity. Enjoy.

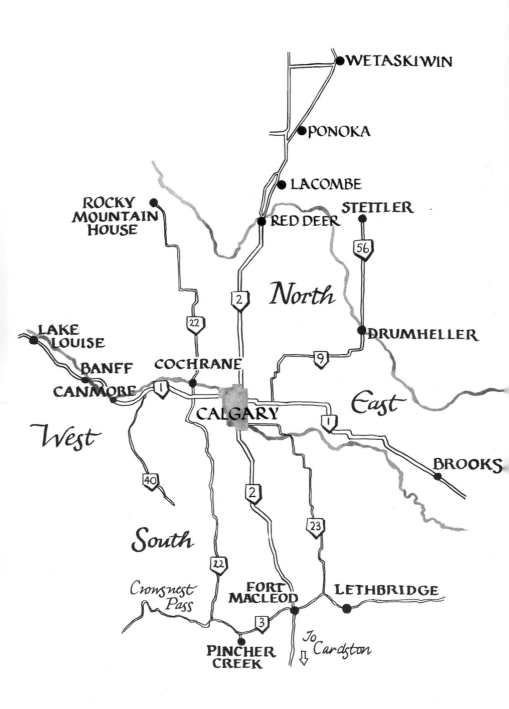

# HOW TO USE THIS GUIDE

The trips in this book are divided into four sections that roughly correspond to the directions of the compass, using Calgary as a centre. Each section begins with a brief overview of the geographical area and what it offers the day tripper. The trips that follow are generally listed in order of their proximity to Calgary. Destinations close to one another are arranged near one another in the book so those who desire longer expeditions can easily combine several trips.

With a few exceptions, all the destinations in this book can be reached within two hours of driving at highway speeds. Anything longer, to my mind, constitutes an overnight trip. Some destinations have sufficient attractions to warrant several day trips or, if you choose, an overnight stay. These include Lethbridge, Brooks, Drumheller, Banff, and Red Deer. In these cases, I usually give a brief introduction to the area, city, or town and then describe several trips, some of which ambitious day trippers or overnight visitors can combine. The major highway approaches to these destinations are also treated as trips.

Each trip report begins with the following information.

**Route:** This describes, often in some detail, the chosen route to a destination or the roads followed on loop trips. Obviously, alternatives are available in many cases, and I encourage people to take detours whenever the urge strikes. Where several trips are grouped in one area, I've tried to provide a different approach or return for each, so as to expose day trippers to as much countryside as possible. All route descriptions begin from that part of Calgary nearest the destination or route.

**Driving Distance:** This is an approximate distance, either one way to a destination or round trip on loop routes. It doesn't include side trips or driving around the destination area. The distance gives day trippers a rough idea of the driving time, a particular concern of parents with young children. In all cases, the distances are measured from the edge of the city, so allow for driving time to and from your point of departure within Calgary.

**Note:** This provides details on the operating hours and seasons of museums, information centres, and other attractions. Remember, this was the information listed at the time of writing. Hours of operation change and attractions that were once free sometimes start charging admission. It's best to phone the listed number in advance or check the website if provided. Hiking distances are also given in this section.

The average family can comfortably manage all the trips. Interpretive walks, on relatively level terrain, are usually no longer than 1.5 kilometres. If a hike is longer and steeper, that is noted.

The trip descriptions are straightforward. The first paragraph or two summarizes what makes the trip worthwhile and lists the highlights. The remainder covers what there is to see and do, not only at the destination but also along the way.

> This icon identifies my favourite places to see and visit. Turn to page 301 for a full listing of my Hot Picks.

# USEFUL INFORMATION

## Phone Numbers and Websites

Travel Alberta
1-800-252-3782   www.travelalberta.com

Kananaskis Country—Canmore head office
403-678-5508

Parks Canada Agency—Calgary regional headquarters
403-292-4401

Banff Information Centre
403-762-1550

Lake Louise Visitor Centre
403-522-3833

Chinook Country Tourist Association—Lethbridge
1-800-661-1222   www.exploresouthwestalberta.ca

Prairies to Peaks Tourism Association—Olds
403-335-7367

Cowboy Trail Tourism Association—High River
1-866-627-3051   www.thecowboytrail.com

Alberta Trail of the Buffalo
1-888-575-0279   www.trailofthebuffalo.com

BoomTown Trail—Camrose
780-672-2710   www.boomtowntrail.com

Travel Drumheller
1-866-823-8100   www.traveldrumheller.com

Tourism Red Deer
403-346-0180   www.tourismreddeer.com

Environment Canada—Calgary-Banff recorded weather
403-299-7878

Alberta Motor Association—24-hour road reports
1-877-262-4997   www.amaroadreports.ca

Government of Alberta toll-free access to provincially run facilities such as the Royal Tyrrell Museum
310-0000 (from anywhere within the province)
*310 (Rogers cellphones)
#310 (Telus and Bell cellphones)

**Note:** Other than toll-free numbers and the Goverment of Alberta numbers listed above, all the phone numbers listed in this book must now be preceded by the 403 area code, whether they are local or long distance calls (the one exception is the Reynolds-Alberta Museum entry, in Wetaskiwin, which has a 780 area code). For those phoning from Calgary, calls to areas in close proximity—such as Airdrie, Okotoks, Cochrane, Strathmore, and Longview—are considered local. Check the start of the residential listings in the Calgary phone directory's white pages for a complete list.

## Trail Reports

For news and updates, check www.billcorbett.ca.

Kananaskis Country Trail Reports
Up-to-date trail conditions and closures:
www.albertaparks.ca/kananaskis-country/advisories-public-safety/
trail-reports.aspx

Banff Trail Reports
www.pc.gc.ca/apps/tcond and click on "Banff National Park"

## Road Maps

While the official Alberta highway map shows all the major and secondary highways mentioned in this book, it's well worth buying *Southern Alberta Range & Township Road Map* (MapArt Publishing). It includes township and range roads and other helpful details, especially for those interested in exploring off the beaten track.

# South

# SOUTH OF CALGARY

For my money, the area stretching south of Calgary has the most diversity to offer the day tripper. Here you can discover prairies, foothills, and the Front Ranges of the Rocky Mountains—sometimes all in one outing. The terrain is undulating and open, providing the sweeping views for which southern Alberta is famous. Southern Alberta is also noted for its chinook winds, which produce dramatic skies and brush the landscape clear of snow much of the winter.

The rolling countryside southwest of Calgary has much to offer those with only a few hours to spare. In less than half a day, you can easily scramble on the Big Rock near Okotoks, tour the aspen parkland of the Cross Conservation Area, visit the historic Turner Valley petroleum fields, marvel at the views from the lofty Leighton Centre, or shop at the Millarville Farmers' Market.

The area west of Highway 2 also contains much of southern Alberta's rich ranching tradition. Most of the early big ranches were located in these rolling plains and foothills, where cattle could graze on lands once roamed by huge herds of buffalo. The big ranches were established in the early 1880s, principally by British or eastern Canadian aristocrats, who could obtain leases of up to 100,000 acres (40,470 hectares) for an annual fee of one cent per acre. While those big spreads were long ago carved up, the ranching heritage is still alive and evident on many of the southwestern trips.

The landscape east of Highway 2 lacks foothills and mountains, but the high plains of the south have much to offer the discerning eye, especially where they're cut by coulees and deep river valleys. This area is also rich in history. The southern plains, once dominated by the Blackfoot Nation, saw the arrival in the late 1860s of the notorious American whisky traders and, soon thereafter, the North West Mounted Police, who cleared the way for settlement. The Lethbridge area was the scene of the first irrigation farming and some of the earliest coal mining in Alberta.

All this history is well told at museums that include the world-class interpretive centre at Head-Smashed-In Buffalo Jump, the Remington Carriage Museum in Cardston, and the Frank Slide Interpretive Centre in the Crowsnest Pass. For those looking for the finest in history and scenery, it would be hard to beat the Crowsnest Pass area.

## ANN AND SANDY CROSS CONSERVATION AREA

**Route:** From its intersection with 37th Street/Secondary 773, drive west on Highway 22X for 6.5 kilometres to 160th Street. A 1.6-kilometre gravel road leads south to a parking area.
**Driving Distance:** 8 kilometres one way.
**Note:** The Cross Conservation Area is open to the public 4 a.m. to 11 p.m., but only by booking online (www.crossconservation.org) at least one day in advance and paying a $2-per-person fee (honour system) when registering at the parking lot kiosk.

Imagine a landscape with substantial tracts of native prairie and dense woodlands populated by elk, deer, and moose. Believe it or not, such a natural preserve exists just five minutes from Calgary's city limits. Better yet, this property with its 20 kilometres of trails and sweeping views is open to the public.

The Ann and Sandy Cross Conservation Area is a 1,943-hectare parcel of rolling foothills parkland southwest of Calgary. In 1987, the Crosses donated the property to the province, adding more land in 1996; it was one of the largest such gifts in Canadian history. The Sandy Cross Conservation Foundation is the property manager,

Taking a walk in the Ann and Sandy Cross Conservation Area.

charged with preserving the area's natural habitats in perpetuity and providing conservation education, primarily to school groups.

The conservation area lies in a transition zone between prairies and foothills. Thus, native grasses and wildflowers on dry, sunny slopes are interspersed with aspen woodlands on shaded aspects. Spruce and willows grow in the moist valley bottoms. This biological diversity provides habitat for a variety of wildlife, including elk, deer, moose, coyote, beaver, the odd bear and cougar, mountain bluebirds, red-tailed hawks, and great horned owls.

Less than 10 percent of Alberta's native fescue grassland is still intact. But the Cross Conservation Area still has slopes of knee-high rough fescue and Parry's oat grass where bison once grazed. Some of these grasslands and most of the native aspen woodlands are still largely intact, thanks to topography and good management.

Once part of the native Stoney territory, the Cross Conservation Area lands were first settled in the 1880s. A succession of farmers ploughed and planted the flat hilltops and wide valley bottoms, where the invasion of non-native brome grasses, used for hay and pasture, is still evident. But the hillsides of this rolling terrain were left largely unploughed.

Sandy Cross bought the property in the 1940s and '50s. As interested in conservation as ranching, he grazed his cattle lightly on the native grasses and delighted in the browsing herds of elk and deer. Sandy, who died in 2003 at the age of 89, came from a well-known Calgary family with extensive ranch holdings south of the city. His father, A. E. Cross, started the A7 Ranch in 1885, later launched the Calgary Brewing and Malting Company, and was one of the four founders of the Calgary Stampede.

The 4.8-kilometre ⚑Fescue Trail is perhaps the most diverse of the several loop walks in the Cross Conservation Area. A rough track, it descends a prairie hillside ablaze in late spring and early summer with such wildflowers as sticky geranium, mouse-eared chickweed, and old man's whiskers. The trail then enters a mature forest of aspen poplar with an understorey of cow parsnip in wet places.

Here, you might encounter a herd of elk, which the Shawnee people called wapitis for their white rumps. Those accustomed to the often-docile beasts along the highway near Banff may be startled by a string of uncivilized cow elk crashing through the trees. In winter, the elk herd can exceed 150 animals. Safe from bow hunters on these protected lands, they can graze on the windswept grasses and retreat to the woods for shelter and to browse on shrubs and the buds (and occasionally the bark) of aspen trees.

The mix of forest and prairie also favours aerial predators such as the red-tailed hawk and great horned owl. Indeed, this area southwest of Calgary is believed to have the highest concentration of red-tailed hawks in North America. These birds usually nest and perch on the edge of woodlands, where they can easily prey on the Richardson's ground squirrels, mice, and voles of the grasslands. The abundance of ground squirrels is obvious to anyone trying to avoid these suicidal animals on country roads in late spring and early summer.

The trail rises out of the forest to a viewpoint overlooking a sprawl of rolling ranchland, the dammed ponds of Pine Creek and, to the west, the Front Ranges of the Rockies. The route then loops back along the crest of the hill past relics of ranching and farming. This is one of the best places in the Calgary area to see mountain bluebirds at close hand. On the return route along a grassy plateau to the parking lot, the view encompasses rural houses to the north, the flattened prairie to the east, and the sprawling suburbs and downtown skyline of Calgary to the northeast.

Other recommended trails are the 3.6-kilometre Aspen loop and a flat gravel trail (1 kilometre, one way) to a mountain view lookout. A more strenuous, 8.7-kilometre loop trail explores Pine Creek and passes an old barn. Remember, these lands have been preserved in a largely natural state by the careful stewardship of previous owners like the Crosses. Treat them with respect by staying on the trails and not picking the wildflowers or native grasses.

# LEIGHTON CENTRE

**Route:** From its intersection with Spruce Meadow Trail (Highway 22X), follow 37th Street/Secondary 773 south. Turn west on 266th Avenue, a winding gravel road that leads to Leighton Centre.
**Driving Distance:** About 22 kilometres one way.
**Note:** Leighton Centre is open to public viewing 10:00 a.m. to 4:00 p.m. Tuesday to Sunday. Admission by donation. Phone 403-931-3633; www.leightoncentre.org.

The stunning view of foothills and mountains from the lawn of Leighton Centre is enough to inspire anyone to reach for a sketchbook and pencil. It's fitting that this centre is dedicated to the fine arts, particularly the depiction of landscape.

This lovely trip just southwest of Calgary requires a few hours at most and will leave you refreshed by its splendour. At Leighton Centre, you can tour the grounds, look in on a children's art class, and view the art collection adorning the rooms of the charming former residence of A.C. and Barbara Leighton. You might even decide to buy a painting by one of the visiting artists.

Leighton Centre is located on 32 hectares of rolling foothills overlooking the Millarville Valley. The view from this lofty perch, at

Canola field en route to the Leighton Centre.

the same elevation as Banff townsite, takes in a panorama of nearly 500 kilometres on a clear day. Because of its height and hills, much of the land was never ploughed and thus retains an impressive cover of native grasses and wildflowers.

Founded by artist Barbara Leighton, the centre is a non-profit organization created in 1974 to celebrate and stimulate landscape art in a natural setting. The centre, run by the Leighton Foundation, offers school and summer camp programs in the restored 1919 Ballyhamage schoolhouse, moved here from a nearby site. Each year, thousands of area children receive instruction in a variety of arts and crafts that usually have a nature theme.

Professionals from around the world attend visiting artist programs, while local amateurs participate in regular art workshops. The Clothesline Art Sale and Festival, in late May, is one of several popular annual sales of work, mostly produced by Alberta artists.

The residence, with its church-like tower, contains an extensive collection of noted artist A.C. Leighton's paintings. Various rooms also showcase the work of other landscape artists, many of them Albertans, and the sale pieces of visiting artists. Barbara Leighton believed people could relate better to paintings displayed in a home rather than in a gallery or museum.

A.C. Leighton was born in England and came to Canada in the 1920s, painting mountain landscapes to promote tourism for the Canadian Pacific Railway. He was later head of the Alberta College of Art in Calgary and was involved in starting the Banff School of Fine Arts. After extensive travelling, A.C. and Barbara returned to live on this land southwest of Calgary until his death in 1965. A reclusive Canadian artist who frequently sketched and painted from his yard, he's best remembered for his mountain watercolours.

Following A.C.'s death, Barbara incorporated his unsold paintings into the Leighton Foundation. She returned to school to earn a diploma in fine arts and later established a school for arts and crafts, a forerunner to today's centre. After her death in 1986, the property, house, and a private art collection were added to the foundation, which is financially assisted by provincial and regional art boards.

## MILLARVILLE LOOP

**Route:** From its intersection with 37th Street/Secondary 773, drive west on Highway 22X for 11.5 kilometres and then south on Highway 22 for 13 kilometres. Secondary 549 east provides access in 2.2 kilometres to the Millarville Race Track and the Farmers' Market. (Map on page 12.)
**Driving Distance:** About 27 kilometres to Millarville and 85 kilometres return.
**Note:** The Millarville Farmers' Market is open Saturdays, 9:00 a.m. to 2:00 p.m, from mid-June to early October. Parking fee. Phone 403-931-2404; www .millarvilleracetrack.com. • The Rothney Astrophysical Observatory is open for visits to its interpretive centre from noon to 4:00 p.m. Monday to Wednesday and for open house programs. Phone 403-931-2366 or 403-220-7977; www.ucalgary.ca/rao.

This is a superb summer outing to the historic ranching community of Millarville. In a short day, you can shop at the famous Millarville

Millarville's Christ Church, with its unusual vertical log construction.

Farmers' Market, visit historic buildings, and walk through the woods of a provincial park. The market is open only on Saturday mornings, and in this early-rising ranching country it's usually crowded by 10:00 a.m.

The Millarville area was first settled by the two Fisher brothers, who lived in a creekside dugout before claiming a homestead in 1884. Despite this primitive beginning, the community that evolved was by no means reminiscent of the Wild West. Many early residents were members of the British upper and middle classes, attracted to the benchlands of Threepoint Creek and the mountain views. These genteel folk loved horses perhaps more than ranching and delighted in the civilized pursuits of polo, horse races, lawn tennis, and dances at Rancher's Hall.

To the south, along the Sheep River, was the Quorn Ranch, established in 1886 by a syndicate of wealthy British sportsmen interested in raising purebred cattle and horses, the latter used for hunting in England. Operated in an extravagant and leisurely manner, the ranch soon failed, and the remainder of its prize stock was sold at a loss to local markets.

While the British gentry have disappeared, their leisure activities have been preserved, including polo at some area ranches. Every year except for two since 1905, the locals have gathered at the Millarville Race Track for the July 1 horse races. The big event is the stock horse challenge, in which area residents race their saddle horses in hopes of winning a silver cup and belt buckle. Much more recent is the Millarville Rodeo, held over three days in late May.

The big attraction, though, is the weekly Millarville Farmers' Market, arguably the most famous in Alberta. This has everything a farmers' market needs: history, diversity, and rural charm. Set among tall poplars on the racetrack grounds, the market offers a wide selection of farm-grown produce and homemade crafts, foods, and other products. At least half the fun is the entertainment. On any given Saturday, there might be wagon rides, llamas on display, a rancher's breakfast, a choir singing on the lawn, or a blacksmith pounding out horseshoes.

About 5 kilometres east of the racetrack on Secondary 549 is Millarville's historic Christ Church, one of the most striking examples of pioneer architecture in Alberta's foothills. Completed in 1896, the church is unique in its use of vertically set spruce logs. Defying the predictions of early skeptics, the church still stands and provides Anglican services every Sunday to congregations of up to a hundred people. Many of the area's early settlers are buried in the adjacent cemetery.

Continue the tour by returning to Highway 22, driving 3.2 kilometres south, and turning west on Secondary 549. This road soon passes Millarville, a growing collection of buildings, and climbs past oil pumpjacks and through more heavily wooded hills of aspen and spruce before descending into rolling ranchland. At an intersection, head north on Secondary 762 for 5.7 kilometres and then turn right on Plummers Road. Continue for 2.9 kilometres to Brown-Lowery Provincial Park, an unexpected refuge of greenery in this ranching country.

The 228-hectare park is a lovely preserve of old-growth spruce and aspen forest with an extensive understorey of wildflowers and other plants. In low-lying areas, marshes fed by tiny streams support wetland vegetation, including cow parsnip. A series of rough trails winds through the property and passes remains of an old cabin and sawmill. The site, donated to the province by Home Oil in 1962, became a provincial park in 1992. Its name honours two pioneers of Alberta's oil industry, Robert Brown Sr. and James Lowery, who took part in the early development of the nearby Turner Valley oil field.

From the park, Plummers Road continues its winding course east. At a junction, turn left to pass through Priddis, located on the banks of Fish Creek. The hamlet, named after settler Charles Priddis, contains a general store, a community hall, and a post office housed in an old schoolhouse. Each July, Priddis hosts a Calgary Stampede breakfast that attracts crowds of some 1,500 people.

The area between Priddis and Bragg Creek, to the west, once contained a glacial lake, formed by melting mountain glaciers ponded in valleys behind the continental ice sheet to the east. Lake deposits from more than 10,000 years ago underlie much of this valley. The rolling hills to the southeast are part of the Priddis Uplands, which emerged from under a cover of ice as the glaciers began to stagnate. The disintegrating ice created the hummocky knob-and-kettle topography one sees today north of Millarville.

Not far from Priddis (on the east side of Highway 22 and a few kilometres south of the Highway 22X junction), the University of

### EATS & DRINKS

Aside from the Saturday fare at the Millarville Farmers' Market, day trippers can stop at the nearby **Corner House Café** (junction of Highway 22 and Secondary 549) for a bison burger or chocolate banana bread pudding. Snacks and groceries are available at the 85-year-old **Millarville General Store** in the hamlet of Millarville. Stop at the nearby **Priddis View & Brew Bistro** for comfort food and desserts or **Priddis Greens Golf & Country Club** for a fine Sunday brunch buffet.

Calgary operates the Rothney Astrophysical Observatory. It boasts a 2,200-square-foot interpretive centre and one of Canada's largest telescopes, ideal for viewing the darkened night sky. Its other telescope is one of a few in the world dedicated to scanning for asteroids that may one day hit the earth.

# OKOTOKS–TURNER VALLEY LOOP

**Route:** From the Highway 22X overpass, drive 12 kilometres south on Highway 2 and then branch off onto Highway 2A for 8 kilometres to Okotoks. Continue south to the end of Southridge Drive and go 7 kilometres west on Highway 7 to the Big Rock. Carry on west through Black Diamond to Turner Valley. Return to Calgary via Highways 22 north and 22X east.
**Driving Distance:** About 90 kilometres return.

This is a wonderful tour of the rolling countryside southwest of Calgary. In a few hours, you can tour the burgeoning town of Okotoks, marvel at an enormous glacial erratic called Big Rock, and glimpse a historic collection of oil industry buildings in Turner Valley.

Situated in the Sheep River Valley, Okotoks is the largest urban centre between Calgary and Lethbridge. As one of Canada's fastest-growing municipalities, its population has more than doubled over the past decade to some 25,000 people, many of them Calgary commuters who enjoy spectacular foothills and mountain scenery a short drive from the big city. Unfortunately, this rapid expansion has cost Okotoks much of its former small-town charm, which has been replaced by the traffic and generic subdivisions and shopping malls typical of much larger places.

Still, Okotoks is a boom town with a difference. It's one of Canada's most environmentally progressive communities—with a population cap of 30,000, a highly energy-efficient sewage treatment plant, a community-wide recycling program, and solar-powered new housing developments and town facilities.

# Okotoks-Millarville

The town's early history is typical for southern Alberta. In the 1880s, Okotoks was an important stopping point on the old Macleod Trail, the horse and wagon route that connected the North West Mounted Police posts of Fort Calgary and Fort Macleod. Here, where wagons crossed the Sheep River, horses were changed and travellers spent the night at a stopping house.

The Macleod Trail, following old Aboriginal routes, fell into disuse in the early 1890s, when the Canadian Pacific Railway built a spur line south from Calgary. The railway brought settlers, businesses, and prosperity to Okotoks. For many years, the main employer in town was the Lineham Lumber Company, which harvested timber from leases on the upper Sheep and Highwood rivers.

Many businesses faltered after the pre–World War I boom, but the railway remained an important link to Calgary, with four passenger trains a day heading for the big city in the 1930s. The passenger service was discontinued in 1971, the victim of a high-speed highway to the east of Okotoks.

While you're in the downtown area, it's worth touring the historic buildings and houses, many built from local sandstone and brick at the turn of the century. Ask for a tour map at the visitor centre, located in the old train station. Perhaps the most interesting building is the former post office, now a French restaurant, its exterior clad with pressed tin.

Many Calgarians make weekend treks to Okotoks to shop and dine. Diners can work off the calories by walking the trails along the floodplain of the Sheep River, long called Sheep Creek by locals. This moist valley bottom supports tall stands of cottonwood trees and an understorey of fragrant wolf willow and saskatoon bushes.

The road southwest of Okotoks passes through magnificent rolling farm- and ranchland sufficiently devoid of trees to offer extensive mountain views. On the right, it's a surprise to suddenly see two huge boulders in the middle of a farmer's field.

This is the famed ⬥Big Rock, the first natural feature in Alberta to be declared a historic site. The other surprise is that the rocks are made of quartzite, which is quite unlike the underlying bedrock of sandstone and shale. The Big Rock is, in fact, an import.

Its story begins some 18,000 years ago, when a landslide near the town of Jasper deposited millions of tons of rocks onto the surface of a glacier advancing east down the Athabasca Valley. Emerging from the mountains, the glacier was deflected southeast along the foothills by the massive Laurentide ice mass, advancing west from the centre of the continent. As the ice melted, tens of thousands of pinkish and purplish quartzite rocks were deposited in a narrow zone from Jasper National Park to south of the U.S. border. Collectively, these rocks are known as the Foothills Erratic Train.

At 16,500 tonnes, the Big Rock is the largest glacial erratic in North America. Aboriginal people, who likely used this landmark as a meeting place, called it *okatoksituktai*, meaning "where the big rock lies." James Hector, the geologist with the Palliser Expedition that explored

Enjoying the view atop the Big Rock near Okotoks.

much of the Canadian west, first noted the erratic in 1863. Today, families, photographers, and even formally attired wedding parties take the short walk from a parking area to admire this fractured, 9-metre-high beauty.

Continuing west, the route crosses the Sheep River again at the western outskirts of Black Diamond, named for its coal-mining past; the excavation scars of an old mine are visible along the banks near the bridge. The mine opened at the turn of the 20th century after a surveyor digging an irrigation ditch discovered a seam of coal, which was primarily used to heat area houses. Today, Black Diamond is a popular destination for city folks out for a drive, a bite to eat, or a visit to Vale's Greenhouse, with its extensive collection of annuals and perennials grown on site.

To the near west is the historic town of Turner Valley, which can also be reached via a 3-kilometre paved walking and cycling trail that parallels the highway and connects the two towns. Seepages of gas found along Sheep Creek prompted the 1914 drilling of a well that produced gas pure enough to fuel cars at the site. The ensuing boom saw the formation of 500 oil companies and wild stock speculation, but it was short-lived. Subsequent discoveries of wet gas in 1924 and oil in 1936 sparked other booms that paved the way for the development of Calgary's oil industry.

On the south side of town, gas seeping around the casing of an early well was lit for safety reasons to produce a constant flame. During earlier boom times, the light from flared and unwanted gas could be seen 50 kilometres away in Calgary. The nearby Turner Valley Gas Plant National Historic Site features tanks, pipelines, domed buildings, and scrubbing chimneys dating back to 1933. While visitors can view this collection of buildings from a nearby road or from an overlook beside the gold course, the site remains closed to the public (for now) because of lingering concerns about contaminants leaking into adjacent water sources.

## EATS & DRINKS

In Okotoks, try **Home Ground Coffee & Roasting House** (22 North Railway Street) for fair trade coffee and baked goods; **Tribal Connection Market** (41 McRae Street) for coffee, tea, and light lunches; and **Bistro Provence** (Tuesday to Saturday for lunch), one of the best French restaurants in Alberta, in an intimate, historical building at 52 N Railway Street. At the nearby **Divine** (42 McRae Street), try the pulled pork sandwich, baked spaghetti, or Asian noodle bowl.

Black Diamond quick stops include **Black Diamond Bakery & Coffee Shop**, a popular local hangout featuring Danish baking, breakfast, and lunch (119 Centre Avenue). Try the big burgers and milkshakes at **Marv's Classic Soda Shop** (121 Centre Avenue).

In Turner Valley, **Coyote Moon Cantina & Espresso Bar** (202 Main Street) offers coffee, all-day breakfasts, and lunches. The nearby **Chuckwagon Café** features elk and buffalo burgers.

# SHEEP RIVER VALLEY

**Route:** From Macleod Trail/Highway 2, at the south end of Calgary, drive 17 kilometres west on Highway 22X and then 27 kilometres south on Highway 22 to Turner Valley. Turn right on Secondary 546 and follow it to its terminus at Junction Creek Campground.
**Driving Distance:** About 85 kilometres one way.
**Note:** Secondary 546 west of the Sandy McNabb Campground is closed December 1 to May 14 to protect the wintering herd of bighorn sheep.

The Sheep River Valley is named for the sizable herds of bighorn sheep that have long frequented its upper slopes. Early Aboriginal people called the area *itou-kai-you*, meaning "sheep at the head of the river." Archaeological evidence indicates these early inhabitants first ventured into the valley more than 7,000 years ago in search of game and shelter.

Today, much of this superb upper valley lies in Kananaskis Country within an hour's drive of Calgary. Summer visitors come here to picnic and fish along the river, watch for grazing sheep, take a short interpretive hike, ramble on high grassy ridges or simply marvel at the area's rugged beauty.

The road west from Turner Valley climbs through rolling foothills dotted with ranches and stands of aspen and spruce forest. Seventy years ago, large sections of these foothills were scarcely treed because of uncontrolled forest fires. These devastating fires nonetheless improved ungulate habitat by removing mature trees and stimulating new growth.

Cattle now graze the rolling grasslands, while beavers maintain dams on creeks, creating low wetlands. The dominant feature throughout is the Sheep River, which carves a deep channel through bedrock as it tumbles out of the low mountains and across the foothills.

A short distance past the Kananaskis Country boundary and visitor centre is the Sandy McNabb Campground. The 1.7-kilometre Sandy McNabb Interpretive Trail loops from a campground parking lot through open forest and willowy bogs to a viewpoint overlooking the

Sheep River Valley. This terrace, carved by glacial meltwaters, stands about 100 metres above the Sheep River.

From its source on Mount Rae, the river descends 1,000 metres to its junction with the Highwood River. This steady descent has resulted in a series of small rapids that downstream are a whitewater kayaker's delight. Farther upstream, the river drops over a succession of sandstone ledges into exquisitely foaming pools.

Just beyond the campground is the eastern boundary of Sheep River Provincial Park, which includes a sanctuary for wintering bighorn sheep that have grazed here for more than 1,000 years. A short trail from the nearby Bighorn day-use area leads to a viewpoint overlooking an expanse of meadows and slopes frequented by sheep.

Swept clear much of the winter by chinook winds, these grasslands provide critical habitat for a herd of bighorn sheep. But some sheep now stay in the sanctuary throughout the year rather than migrate up the valley to much larger summer ranges. This has resulted in overgrazing and crowding. Consequently more parasitic lungworm infections have reduced the herd from 150 to some 60 animals over the past two decades. To help preserve wildlife habitat and to connect migration routes, two additional parks have been created: Bluerock Wildland Provincial Park and Elbow-Sheep Wildland Park.

Within the Sheep River Valley's three parks, more than 30 Aboriginal archaeological sites have been uncovered, including one that indicates 10,000 years of human occupation in the area. The majority of these are prehistoric campsites, typically containing remnants of flaked stone tools, hearths, and bones.

Farther west along the road is Sheep River Falls, a good stopping place though crowded with picnickers on hot summer weekends. A short walk downstream leads to the falls, an impressive plunge over a sandstone ledge into a deep pool. Viewers should take care to not venture too close to the rocky overlook.

Near the road's end is Bluerock Campground. A 2-kilometre interpretive loop climbs steadily from the campground along Bluerock Creek to the site of an old sawmill. The grassy, flower-covered

Overlooking Sheep River Falls.

hillside on the right contrasts sharply with the mossy forest on the steep opposite bank. The latter is sheltered from sun and wind and thus retains its moisture.

A sawmill operated briefly here in the 1940s under the stewardship of Napp Lefavre. Many such logging camps suffered from poor markets and difficulties in hauling timber out of the valley on steep, narrow roads. Rusty bolts, bits of boards, and an old bridge in the grassy clearing below are all that remain of Lefavre's abandoned sawmill.

Across the valley in Junction Creek, John Lineman established one of several logging camps at the turn of the century. The logs were floated down the river to his mill in Okotoks, an often-treacherous operation that claimed several lives. Forest fires, not poor markets, halted his activities here in 1910.

While the Sheep Valley's resources of timber, coal, and oil were keenly sought, the rugged terrain, along with market vagaries, outlasted all entrepreneurs. For example, Pat Burns, a wealthy Calgarian, opened a coal mine in 1913, but the expected Calgary and Southern Railway was never built into this valley. Instead, the coal was hauled out by wagon until the mine closed in 1923. Today, the only human activity in these upper reaches is the pilgrimage of nature-loving visitors.

# HIGHWOOD PASS LOOP

**Route:** From Macleod Trail/Highway 2, near the south end of Calgary, take Highway 22X west for 17 kilometres. Drive south on Highway 22 for 49 kilometres to Longview and then west on Highway 541 for 44 kilometres to Highwood Junction. Turn north on Highway 40, then follow it over Highwood Pass for 105 kilometres to the Trans-Canada Highway. Head east for 60 kilometres to reach the western outskirts of Calgary.
**Driving Distance:** About 275 kilometres return.
**Note:** Highway 40 from Highwood Junction to the Kananaskis Trail junction is closed from December 1 to June 15 to protect wintering herds of bighorn sheep.

This is one of the finest and most diversified driving tours in Canada. It journeys through the heart of southern Alberta's ranching country and then climbs past forested foothills and folded mountains to cross the highest driveable pass in Canada. From this lofty spot, you can take a superb alpine hike or a shorter interpretive walk.

The trip begins by passing through the rolling landscape southwest of Calgary. This is ranching country, ranging from the splendid stables and show jumping grounds of Spruce Meadows to foothill spreads that have been producing some of Canada's finest beef for over a century. This is also prime real estate, commanding high prices for suburban acreages that offer short commutes and spectacular scenery. For the motorist, the foothill and mountain vistas seem to improve over every rise on the way to Longview.

The route heads west at the outskirts of Longview, a village of 300 people that serves the ranching and petroleum industries. Area oil discoveries in 1936 sparked a boom, prompting the sudden emergence of Little New York and Little Chicago, each with an instant population of more than 1,500. The discovery of oil at Leduc in

1947 signalled the end of Little Chicago, but Little New York, earlier renamed Longview, still survives on a much smaller scale.

In these foothills, cattle grazing extends up the Highwood Valley well into Kananaskis Country, as is evident from the cows, and their deposits, on the road. Since the late 1800s, ranchers have been moving their herds in spring along the flat river terraces to the high country, where the cattle graze on grassy slopes until fall. The cattle drives follow the same trails up the Highwood Valley as those used by the Stoney First Nation, explorers, and, later, coal prospectors and loggers.

The Highwood Valley also provides a migration corridor and critical habitat for wildlife. In winter, warm chinook winds sweep the snow off open slopes, allowing elk, bighorn sheep, and deer to feed on exposed grasses. While much elk habitat has elsewhere been destroyed, undisturbed grassy slopes in the Highwood Valley help sustain a group of some 600 animals, the largest herd in Kananaskis Country. The valley's upper reaches also support small populations of such threatened predators as cougars, wolverines, wolves, and grizzly bears.

North of Highwood Junction, Highway 40 begins a steady climb between the Elk Range on the left and the Misty Range on the right. George Dawson named the latter for the inclement weather shrouding the peaks during his geological explorations of the mid-1880s.

Notice the exaggerated folding on the faces of some of these mountains. This wavy appearance was caused during mountain building between 80 million and 40 million years ago, when land forces from the west caused horizontal layers here to fold and fracture.

The climb levels off at the summit of ▲Highwood Pass, which at 2,206 metres is the highest paved road in Canada. The pass was used for thousands of years by Aboriginal peoples and, later, by fur traders and explorers, as a means of moving between the Highwood and Kananaskis valleys.

Here, you can step from the car to be immediately surrounded by wildflowers in a subalpine meadow near the treeline. This is a fascinating and harsh landscape, where the growing season is compressed into less than three months and trees take hundreds of years

Looking down on Highwood Pass from Pocaterra Ridge.

to reach a modest height, despite an annual precipitation of some 200 centimetres.

The lofty elevation here, near the Continental Divide, has also been a biological blessing. The sudden change in the slope angle along the Elk Range to the northeast marks the high point reached by scouring ice during glaciation. In the higher, ice-free areas, called nunataks, unique alpine grasses and rock crawlers, ancient ancestors of today's grasshopper, survived the ice age. The diversity of vegetation here is also enhanced by the absence in the underlying bedrock of calcium-rich limestone, which limits the growth of many subalpine plants.

To learn more about this landscape, take the Highwood Meadows Interpretive Trail, a 500-metre walk from the Highwood Pass parking lot. The trail is on a boardwalk built to protect the fragile soils and plants from the damaging impact of foot traffic. Despite their diminutive stature, some of the larch and fir trees along the trail are more than 350 years old.

Across the highway is the ⚑ Ptarmigan Cirque Trail, one of the finer short hikes in the Rockies and a quick approach to alpine terrain. The

2.5-kilometre trail initially climbs steeply as it passes through mature stands of alpine fir, Engelmann spruce, and subalpine larch. But after a kilometre, it quickly levels out into a sublime alpine meadow, which in summer is covered in wildflowers and ground-hugging plants that make the most of the short growing season.

At this elevation, it might seem strange to see fossilized marine life, such as horned corals, in the rocks. The corals, once growing in an inland sea, were preserved in sedimentary rocks thrust to these heights during the process of mountain building. Those tremendous forces are clearly visible in the folded rocks and vertical bedding planes of nearby Mount Arethusa.

Ptarmigan Cirque is named for the hardy white-tailed ptarmigan that live here year-round. Their speckled coats, which blend into the rocky landscape, turn white in the fall to match the winter snow cover. The bowl shape of the cirque was carved by mountain glaciers. Along the interpretive trail, a well-beaten path leads through scree to the rubbly top of a moraine left by the retreating glacier. From here, you can gaze up at the barren bowl protected by Mount Rae, the highest peak in the area.

Back in the car, the descent is swift and steady from Highwood Pass into the Kananaskis Valley. Just beyond the pass is another short interpretive walk, the Rock Glacier, so called because the jumbled rocks move in a similar manner to an advancing ice glacier. More impressive rock is found farther along on the right, where the limestone faces of Mount Elpoca and Mount Wintour have been severely weathered into a jagged appearance.

A few kilometres beyond Highwood Pass is a 1-kilometre trail that leads to Elbow Lake, a pleasant destination for a short hike and picnic. Above the lake, the small glacier on the north face of Mount Rae is the principal source of the Elbow River, which provides Calgary with nearly half its drinking water.

The road levels out as it proceeds north up the Kananaskis Valley. The relative quiet of Highwood Pass, protected within Peter Lougheed Provincial Park, is replaced in this busy valley by such recreational facilities as stocked trout ponds, a recreational vehicle park, numerous campgrounds, an alpine village, two golf courses, and a ski resort. For more information, see the Kananaskis Valley trip description on pages 236–41.

> ### EATS & DRINKS
>
> In Longview, pick up coffee at folk-musician-turned-rancher Ian Tyson's **Navajo Mug** or enjoy some sublime beef in the heart of cattle country at **Longview Steakhouse**. They're both located along a short stretch of Highway 22.

# BAR U RANCH NATIONAL HISTORIC SITE

**Route:** From Macleod Trail/Highway 2 near the south end of Calgary, take Highway 22X west for 17 kilometres. Drive about 60 kilometres south on Highway 22 past Longview to the signed Bar U Ranch turnoff to the west.
**Driving Distance:** About 80 kilometres one way.
**Note:** The historic site is open daily 9:00 a.m. to 5:00 p.m. from late May to late September. Admission charged. Phone 1-888-773-8888 or 403-395-2331.

The golden era of the 100,000-acre (40,470-hectare) ranches in Alberta's foothills is long gone. But this century-old story lives on at the Bar U Ranch National Historic Site, where remnants of one of the earliest and most enduring of these massive spreads have been preserved. There, interpreters dressed in jeans and cowboy hats walk visitors through restored and restocked historic ranch buildings.

The Bar U was one of the four big southern Alberta ranches that emerged from the Dominion Lands Act of 1872, which allowed wealthy eastern investors to lease up to 100,000 acres of rangeland for one cent per acre. These business people included the Allan family of Montreal, which teamed up with Quebec stockman Fred Stimson to form the North West Cattle Company, better known for its Bar U brand.

Riding in grass up to his horse's belly, Stimson arrived in 1881 at the site of the Bar U Ranch, along the banks of Pekisko Creek. A year later, the federal lease was granted and 3,000 head of Durham Shorthorn cattle were trailed up from Idaho. By the end of the decade, the Bar U had grown to nearly 158,000 acres (63,940 hectares), with more than 10,000 cattle, 800 horses, and enough people to make it the largest settlement between Calgary and Fort Macleod. (In 1891, the ranch population included a horse breaker named Harry Longabaugh, better known as the Sundance Kid.) Cattle were sold for domestic consumption and to markets as far afield as England.

Besides vast expanses of cheap land, the early foothills cattlemen were blessed by sufficient rainfall and, in winter, sheltering coulees and warming chinook winds that exposed the rough fescue grasses. Called the queen of grasses, in part because the base of its barbed blades is a royal purple, rough fescue provided bountiful winter protein if not overgrazed.

But winter wasn't always benign. Foothill ranchers suffered terrible losses in 1886–87 and in 1906–07 (16,000 imported Mexican cattle perished on the Bar U in the latter winter), forcing those who survived to invest in fencing and haying. By then, railway lines, irrigation ditches, and the growing pressure of farming were already carving up the open range. The North West Cattle Company had taken advantage of an 1892 provision allowing ranchers to buy up to 10 percent of their leased lands for $1.25 an acre. It thus owned 15,000 acres (6,070 hectares) in addition to leased lands.

In 1902, the Bar U was sold for $220,000 to a group that included its one-time foreman, George Lane. He soon began importing French purebred Percherons, which were bred for sale to area settlers as draft horses and won numerous international awards. During Lane's reign, the Prince of Wales came for a visit and later bought the EP Ranch, which still operates under local ownership just west of the Bar U. Following Lane's death in 1925, the Bar U was sold to cattle and meat-packing baron Pat Burns, who was then said to be able to ride from Calgary to the U.S. border without once leaving his property.

Restored buildings at Bar U Ranch National Historic Site.

Under the Burns family stewardship, the ranch introduced modern technology, increased its grain acreage, and replaced the Shorthorn cattle with more durable Herefords.

In 1950, the Bar U's original holdings were split up and sold to area ranchers, ending a storied era. Four decades later, part of the ranch returned to its original grantor when Parks Canada acquired 148 hectares of the original headquarters and some surrounding rangeland to create a National Historic Site commemorating the evolution of Canada's ranching industry.

At the site's orientation centre, visitors can tour exhibits, watch a video, and browse through a general store. Outside, it's easy to spend a couple of hours touring the 35 historic structures that include an 1882 saddle horse barn, a cookhouse, blacksmith and harness repair shops, and a Percheron barn. Many of these buildings have been restored and furnished with period artifacts. From spring to fall, there are special events such as roping and branding demonstrations, polo games, old-time rodeos, and competitions for blacksmiths and ranch horses. Parks Canada also offers a volunteer program, allowing participants to help handle horses and dig for artifacts.

## HIGH RIVER AND FRANK LAKE

**Route:** From the Highway 22X overpass, drive 41 kilometres south on Highway 2 and then a couple of kilometres west on Highway 23 to reach High River. From the same Highway 2 exit, drive about 6 kilometres east on Highway 23 to reach Frank Lake, with the final access to the parking lot and viewing area on a marked gravel road to the right. When the gate to the viewing area is closed, add another kilometre or so on foot to the access.
**Driving Distance:** About 50 kilometres one way.
**Note:** The Museum of the Highwood (4th Avenue and 1st Street West) is open 9:00 a.m. to 4:30 p.m. Monday to Saturday and noon to 4:00 p.m. Sunday year round. Donations welcome. Phone 403-652-7156; www.highriver.ca.

Almost unnoticed, High River has grown to a population of 13,000, thanks in part to its commuting proximity to Calgary. Yet it's still sufficiently far from the big city to retain a small-town atmosphere. It makes a nice half-day's destination, especially when combined with a visit to nearby Frank Lake, arguably the best birdwatching spot in southern Alberta.

There's no urban sprawl creeping out from High River. Instead, it suddenly pops into view, surrounded by golden crops in midsummer. This is clearly farming and ranching country, a fact accentuated by the looming presence of the $50-million Cargill meat-processing plant just north of town.

But High River, the birthplace of former prime minister Joe Clark, is scarcely bald prairie and hardly a utilitarian farm centre. Indeed, the tall, shady trees, stately old homes and buildings, and abundance of parks and pathways are evidence that this quietly dignified community has been around a long time.

The Blackfoot called the Highwood River, which flows through town, *ispitsi*, for the tall cottonwood trees that grow along its banks. The most sacred of these was the Medicine Tree, a sacred double cottonwood, where they would leave offerings of food, tobacco, and arrowheads. The Medicine Tree is long gone, but a remnant of its trunk is attached to an archway at George Lane Memorial Park in the centre of town.

In 1800, explorer David Thompson camped near here along the river. Seventy years later, Americans Dave Akers and "Liver Eating" Johnston built the nearby Spitzee Post to trade whisky to native people in exchange for buffalo hides and furs. This and two subsequent posts were short-lived. By the mid-1870s, the North West Mounted Police had shut down the illegal whisky trade in present-day southern Alberta.

With the signing of the Aboriginal treaties in 1877, the land around High River became available for ranching. One of southern Alberta's four big early ranches, the North West Cattle Company was formed west along the Highwood River in 1882. Better known by its brand, Bar U, the ranch prospered under the management of Fred Stimson and later George Lane, one of the founders of the Calgary Stampede. See pages 23–26 for details on the Bar U.

High River celebrates this Western heritage with two annual rodeos. In mid-June, Guy Weadick Days—commemorating another Calgary Stampede founder—features professional chuckwagon racing, while the Little Britches Rodeo and Parade (late May) focuses on cowhands aged 2 to 16.

High River began life in the 1880s as a stopping place on the trail between Fort Macleod and Calgary. It was first known as The Crossing, the spot where wagon trains crossed the Highwood River. A

One of 16 murals in downtown High River.

subsequent village was incorporated as a town in 1906. Some of the area's oldest buildings are housed at Sheppard Family Park, a former farmstead on the south edge of town that contains a restored and furnished 1882 log cabin, an 1899 house, and a century-old barn.

Visitors to High River can learn more about the town's history by visiting the Museum of the Highwood, housed in the town's original train station built from sandstone blocks recycled from an earlier Calgary train station. A walking tour through downtown also reveals the area's history through 16 murals painted on building walls. En route, look for the old Wales Theatre, built in 1927, which has a free-standing balcony and still screens films daily.

Another downtown walking tour showcases the work of local artists, displayed at businesses throughout the summer. Those seeking further exercise can stretch their legs on a 17-kilometre network of trails that follow the shaded Highwood River and connect several town parks. Paths also lead through the Highwood Wildlife Sanctuary, in northeast High River, which attracts pheasants, Hungarian partridge, ducks, geese, and deer.

The real prize for birdwatchers is ◈Frank Lake, just east of High River. Considered the most important wetland for waterfowl in southwest Alberta, the lake and its surrounding marshes attract scores of nesting and migrating birds. During one visit, a sharp-eyed birder reported 78 species, including various ducks, geese, grebes, ibis, owls, wrens, and harriers. Early morning and evening are the best viewing times, particularly during the spring and fall migrations, when the sky can be black with noisy waterfowl. A bird blind provides up-close viewing.

Frank Lake has dried up a couple of times in the past century. A Ducks Unlimited project in 1989 created a larger wetland that now includes three basins. The key to ensuring sustainable water levels was piping in treated waste water from High River and the Cargill plant; the wetland further purifies the water.

If time permits, a drive 10 kilometres to the east on Highway 23 and then 5 kilometres south leads to the Frankburg Mormon Pioneer Cemetery. It's all that remains of a Mormon community established in 1902, when Christopher Frank led a group of settlers here from Utah. Frankburg was abandoned in the mid-1930s, a victim of the Great Depression.

---

### EATS & DRINKS

◈ High River's cuisine has improved considerably in recent years. **Colossi's Coffee House** (114–4th Avenue SW) offers fresh-roasted coffee, premium loose teas, and bagels. Enjoy a unique breakfast or lunch experience in the **Whistle Stop Café** (4th Avenue and 1st Street), a refurbished 1960s rail dining car. **Evelyn's Memory Lane Café** (118–4th Avenue SW), a 1950s-style diner complete with swivelling stools features homemade ice cream, roast chicken sandwiches, and deep-dish pies. Try the omelettes, hamburger soup, and homemade biscuits at the **South Fork** restaurant (110–1st Street W) and the sirloin burgers or steak sandwiches at **Cast Iron Grill** (240 Macleod Trail SW).

# NANTON AND CHAIN LAKES
# PROVINCIAL PARK

**Route:** From the Highway 22X overpass, drive 68 kilometres south on Highway 2 to Nanton. To reach Chain Lakes Provincial Park, take Secondary 533, from the southern outskirts of Nanton, for 38 kilometres west to its intersection with Highway 22 and the park entrance. Return to Calgary by driving 25 kilometres north on Highway 22, 31 kilometres east on Secondary 540, and north on Highway 2A to regain Highway 2 near High River.

**Driving Distance:** About 220 kilometres return.

**Note:** Visit the town's website at www.town.nanton.ab.ca.

This lovely tour rises from the prairie flats through exquisitely rolling hills to Chain Lakes Provincial Park, a popular destination for fishing and picnicking. Along the way, you can test Alberta's version of a magnetic hill.

Little of the countryside along this trip is still natural. The prairies en route to Nanton are ploughed and often irrigated, the hills dotted with grazing cattle, and the Chain Lakes are dammed and stocked with trout. Yet the landscape, with its undulating topography and mountain views, retains a bucolic charm largely undiminished by human activities.

Contrary to first impressions, there's more to Nanton than twin strips of highway flanked by businesses catering to the motorist. Away from the double-lane asphalt, this is one of the more pleasant small communities south of Calgary. Nanton was long known for its pure spring water, which bubbled up in foothills to the west and was piped to a tap along Highway 2, where visitors could sample it. Nanton spring water is still bottled by a local company and sold to distant markets.

The area's first farmers settled in the late 1800s along Mosquito Creek, near a crossing of the wagon trail between Fort Macleod and Calgary. A village was formed in 1903 and named for Sir Augustus Nanton, an Ontario businessman who helped arrange financing for the Calgary and Edmonton Railway.

In town, it's well worth visiting the Bomber Command Museum of Canada (see pages 33–35) and strolling along the downtown Antique and Art Walk, which features shops housed in restored heritage buildings. Historic buildings include a 1902 hotel and a restored 1906 yellow school building that now serves as the town's visitor centre.

The route west from Nanton is one of the finest short drives in southern Alberta. It passes over the northern section of the Porcupine Hills, which separates the parallel valleys that contain Highways 2 and 22.

Just west of Nanton, the road crosses the old Macleod Trail, a north-south route that once extended from Fort Edmonton to Fort Benton in Montana. The route was used for centuries by Aboriginal peoples, early white traders, 19th-century cattle drivers, and North West Mounted Police patrols. Though the fences of homesteaders cut the route off after 1900, vestiges of the deep wagon ruts can still be seen in farmers' fields.

Where the road bends south just before an abrupt rise of hills, it's worth taking a short detour by continuing west for a couple of kilometres. Along the north side of a narrow valley are some fine examples of sandstone outcrops. Back on Secondary 533, the road passes through an impressive line of hills cut by a network of ravines or coulees.

At 24 kilometres from Highway 2, a short road leads to an advertised "magnetic hill," where a car in neutral will provide a mild sensation of coasting uphill. The real highlight is at the end of this road, where a lookout affords a magnificent view across the creased hills to the prairie expanse. A plaque here commemorates ranching pioneer and Calgary entrepreneur A. E. Cross, whose descendants still own considerable ranchlands in the area.

The same success wasn't enjoyed by the Oxley Ranch, which held extensive lands along nearby Willow Creek. Formed in 1882 as one of the four big ranches in southern Alberta, the Oxley suffered from internal squabbling between its manager and aristocratic shareholders in Britain. Reorganized once, it was sold in 1903.

The final stretch of highway, on a good gravel surface, follows Willow Creek, which meanders, appropriately enough, through thickets of willows. Despite its diminutive size, the creek is a major water source, meeting the irrigation needs of farmers and the towns of Claresholm and Granum to the southeast. Its small but steady flow is assured by a nearby dam that backs the creek's flow into Chain Lakes Reservoir, formerly a series of shallow, spring-fed lakes from which the name derives.

Completed in the mid-1960s, the long, narrow reservoir initiated the creation several years later of Chain Lakes Provincial Park. The park is an interesting blend of ecosystems, where fescue grasses and prairie crocuses can be found alongside higher-elevation species like western wood lily and mountain fleabane. A marsh below the dam is home to a diversity of wetland plants as well as great blue herons, common loons, warblers, and shorebirds.

Historically, the valley bottom here was used for grazing cattle and growing substantial hay crops. Visitors today can see an interesting collection of munching horses, cows, and sheep, used as a management tool to reduce an escalating fire hazard. Controlled burns are also being used to remove old grasses and willows and allow new growth that will feed the area's moose and elk.

The park is a pleasant place to have a lakeside picnic, take a short stroll, or simply admire the views of the nearby Livingstone Range. But it's most popular as a place to fish for stocked rainbow trout, which can reach weights of more than three kilograms. It's not unusual to see many anglers casting into the murky waters from shore or boats or, in winter, dangling a baited hook through a hole in the ice.

Return to Calgary by heading north and then taking Secondary 540 east toward Highway 2A. This quiet and highly scenic route offers superb views of the mountains and the amazingly deep valley of Pekisko Creek as it angles northeast to join the Highwood River.

# AEROSPACE TOUR

**Route:** From the Highway 22X overpass, drive 68 kilometres south on Highway 2 to Nanton. From Nanton, go 29 kilometres east on Secondary 533 and then 2.5 kilometres south and east to the RCAF Vulcan Aerodrome. It's another 13 kilometres east and north on mostly gravel roads to reach Vulcan. The return to Calgary, via your choice of primary and secondary highways, is about 100 kilometres.

**Driving Distance:** About 215 kilometres return.

**Note:** The Bomber Command Museum of Canada is open 9:00 a.m. to 5:00 p.m. daily from mid-April to mid-October and 10:00 a.m. to 4:00 p.m. on weekends the rest of the year. Phone 403-646-2270; www.bombercommandmuseum.ca. • The Vulcan Tourism and Trek Station is open 9:00 a.m. to 6:00 p.m. Monday to Friday and 10:00 p.m. to 6:00 p.m. weekends from May to early September, with reduced hours the rest of the year. Phone 403-485-2994; www.vulcantourism.com.

What do World War II bombers and science fiction spaceships have in common with small-town southern Alberta? More than you might think. In this back-to-the-future aerospace tour, you can crawl through the fuselage of a hulking Lancaster bomber, stare at the prairie ruins of a World War II air training school, and visit a town dedicated to the space-age trappings of the television show *Star Trek*.

The tour begins with a drive south to Nanton, a charming prairie town and home of the ◖Bomber Command Museum of Canada. The museum opened in 1992 to honour the Canadian and British flyers who served in the dangerous Bomber Command during World War II; more than 10,000 Canadians died in the aerial battle over Europe. It also pays tribute to the southern Alberta communities that provided bases for training Commonwealth pilots during the war.

The museum's recently expanded display space houses an impressive collection of period airplanes, including a Blenheim bomber, a Fleet Fawn, and a Tiger Moth. The showpiece is a restored Lancaster bomber, the Canadian-made workhorse of Bomber Command. Visitors can squeeze through the sparse and narrow fuselage and imagine flying this defenceless black monster on bombing missions into enemy territory, protected only by speed and darkness.

More than 7,000 Lancasters were built during World War II. Fewer than 20 remain intact worldwide. The bomber on display in Nanton nearly shared the same fate, vandalized and rusting away in a farmer's field near Vulcan after being retired from active duty in 1959. Several enterprising locals rescued the Lancaster and hauled it across fields to Nanton, where it continued to deteriorate for 25 years until a restoration and museum plan was finally hatched.

From Nanton, the aerospace tour heads east on Secondary 533 through level farmland. Just after crossing the Little Bow River, the main road bends north to become Secondary 804. Instead, continue east on slightly rougher pavement and then follow the signs south and east to reach the strange sight of half a dozen large, dilapidated buildings on the bald prairie, overlooking the Little Bow Valley.

The skeletons of these hangars and grass-infested runways are all that remain of the RCAF Vulcan Aerodrome, where, during World War II, more than 1,000 Allied students received flight training at one of many Canadian schools under the British Commonwealth Air Training Plan. Tutored to fly the twin-engine Anson II aircraft, graduates from the Vulcan school were destined for Bomber Command in England. While relations with area farmers were generally good, one aerodrome report talks of an airplane becoming entangled in a nearby barbwire fence and an "aged lady" forcing repairs to be made, "using a shotgun for emphasis."

From the aerodrome, head northeast on good gravel roads to Vulcan, which housed most of these wartime pilot trainees. Today,

Lancaster bomber at the Bomber Command Museum of Canada.

Vulcan's aerial interests are focused on the fictitious future. Although named for the Roman god of fire, the town in the early 1990s cleverly tied its tourism fortunes to the fictitious planet of Vulcan, the home of Mr. Spock in the long-running TV show *Star Trek*. Soon thereafter, businesses on Vulcan's main street began sporting window paintings of the sharp-eared Spock and other crew members.

Things really got serious in the late 1990s with the construction of a 9.5-metre-long replica starship, loosely based on the USS *Enterprise*, and a space station that now houses the town's tourism office and sells Star Trek memorabilia, including clothing. A costumed captain and crew members greet visitors and answer questions about the station and the town.

Not all of Vulcan's passion for outer space is based on fantasy. In 1962, a 20-kilogram meteorite believed to be from the Mars-Jupiter asteroid belt was found in a field near Vulcan. Now, the local Big Sky Astronomical Society (www.bigsky.ab.ca) has opened an observatory, which is adjacent to Twin Valley Dam, off Secondary 529, southwest of Vulcan. Its telescope offers views of more than 1,000 stars on clear nights and perhaps one day may spot a passing spaceship.

# WILLOW CREEK MUNICIPAL PARK

**Route:** From the Highway 22X overpass, drive 92 kilometres south on Highway 2. Turn right on Secondary 527 west, then follow it for 15.5 kilometres to Willow Creek Municipal Park.
**Driving Distance:** About 110 kilometres one way.

Willow Creek Municipal Park is a small prairie jewel tucked away in a sheltered valley beneath the Porcupine Hills. The lovely drive and shaded creek make this an excellent destination for an afternoon picnic and a short grasslands stroll.

The approach from Calgary provides no clue to what lies ahead. The prairie terrain is mainly level, relieved only by the distant rise of western foothills and mountains. Secondary 527 angles southwest towards these hills and away from busy Highway 2.

At 5 kilometres along 527, the road crosses the old Macleod Trail, the north-south route used by travellers for centuries before the arrival of the railway. In some places, traces of wagon ruts can still be seen among the prairie grasses and farmlands.

The road soon crosses Pine Coulee Reservoir, a 13-kilometre-long body of water that attracts plenty of boaters fishing for stocked walleye and burbot. The reservoir was created in the late 1990s to help secure drinking and irrigation water supplies in the Willow Creek drainage. Although an upstream dam already existed at Chain Lakes Reservoir, increasing water demands coupled with drought conditions in the 1980s prompted the construction of this $100-million diversion project. Ironically, Willow Creek Park's day-use and campground facilities were closed in 2006 because of flood damage caused a year earlier.

The road becomes more enchanting with each passing kilometre, as it dips through grassy draws grazed by cows and passes beneath foothill ridges studded with sandstone outcrops. Where it swings south, it's tempting to continue endlessly west on gravel roads that climb through rolling ranchland into the Porcupine Hills. After all, the most interesting trips are usually spontaneous explorations off the beaten track.

Soon enough, the road reaches Willow Creek Municipal Park. This 109-hectare park lies in a large valley, once a runoff channel for a glacial lake. The lake was created when glacial meltwaters from the mountains backed up against the continental ice sheet. When the ice sheet retreated, the lake drained.

Today, the park is an oasis in the otherwise dry prairie. The sheltered valley is fed by Willow Creek, creating a rich and diverse habitat. The moist floodplain supports stands of balsam poplar, black cottonwood, and narrowleaf cottonwood, the last not commonly found in Alberta. The shaded creek attracts populations of mule and white-tailed deer, beavers, coyotes, weasels, and occasionally moose.

This lush environment is in stark contrast to the dry grasslands on the bench above the creek, where rough fescues, other native grasses, and sagebrush predominate. A short trail leads up the hillside past the preserved remains of an Aboriginal teepee ring. The ring of rocks, once used to hold down a skin teepee, was left behind when the camp was moved. The trail continues to the top of the bench, offering stel-

Looking southwest from Willow Creek Municipal Park.

lar views over the Willow Creek Valley and southwest towards the Porcupine Hills.

A buffalo jump and the site of a major hunting camp are located just east of the park. Blackfoot, Peigan, and Blood tribes were attracted to this valley by the buffalo, berries, and winter shelter it offered. They also considered the cottonwoods, which grew along the floodplain, sacred.

Settlers and later residents, particularly from the nearby town of Stavely, were attracted to this site for recreation. They picnicked along the creek and held dances in a hall constructed on an old saw-mill loading platform. The dance hall was damaged beyond repair when Willow Creek flooded in 1963. Such floods have since been reduced by the construction upstream of the dam that created Chain Lakes Reservoir.

Willow Creek Park, established in 1957, still attracts overnight campers, picnickers, and nature lovers. Birdwatchers often flock to the area in search of great blue herons, belted kingfishers, northern orioles, meadowlarks, kestrels, and cliff swallows—the latter nesting along the steep creek banks. Near one campsite is a nice stretch of flat-rock beach, where families often frolic and wade into the creek.

## CLARESHOLM AND PORCUPINE HILLS

**Route:** From the Highway 22X overpass, drive 108 kilometres south on Highway 2 to Claresholm. Head west on Secondary 520 over the Porcupine Hills to Highway 22 and follow it north back toward Calgary.
**Driving Distance:** About 300 kilometres return.
**Note:** The Claresholm Museum, on Railway Avenue, is open daily 9:30 a.m. to 5:00 p.m. from mid-May to late August and reduced hours in winter. Phone 403-625-3131; www.townoclaresholm.com.

The Porcupine Hills are an unusual rise of land in southwest Alberta, which at their crest have never been covered by glacial ice. This excellent day trip climbs to the height of these hills and offers a short

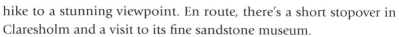

hike to a stunning viewpoint. En route, there's a short stopover in Claresholm and a visit to its fine sandstone museum.

The approach from Calgary follows Highway 2 through gently rolling prairie, intermittently bisected by the small valleys of the Sheep and Highwood rivers and smaller drainages. To the west, the forested Porcupine Hills parallel much of the highway, rising southwest of Claresholm.

Although the old Macleod Trail passed through the area, it was the southward extension of the Calgary and Edmonton Railway in 1891 that put Claresholm on the map. Named by the railway, Claresholm was located in a low spot, where collected water could feed the steam engines and railway cars wouldn't roll away.

In 1902, O. J. Amundsen had the townsite surveyed and convinced 25 settlers from North Dakota to move here. Surrounded by good agricultural land, the town quickly grew. By 1910, a row of wood frame buildings lined the main street along the railway line. Visitors today can take a self-guided walking tour of historic downtown buildings and view several murals. A tour map is available in the visitor information centre, located in the Claresholm Museum.

The museum is housed in the old sandstone train station, Claresholm's architectural jewel, which has been designated a provincial historic resource. The building was originally part of a larger station built in 1886 and located on 9th Avenue in Calgary. When that station was being replaced, it was dismantled, with its sandstone blocks going to Claresholm and High River to build new train staions around 1912. This station was converted to a museum in 1969, a year after the passenger train service stopped. Beside the museum are a 1903 one-room school and a heritage log cabin, with a 1918 Model T school bus featured in a new facility that contains many more artifacts.

A lovely garden in front of the museum honours Louise McKinney, a prominent local politician, temperance promoter, and religious activist in the Methodist Church. In the 1917 provincial election, she ran successfully for the agrarian Non-Partisan League,

The Louise McKinney Garden at Claresholm Museum.

becoming one of the first two women elected to a Canadian legislature. She was also one of five women in the famous Persons Case, which in 1929 established women as "persons" who could hold office as Canadian senators.

West of Claresholm, Secondary 520 soon crosses Willow Creek. An upstream dam on the creek at Chain Lakes Reservoir provides a steady supply of water to Claresholm, Granum, and area farmers. Within 15 kilometres, the road begins to climb into the Porcupine Hills, cut by coulees and dotted with ranches.

The name Porcupine Hills refers to a Blackfoot description of the spiny, tree-lined ridges that resemble a porcupine in profile. Fur trade explorer Peter Fidler was likely the first European to visit the Porcupine Hills, travelling there in the early 1790s with a band of Peigans, one of the Blackfoot Confederacy tribes.

During glacial advances, continental ice sheets flowed around much of this area, leaving these high hills standing above the prairies. In fact, the height of the Porcupine Hills is one of the few areas in Alberta untouched by glaciation. At the end of the last ice age, the draining of the glaciated valley to the west carved a channel that separated the Porcupine Hills from the foothills.

The Porcupine Hills weren't completely untouched by glaciation. On their lower eastern slopes, for example, sizable meltwater channels were formed against the edge of the receding continental ice sheet. When the ice melted, these channels, running at a level elevation along the side of the hills, were left high and dry above the valley floor. One such channel, called the Canyon, can be seen west of Claresholm.

Geologically, it could be argued that the Porcupine Hills aren't part of the foothills. While the foothills exhibit the same subsurface folding and thrust faulting as the mountains, the beds of sandstone and shale that underlie the Porcupine Hills dip gently, in the manner of the plains to the east.

Where the Porcupine Hills reach their height along Secondary 520, drive 1.8 kilometres south on the Skyline Road. Park at a low point in the road, cross a fence to the west, and hike north on a rough track that parallels the fence line. Close any gates you open, as this walk is on a crown-owned grazing lease. Within a kilometre, a hilltop dotted with immense old Douglas firs appears. The main ridge of the Porcupine Hills, with its considerable variation in elevation and topography, contains ecosystems of the montane, subalpine, and boreal forests as well as those of the aspen parkland and prairie grassland.

This lofty perch provides exceptional views west to the Livingstone and High Rock ranges. Below is Happy Valley, which contains Highway 22 and grazing cattle. These lush lands are part of the Waldron Grazing Cooperative, a syndicate of ranchers that carries on the tradition of the famous Walrond Ranche.

Created in 1883, the Walrond was one of the four big ranches that briefly ruled southern Alberta. Named after its principal investor, Sir John Walrond of Britain, the ranch was at first a prosperous undertaking along the northern reaches of the Oldman River. But after the severe winter of 1907, the herd was sold and its lease relinquished. More recently, many of its former lands have been acquired by the co-op. The 1894 Walrond Ranche House was moved in the

1980s to the Kootenai Brown Pioneer Village in Pincher Creek, where it can be viewed today (see page 58).

From this height of land, Secondary 520 descends quickly to reach Highway 22, the return route north to Calgary. West of this junction is the Whaleback, a long, heavily treed ridge that parallels the highway for some distance. The Whaleback contains Alberta's largest and most undisturbed area of montane landscape, characterized here by open forests and grasslands and frequented by elk and deer. A portion of the Whaleback Ridge is protected within the Upper Bob Creek Ecological Reserve, to the southwest (see pages 45–48).

## EATS & DRINKS

In Claresholm, **Latte-Da Espresso & Pastry Bar** (squeezed between a laundromat and a car wash at 4416–1st Street W) serves coffee and baked goods. **A & B Bakery** (129–50th Avenue W) features cinnamon swirls and cheese buns. Check out the Sunday brunch at **The Bridges at Claresholm Golf Club** (349–39th Avenue W).

# FOOTHILLS TOUR

**Route:** From Macleod Trail/Highway 2, at the south end of Calgary, drive 17 kilometres west on Highway 22X and then 77 kilometres south on Highway 22. Just north of Chain Lakes Reservoir, turn west on Secondary 532 and follow it for 26 kilometres to its junction with Secondary 40, the Forestry Trunk Road. Drive 39 kilometres south on Secondary 40 and then 22 kilometres east on Secondary 517 to rejoin Highway 22, following it north towards Calgary.

**Driving Distance:** About 320 kilometres return.

**Note:** Secondary 532 west from Chain Lakes is a rough gravel road that adds a rugged dimension to this trip. It's certainly passable by passenger vehicles when reasonably dry. This section can be avoided by taking paved Secondary 541 west from Longview and then heading south on Secondary 40/Forestry Trunk Road, a much smoother gravel road.

The Calgary area is celebrated for its mountains, prairies, and low rolling ranchlands. All are thinly treed, allowing the distant vistas for which southern Alberta is famous. For a change of pace, how about a trip that features the heavier forests of its foothills and lower mountain slopes? This route rises over the rugged foothills of southern Alberta and then follows the Oldman River out of the dense forests and back onto the edge of the plains. Along the way there's a refreshing stop at the lovely Livingstone Falls.

The drive south from Calgary roughly follows the eastern edge of southern Alberta's foothills, a thin belt that parallels the Rocky Mountains on a northwest-southeast alignment. Highway 22 south of Longview actually marks the geological boundary between the foothill formations to the west and the plains to the east.

While sedimentary layers of primarily sandstones and shales underlie both, the plains strata have remained fairly horizontal. The foothills structures, by contrast, were shaped some 50 million years ago by the same forces that earlier created the mountains to the west. Their layers have thus been intricately folded, causing older rocks to be stacked on top of younger ones.

Drilling for natural gas and oil in the Turner Valley field has revealed highly complex rock structures beneath the surface. Clues to these underground structures can be found along riverbanks where the bedrock has been exposed. The north bank of the Highwood River near Longview is a good place to look for these features.

The reason these complex structures aren't revealed at the surface is that the bedrock of sandstones and shales is fairly soft and has eroded over the years into the gentler slopes of the foothills. Sandstone, however, is more resistant than shale and forms the parallel ridges one finds in the foothills. Where exposed as outcrops, these sandstone ridges are called hogbacks. Softer shales usually underlie the dips or valleys between the ridges.

Just north of Chain Lakes Reservoir, the route swings west to climb through the foothills and into the Front Ranges of the Rockies. The road initially follows the headwaters of Willow Creek and

Hiking along Windy Peak Hills.

then starts a roller-coaster ride through aspen forest that soon gives way to pine and spruce.

Higher up, the valley walls become more steep-sided and several drainages descend from a rockier ridge, the first evidence of a transition to a mountain environment. The road climbs steeply to a divide that provides superb views back down the valley and over the contorted hills to flatter lands beyond.

From a small parking lot on the left, adventurous hikers can follow a rough trail south along an open, broad ridge—the aptly named Windy Peak Hills. In mid- to late fall, this is often a superb place to watch, up close, the southern migration of golden eagles (see pages 241–45).

Back in the vehicle, you quickly descend into heavier coniferous forest, a steady companion the length of the Forestry Trunk Road. Ten kilometres south on this road, it's well worth stopping for a picnic or stroll at the Livingstone Falls Campground, set amid well-spaced trees. The river here and the mountain range to the east are named for the famous African explorer and missionary David Livingstone.

Although small, Livingstone Falls is unique. A rock ledge has been thrust up into the current, allowing the water to slide elegantly down its surface, rather than falling off it. The tiny river divides into two channels here, forming closely spaced waterfalls over the same ledge.

Beyond the campground, the road soon follows the Oldman River, which tumbles out of mountains to the west and heads south along this valley. The river's name comes from a Blackfoot word that means "the river the Old Man played upon." According to legend, the Blackfoot god Old Man Napi created a playing field near where the river is joined by the tributary Livingstone River.

The Oldman River suddenly swings east through the Livingstone Range at a spectacular canyon known as the Gap. The route follows the canyon east along Secondary 517. It's believed this slash in the mountain flank was initially carved by an ancient Oldman River and subsequently enlarged by glaciation. In much more recent times, the Gap has also been an important transportation corridor for moving cattle to and from summer ranges in the high country.

Beyond the Gap, the road suddenly emerges into rolling hills that are largely naked. There are, however, patches of aspen in sheltered spots and thick stands of Douglas fir on slopes to the south. The lower foothills south of the Bow River are actually a southern extension of aspen parkland, more commonly found in central Alberta. A mixture of aspen forest and prairie grassland dominates this ecosystem.

# WHALEBACK

**Route:** Perhaps the most direct route is to drive, from the Highway 22X overpass, 68 kilometres south on Highway 2 to Nanton. From the south end of town, go 38 kilometres west on Secondary 533 to Highway 22 and then 30 kilometres south to a small pull-off on the right (it's 4 kilometres south of the Secondary 520 junction). Park beside a gate and hike a rocky track ascending a hill to the west. A lovely return route is via Highway 22 north.
**Driving Distance:** About 140 kilometres one way.
**Note:** Hiking time is about four to five hours return, with 375 metres elevation gain. To reach the Whaleback, you must cross private and then leased crown land. Park

at the highway and proceed on foot, sticking to existing tracks wherever possible and taking care not to disturb grazing cattle.

From spring through fall, it's well worth visiting this unique foothills landscape in the midst of southwestern Alberta's rolling cattle country. This trip describes a half-day excursion (wear sturdy hiking footwear) along the northern portion of Whaleback Ridge. From this lofty perch, surrounded by stands of ancient Douglas fir and gnarled limber pine, you can gaze across sheltered valleys and smaller ridges to the nearby peaks of the Livingstone Range.

The Whaleback—named for its series of spine-like ridges—boasts Canada's largest and healthiest montane landscape, characterized by a relatively dry climate and a patchwork of grassy slopes and dense forest. A rare environment in Alberta, montane landscape is most commonly found in mountain valleys, such as along the Bow River in Banff National Park, where it has been largely carved up by roads, railways, and commercial development.

At 235 square kilometres, the roadless Whaleback remains largely intact. Its mix of open grass slopes, heavy timber, and wetlands offers a rich habitat for elk, cougar, grizzly bears, wolves, eagles, songbirds, and an abundance of wildflowers. It also harbours magnificent stands of Douglas fir and, on exposed upper slopes and ridges, limber pine bent by centuries of chinook winds.

In mid-1999, the Alberta government granted the Whaleback full environmental protection under its Special Places 2000 program. The resulting Bob Creek Wildland and the subsequent creation of the Black Creek Heritage Rangeland now protect some 29,000 hectares of the Whaleback that were previously threatened by petroleum and other development.

From the highway, the route ascends a short hill and passes a large pond frequented by cattle. These lands were once part of the vast cattle empire of the Walrond Ranche, formed in 1883 and prosperous until winter blizzards hastened its demise in the early 1900s. Much of its original property was acquired in the 1960s by the Waldron Grazing Cooperative, a syndicate of ranchers that owns or leases most of the southern half of Whaleback Ridge. During the summer, several thousand cattle, most of them yearling steers castrated as calves, graze the Whaleback area. Visitors perturbed by the wanderings and droppings of these animals should consider that area ranchers have, by lightly grazing their cattle on the rough fescue grasses over the decades, helped keep this spectacular landscape intact.

The track soon cuts through the thickly wooded lower slopes of Black Mountain, offering views back east to the Porcupine Hills and the first good look ahead to Whaleback Ridge. The undulating ridge is 30 kilometres long, with open, grassy slopes in the south giving way to denser forests of Douglas fir, white spruce, aspen, and limber pine to the north. This mixture of exposed grasses and sheltering woods provides critical wintering habitat for about 2,000 elk, the second-largest herd in southern Alberta.

The route continues straight ahead, bypassing a track leading south. Just beyond, where the road turns north, step across a tiny creek and work your way northwest towards a prominent coulee, sticking to trails where you can find them. En route, you'll pass beneath a controversial power line, erected in the 1980s, and skirt a small wetland that contains a diversity of nesting songbirds. Beyond, follow a trail up the coulee until you can angle right up the final grassy slopes to the ridge.

The view that awaits is stunning: the Bob Creek Valley below and a succession of ridges rising to the Front Ranges of the Rocky Mountains. On the far side of Bob Creek is Little Whaleback Ridge, near where the sour gas well and access road were proposed. In the skies above, hawks and occasionally golden eagles ride the thermal currents.

As best you can, follow the ridgeline north, dropping down here and there to bypass narrow bits of fractured and exposed Belly River sandstone. Soon enough, you'll reach a barbwire fence marking the southern boundary of the small Upper Bob Creek Ecological Reserve, which offers slightly greater environmental protection than the rest of the Whaleback Ridge. From the reserve's edge, a rough

The Whaleback boasts Canada's largest montane landscape.

road descends steeply into Breeders Valley, where a track leads south back to the approach route.

To explore the numerous other hikes in the area, consult *The Whaleback: A Walking Guide* by Bob Blaxley (Calgary: Rocky Mountain Books).

## HEAD-SMASHED-IN BUFFALO JUMP

**Route:** From the Highway 22X overpass at Calgary's southern outskirts, drive 143 kilometres south on Highway 2. Follow the Head-Smashed-In Buffalo Jump signs west on Secondary 785 for 16 kilometres.

**Driving Distance:** About 160 kilometres one way.

**Note:** The interpretive centre is open daily 9:00 a.m. to 6:00 p.m. from July 1 to Labour Day and 10:00 a.m. to 5:00 p.m. the rest of the year. Admission charged. For information or to book tours, phone 403-553-2731; www.history.alberta.ca/headsmashedin.

Head-Smashed-In Buffalo Jump is one of the oldest, largest, and best-preserved buffalo jumps in North America. For thousands of years, Plains Aboriginals hunted buffalo by driving them over a cliff at the edge of the Porcupine Hills. The vivid name refers to the legend of a young Peigan man who watched the hunt from below the cliff and was found, with his skull crushed, under a pile of dead buffalo.

Today, Head-Smashed-In is a UNESCO World Heritage Site and one of the subtle wonders of Alberta. A $10-million interpretive centre, sensitively built to blend into the sandstone cliff, tells the story of the prehistoric Plains peoples and their relationship with the buffalo. The surrounding grasslands and cliffs also harbour many secrets of this rich and ancient culture.

Although the Alberta government built the centre and operates it, the interpretive staff are local Peigans and Bloods, fluent in English and Blackfoot and well versed in their ancestral legends and traditions. (The Peigan, Blood, and Blackfoot are the three tribes, or nations, that constitute the historic Blackfoot Confederacy of south-central Alberta and Montana.) The story these descendants of the buffalo hunters tell on their group tours goes beyond conventional history into prehistory.

This was no primitive society. Hunting the massive, unpredictable buffalo without horses or guns required complex organizational skills involving hundreds of people. In years when buffalo grazed in the expansive basins above the cliffs, young men disguised under wolf and buffalo calf skins would lure and then push the herding animals into narrow drive lanes marked by stone cairns, some still evident. Farther along, hunters hidden behind brush piles would jump up, shouting and waving buffalo robes to keep the animals on course towards the cliff.

The hunters pressing from behind were aided by a visual deception that made the land above and below the cliff appear as an unbroken line of grassland. By the time the buffalo reached the precipice, they were at full gallop, unable to stop or veer to the side to avoid the fatal plunge.

Teepee camping offered at Head-Smashed-In Buffalo Jump.

As visitors overlooking the cliff might guess, the 10-metre drop often didn't kill the animals outright. Deposits at the cliff base contain countless thousands of arrowheads, confirming that hunters armed with spears and arrows finished off the many survivors. The carcasses were then dragged to the flats near the teepee campsites for butchering.

Some cuts were eaten fresh, while other meat was dried and mixed with fat and berries to produce long-lasting pemmican. Over the centuries, some 3 million kilograms of rocks were hauled more than a kilometre to the teepee campsites, where they were heated in fires and dumped into water-filled pits to boil the meat and render grease. Almost nothing was wasted. Bones were fashioned into tools, horns into containers, and hooves into rattles. Hides became blankets and teepee covers, while skulls were painted and used in religious ceremonies and pre-hunt rituals.

It was, by and large, a good life that lasted for thousands of years. It ended in little more than a century. The arrival of the horse and gun around 1730 soon made buffalo jumps obsolete; Head-Smashed-In

Below the bison-hunting cliff at Head-Smashed-In Buffalo Jump.

was last used in the early 1800s. And by 1880, the herds of prairie bison that had once roamed the Canadian prairies in the tens of millions were wiped out.

As the Plains tribes kept no written records, the story of the prehistoric hunt has been pieced together by archaeologists delving through the rich bone beds. Scientists know, for example, that the site was likely first used as a buffalo jump 5,700 years ago, well before the first Egyptian pyramid was built.

Many of the archaeological prizes—including skulls, stone projectile points, hide scrapers, and a rare leather pouch—have been added to displays in the interpretive centre. The displays are a mixture of legend, artifacts, and a bit of artifice. As visitors enter the front door, they're confronted by a 12-metre cliff built with three stuffed buffalo poised at its edge above a reconstructed archaeological pit below. Nearby is a theatre, where a film recreating the hunt appears so lifelike that some viewers believe live buffalo are being driven off the cliff.

Visitors enter the centre at the cliff base and ascend to the top, where they emerge above the cliff. After taking a short walk to a viewpoint overlooking the jump, they return to tour the building from top to bottom via a series of terraces, each with a theme. The top level orients the visitor to the ecology of the prehistoric plains and introduces the Blackfoot account of the origin of man. The second level surveys how early Plains peoples lived, and the third describes the hunt, including its spiritual significance. The fourth level depicts how the arrival of Europeans dramatically altered this ancient culture, and the fifth shows how archaeology has been used to uncover the past.

During the summer, Head-Smashed-In offers a variety of special events. On Wednesdays, traditional drumming and dancing demonstrations are performed twice a day on the interpretive centre's plaza. On the first Saturday of the month, visitors can sign up for a hike into the buffalo-hunting drive lanes or take a hands-on workshop to, say, make a hand drum, practise moccasin making, or see how ancient weapons were built and used.

### EATS & DRINKS

The **Head-Smashed-In Café** features native cuisine.

## ◆ FORT MACLEOD

**Route:** From the Highway 22X overpass, drive 145 kilometres south on Highway 2 and 4 kilometres east on Highway 3 to Fort Macleod.
**Driving Distance:** About 150 kilometres one way.
**Note:** The Fort Museum of the North West Mounted Police (219 Jerry Potts Boulevard) is open daily 9:00 a.m. to 6:00 p.m. from early July to early September, with reduced hours in spring and fall. Admission charged. Phone toll free 1-866-273-6841 or 403-553-4703; www.nwmpmuseum.com. • For information about other Fort Macleod attractions, see www.fortmacleod.com.

The arrival of the North West Mounted Police (NWMP) on the prairies in 1874 paved the way for the orderly settlement of southern Alberta. From their base in Fort Macleod, the redcoats quickly rousted the American whisky traders, helped native people make the transition to reserves, and assisted new settlers.

This trip to southern Alberta's oldest community visits reconstructions of the original NWMP forts and features daily performances of the Mounties' famous musical ride on horseback. It also includes a tour of the finest restoration of historic downtown buildings in small-town Alberta.

The highway between Calgary and Fort Macleod roughly follows the old Macleod Trail, used for centuries as a north-south route by natives and, later, white explorers and traders. The four-lane highway takes the straightest line possible. By contrast, the Macleod Trail took a meandering route, following the lay of the land and the line of least resistance.

The trail was perhaps a migratory route for prehistoric peoples arriving in North America. Later, the Algonquin and then the Blackfoot nations used it. Among the first white travellers were traders in the 1860s, who hauled supplies by wagon from Fort Benton in Montana to Fort Edmonton. Cattle herds from Montana were also driven this way in the early 1880s. First known as Blackfoot Trail, the name was changed to Macleod Trail to reflect the mounted police who patrolled this route from Fort Macleod. The historic trail finally fell into disuse with the construction of a railway between Calgary and Fort Macleod in the early 1890s.

Fenced off by homesteaders at the beginning of the 20th century, the abandoned route has largely disappeared under a cover of grass. Traces of the deep ruts made by heavy wagons are still visible in some places. On some roads leading west of Highway 2, local groups have erected commemorative wagon wheels where the old trail passed.

While the Macleod Trail is long gone, its influence remains in the towns along the highway. When 19th-century wagons made their way north from Fort Benton, they covered 16 to 20 kilometres a day. They required regularly spaced stopping houses along the way, where horses could be changed and passengers and drivers could spend the night. The houses were often located at river crossings, such as the one on the Sheep River at Okotoks. Reinforced by the arrival of the railway, the stopping houses led to such towns as High River, Nanton, and Claresholm.

Not all such places survived. In the 1870s, buffalo hunter Henry Kountz built a stopping house along Willow Creek (northwest of present-day Claresholm) called The Leavings, in reference to where the wagons and stages left the creek. The North West Mounted Police established a detachment there in 1886. Bypassed by the railway, the site was abandoned in 1903.

Previously known as Blackfoot Crossing, Fort Macleod was founded in 1874 when Metis guide Jerry Potts led a troop of 150 North West Mounted policemen to an island in the Oldman River. Here, following their long trek across the prairies, the men erected a fort, or barracks, named after their commander, Colonel James Macleod. Exposed to flooding, it was soon moved 3 kilometres west to higher ground.

In 2005, the North West Mounted Police 1884 Barracks was unveiled as a provincial historic site at this location, along Highway 3 near Fort Macleod's western outskirts. The facility houses several reconstructed buildings with period displays of a saddlery, a prison and gallows, and a medicine room.

Not far away is the Fort Museum of the North West Mounted Police, a representation of the long-standing fort, complete with thick log walls and palisades. Displays in buildings around the fort's perimeter tell the story of the Mounties, the Aboriginal peoples of southern Alberta, and early settlers.

Among the buildings are a sod-roofed storehouse and the restored office of local lawyer Frederick Haultain, who became premier of the North-West Territories before the formation of Alberta and Saskatchewan as provinces in 1905. For many visitors, the highlight of a

Walking through historic downtown Fort Macleod.

museum visit is the musical ride, performed four times daily in summer by a mounted patrol dressed in replica 1878 NWMP uniforms.

While in Fort Macleod, it's well worth taking a walking tour of the impressively restored buildings of the historic downtown, a designated provincial historic area. (Tour brochures are available at the Fort Museum.) The tour covers nearly 30 buildings, including wood frame structures built in the late 1890s and brick and sandstone buildings from the early 1900s. The highlight is the 1912 Empress Theatre, the oldest operating theatre in Alberta. Renovated at a cost of nearly $1 million, the theatre features one original leather seat and the decorative neon tulips installed on the pressed tin ceiling in 1938.

For further exercise away from civilization, visit River Valley Wilderness Park, one of the few places where the narrow-leaf cottonwood tree survives. To reach the park, drive north on 6th Avenue, cross the Oldman River on a green bridge, and take the first left.

The town of Fort Macleod was incorporated in 1892. Stimulated by the development of a railway and coal mines in the nearby Crowsnest Pass, the town's population reached 2,500 by 1910. In the boom before World War I, Fort Macleod was promoted as the Winnipeg of the West and had rivalries with Lethbridge and even Calgary. But its promise never materialized, and today Fort Macleod is only slightly larger than it was in 1910, even though it claims the highest number of sunlight hours in Canada.

---

### EATS & DRINKS

If you like history with your meal, several restaurants have moved into renovated historic buildings in downtown Fort Macleod. For example, the **Silver Grill Restaurant** (246–24th Street) has a pressed metal ceiling to complement its Chinese food, while **Rahn's Bakery & Café** (228–24th Street) serves an early breakfast in a 1907 building; I also recommend picking up a freshly baked apple turnover or butterhorn.

---

# PINCHER CREEK

**Route:** From Macleod Trail/Highway 2, at Calgary's south end, drive 17 kilometres west on Highway 22X and then 160 kilometres south on Highway 22. Head east on Highway 3 for 20 kilometres and then 3 kilometres south on Highway 6. Pincher Creek can also be reached by Highway 2 south to near Fort Macleod and then Highway 3 west.

**Driving Distance:** About 200 kilometres one way.

**Note:** Kootenai Brown Pioneer Village (1037 Bev McLachlin Drive) is open 10:00 a.m. to 8:00 p.m. daily from late May through August, with reduced hours the rest of the year. Admission charged. Phone 403-627-3684; www.kootenaibrown.org.

Pincher Creek is the centre of one of southern Alberta's oldest ranching areas. It also sits amid a spectacular landscape, where the plains and foothills rise dramatically into the mountains. The scenery alone justifies the drive from Calgary. This trip tours the countryside and stops at one of the most diversified small museums in Alberta.

After the drive from Calgary, it's worth taking a short detour off Highway 3 to Lundbreck Falls, where you can stretch your legs and admire this impressive plunge in the Crowsnest River. Anglers from around the world come to the Crowsnest, a rare combination of a small, clear river with sizable trout in a spectacular setting.

From Lundbreck Falls, proceed directly to Pincher Creek or take the scenic, roundabout route via Burmis and Beaver Mines. The latter is a hilly approach that crosses the Crowsnest and Castle rivers.

Pincher Creek is named for a pair of horse trimming pincers apparently found on the creek bank by a North West Mounted Police patrol. Its population of 3,600 makes this the largest community along the southern foothills and a rare town to have survived being bypassed by a rail line. Although a large gas reservoir helps feed the economy, Pincher Creek owes its continued existence to a strong ranching tradition that dates back to the late 1870s.

These high plains and rolling foothills provided ideal conditions for raising cattle. The often fierce chinook winds that blew through Crowsnest Pass kept the range clear of snow much of the winter. Cattle could also escape occasional cold snaps and blizzards in coulees and stands of trees.

The area's excellent grasslands convinced the North West Mounted Police at nearby Fort Macleod to set up a farm here for feeding and raising the force's horses. From that base grew a vibrant community of settlers and ranchers, some of them retired Mounties. The largest early ranch near Pincher Creek was the Stewart Ranche, owned by a member of an Ontario lumber family and sold in 1888.

There are still some sizable ranches in the area, including one spread owned by investors from France. Pincher Creek's continued ranching strength is celebrated by an annual rodeo and cowboy poetry competition. Pincher Creek's ranchlands also support a growing number of tall, three-bladed wind turbines used to generate electricity. The area is now Canada's wind energy capital, with some 200 turbines— and counting—providing power for local and export markets.

Wind turbines near Pincher Creek.

Kootenai Brown Pioneer Village contains an unusual and impressive collection of log buildings dating back to the early 1880s. Here is the transplanted log home (circa 1880) of the Irish-born Kootenai Brown. His remarkable resumé included the following careers: soldier, miner, buffalo and wolf hunter, whisky trader, guide and scout, gold prospector, and dispatch rider. He was twice married to Aboriginal women, once escaped the capture of Sitting Bull, and was acquitted of a U.S. murder charge. Yet he's best known as a prime mover in the creation of a national park at Waterton Lakes, where he lived for many years.

In 1885, another remarkable man, Oblate missionary Albert Lacombe, built a temporary church in Pincher Creek that's now located in the park. Father Lacombe was an important influence on the Blackfoot and Cree and lobbied tirelessly for native aid programs and government-sponsored Catholic schools.

Pincher Creek still has a strong French Catholic community, thanks to the efforts of Quebec missionaries who encouraged western settlement. The first German settlers in Alberta also came to the Pincher Creek area in 1883. In 1916, Doukhobors from British

Columbia established several nearby colonies, where they hoped to quietly farm and pursue their pacifist religious beliefs. A Doukhobor barn and bathhouse from near Cowley have been relocated to Kootenai Brown Pioneer Village.

On the return to Calgary, consider taking a back route north on Secondary 785. Nearby, the flow of three rivers—the Oldman, Crowsnest, and Castle—has been harnessed at the Oldman Dam and reservoir, one of the most controversial developments in Alberta's history. Nearby are the Three Rivers Rock and Fossil Museum—housing a private collection of more than 3,500 rocks, fossils, and minerals; call 403-627-2206—and Heritage Acres Museum (www.heritageacres .org). The latter features an unusual "village" of miniature buildings constructed from glass telephone insulators, as well as antique farm machinery, a restored Doukhobor barn, and a relocated, full-size grain elevator.

Continue north and east on this gravel road, which leads through some of the most spectacular rolling ranchlands in southern Alberta. The road eventually passes Head-Smashed-In Buffalo Jump en route to Highway 2.

---

### EATS & DRINKS

In Pincher Creek, try **Denise's Bistro** (967 Main Street) for coffee, lunch, and pastries and **Bright Pearl Restaurant & Bar** (745 Main Street) for a good Chinese buffet lunch. Two kilometres west of Pincher Creek on Secondary 507, **September Springs Ranch** has the **Memories Café & Tea Room**, offering lunch specials and scones with Devonshire cream. The old **Blairmore ski club lodge**, still equipped, is also on the premises, offering magnificent mountain views.

## Pincher Creek Hutterite Colony

**Route:** From Highway 6, at the northern edge of Pincher Creek, take Secondary 507 west for 1 kilometre and then go right (sign) on a gravel road for 2 kilometres to the Pincher Creek Hutterite Colony.

**Note:** Group tours of the Pincher Creek Hutterite Colony are available, for a reasonable fee, every day except Sunday and usually include lunch or dinner with colony members. Tours must be booked in advance. Phone Rosa Gross at 403-627-4021.

There are some 170 Hutterite colonies in Alberta, covering a large and growing chunk of rural landscape. Yet most Albertans have only a fleeting acquaintance with the distinctively clad Hutterites. This tour offers a rare, intimate glimpse into the everyday lives of this fascinating and often misunderstood religious group.

It's largely because of misperceptions that the Pincher Creek Colony decided to unveil the usually private world of these communal colonies. "We're normal people," says guide Rosa Gross. "We're not that different from everyone else."

Well, they're a lot tidier, for one thing. The tour of kitchen, dining areas, and even livestock processing areas reveals a world of immaculately scrubbed surfaces. There's also a clear segregation of well-defined duties along gender lines—with men making the major decisions, women undertaking domestic duties, and the two sitting separately in the dining room and in church. The prescribed dress code has men (bearded if married) in dark clothing and the women in ankle-length skirts and polka-dotted scarves.

Despite the conservative dress and Old World customs, colony members warmly greet visitors, which include several hundred German tourists a year (among themselves, Hutterites speak an Austrian dialect of German, though standard German is used in church services). Their polite children exude innocence and joy, whether at play or in their one-room school, which provides education, following the Alberta curriculum, to the age of 15. Though some pursue further education, most are assigned jobs in the colony.

Touring the Pincher Creek Hutterite Colony.

The Pincher Creek Colony, established in 1926, embraces modern farming technologies. There are three new combines in the yard, and computers monitor various livestock operations, including a dairy and barns for chickens, hogs, domestic geese, ducks, and turkeys. It all adds up to a large, prosperous farming operation that embraces 8,000 acres of owned and a few thousand acres of rented land, most of it under cultivation to produce grain and hay crops and vegetables. What's not used to feed the colony of 112 people is sold to markets in Alberta and B.C. One section of colony farmland is rented to a company that operates 60 large windmills.

An Anabaptist (meaning adult baptism) Christian sect formed in Austria in the 1500s and named after leader Jacob Hutter, the Hutterites moved several times around eastern Europe to escape religious persecution, finally leaving the Ukraine in the 1870s to settle in South Dakota. Their pacifist ways and German tongue, however, were very unpopular during World War I, and they soon moved to the Canadian Prairies, though colonies have since been established in Midwest and Western U.S. states.

As in all Hutterite colonies, the Pincher Creek members live communally (though in separate, familial houses) and own all property and goods collectively. Typically, when a colony reaches a population of up to 150, about half its members are chosen to form a new colony. In 1956 and again in 1970, Pincher Creek formed offshoot colonies in the state of Washington but is likely at least a decade away from another division.

## CROWSNEST PASS

**Route:** From Macleod Trail/Highway 2, at Calgary's south end, drive 17 kilometres west on Highway 22X and 160 kilometres south on Highway 22. At the Highway 3 junction, turn right and drive 10 kilometres west to reach the Leitch Collieries and the beginning of the Crowsnest Pass tour.
**Driving Distance:** About 200 kilometres one way.
**Note:** The Frank Slide Interpretive Centre is open daily 9:00 a.m. to 6:00 p.m. from July 1 to Labour Day and 10:00 a.m. to 5:00 p.m. the rest of the year. Phone 403-562-7388; www.history.alberta.ca/frankslide. • The Bellevue Underground Mine tours (www.bellevueundergroundmine.org) operate 10:00 a.m. to 6:30 p.m. from mid-May to early September. Phone 403-564-4700. Admission charged for both.

The Crowsnest Pass is one of the finest destinations in Alberta. The windswept foothills provide a dramatic foreground to the sudden rise of the Rocky Mountains, which frame the long, low Crowsnest Pass (elevation 1,358 metres). The pass is also rich in coal-mining history, tinged with the tragedies of the Frank Slide and the Hillcrest explosion, the worst mine disaster in Canadian history. Though the coal-mining era is over, its history is well preserved at excellent museums and interpretive stops.

A day trip hardly does the area justice. If time is limited, head for the refurbished Frank Slide Interpretive Centre, which gives a fine overview of Crowsnest Pass history. You can also do a self-guided heritage driving tour through the pass, following road signs and a detailed brochure, available at the interpretive centre.

Interpretive trail through the massive boulders of Frank Slide.

The alternative is to stay overnight. The area is well stocked with motels and good campsites, the finest of which is at Beauvais Lake Provincial Park to the near south.

Located 40 kilometres north of the U.S. border, the Crowsnest Pass is the most southerly highway and railway corridor through Canada's Rocky Mountains. There are five communities strung along this 32-kilometre corridor to the B.C. border, which marks the Continental Divide. In 1979, these towns were amalgamated into the Municipality of Crowsnest Pass, with a collective population today of some 5,700 people.

Archaeological surveys indicate extensive use of the pass by prehistoric cultures, dating back perhaps 10,000 years. One Kootenai summer campsite discovered at Crowsnest Lake is 8,500 years old.

Among the early white visitors were members of the Palliser Expedition (1857–60), who explored the area extensively as part of their reconnaissance mission through Canada's prairie regions. Large deposits of coal were noted by G. W. Dawson in an 1882 survey conducted for the Geological Survey of Canada. But the first industrial activity was the establishment of a sawmill around 1880.

The real impetus for development in the Crowsnest Pass was the arrival in 1898 of a Canadian Pacific Railway line, built to serve the lead, copper, and zinc mines of southeast British Columbia. The deposits of soft bituminous coal were perfectly situated to fuel the railway's steam engines and to heat the homes of an influx of prairie settlers.

The boom was on, and soon the Crowsnest Pass developed into Alberta's largest coal-mining region. The five communities that exist today were formed between 1898 and 1905, as were numerous coal-mining ventures. Not all survived.

Leitch Collieries, located at the east end of Crowsnest Pass, was one such failure. Established in 1907 as one of the largest mines in the pass, it suffered from strikes and poor markets and went out of business in 1915. When the mine closed, the buildings from the nearby company town of Passburg were moved to surviving communities. Fortunately, the remains of the mine manager's house, the powerhouse, the coal washery, the tipple, and a row of 101 coke ovens have survived. They're preserved as a provincial historic site at the Collieries, which can be toured on foot.

On the other side of the highway is the pretty community of Hillcrest, where a large cemetery graphically tells the town's sad history. In 1914, a huge explosion ripped through the tunnels of Hillcrest Mine, killing 189 men and boys and leaving more than 500 widows and children behind.

Such tragedies weren't uncommon in the area's coal mines, where the high concentrations of methane gas and coal dust were a lethal mix. Between 1902 and 1912, more than 350 people died from explosions, helping the coal mines of Alberta and British Columbia earn the world's worst safety records at the time.

The Crowsnest Pass's most famous tragedy wasn't an underground explosion, but the Frank Slide. In the early morning of April 29, 1903, more than 80 million tonnes of limestone slid off the face of Turtle

The famous Burmis Tree at the east entrance of Crowsnest Pass.

Mountain, sweeping across part of the sleeping town of Frank and continuing well up the other side of the valley. About 70 people were killed. Many scientists believe the slide was likely triggered by coal-mining tunnels in a mountainside already inherently unstable; Aboriginal peoples had long called Turtle "the mountain that moves." Perhaps not surprising in such a deadly industry, the mine reopened 30 days later, only to close for good in 1917.

Today, visitors flock to the Frank Slide site to marvel at the enormous jumble of boulders that litters the valley. The Frank Slide Interpretive Centre has been extensively renovated and updated, incorporating the latest in interactive displays to tell the history of the famous slide and of coal mining in the pass.

While at the interpretive centre, it's well worth taking a 1.5-kilometre interpretive loop walk through the debris on the Frank Slide Trail. Living among the boulders are pikas and golden-mantled ground squirrels, both usually found in rocky terrain at higher elevations.

Although all the coal mines in the Crowsnest Pass are now closed, visitors can don a miner's helmet and lamp and follow guides through part of the nearby Bellevue Underground Mine. The mine, originally owned by a company based in Lille, France, opened in 1903 and operated until 1962.

Another industry that prospered briefly in the Crowsnest Pass was rum-running. During Alberta's Prohibition era from 1916 to 1923, liquor was smuggled across the border from British Columbia and sometimes Montana in fast cars and then bootlegged to thirsty patrons. One of the ringleaders was Emilio Picariello, known as Emperor Pick, who owned the Alberta Hotel, now a pharmacy in ⚑Blairmore. Cases of smuggled liquor were apparently taken from the hotel through a tunnel under the road and loaded onto railway cars. Picariello was hanged in 1923 after a policeman was killed in a shootout.

The westernmost community in the Crowsnest Pass is the sizable Coleman, where many old downtown buildings, such as a theatre and police barracks, are being restored to their coal-era grandeur. Visitors can also tour the Crowsnest Museum. While in Coleman, it's worth taking a walk on the ⚑Miners' Path, a 1-kilometre trail (one way) that follows a tiny stream past towering Douglas firs to a small waterfall and then climbs to a bench with views of Crowsnest Mountain and the adjacent spires of the Seven Sisters. Just beyond Coleman

## EATS & DRINKS

You can get fat in a hurry grazing through Crowsnest Pass. In Bellevue, **Old Dairy Ice Cream Shoppe** (2501–213th Street), located in a former dairy, boasts more than 70 flavours of hard and soft ice cream. In ⚑Blairmore, **Stone's Throw Café** (13019–20th Avenue) features creative, all-day breakfasts and tasty pita melts, while **Tin Roof Bistro** (12849–20th Avenue) offers more upscale fare. There are several fine stops along Highway 3 in Coleman: **Cinnamon Bear Bakery & Café** (8342–20th Avenue) has fabulous fresh scones and muffins, **Crowsnest Café & Fly Shop** is a unique combination of fly-fishing gear and organic coffee and meals, and **Popiel's Restaurant** (8329–20th Avenue) is a popular family-run place with big portions. Away from the highway, **Chris' Restaurant** (7802–17th Avenue) is a local hangout featuring eggs and large pancakes.

are outcroppings of 93-million-year-old volcanic rock, one of the few places providing surface evidence of volcanic activity in Alberta.

## SUNDIAL HILL MEDICINE WHEEL

**Route:** From the Highway 22X overpass at Calgary's southern outskirts, drive south on Highway 2 for 83 kilometres. Just past Parkland, head east on Secondary 529 for 36 kilometres and then south on Highway 23 for 16 kilometres to Carmangay. Drive through the town to its northeast corner and then go 30 kilometres east on a good gravel road. Just before a big transmission line, turn south and drive 800 metres on a small road to a cattle guard. Proceed straight ahead up a rough, rocky track (watch your oil pan on passenger cars) to the fenced Sundial Butte.

**Driving Distance:** About 165 kilometres one way.

**Note:** Although accessible to the public, Sundial Hill Medicine Wheel is an archaeological site protected by law under the Historical Resources Act of Alberta. Don't disturb it in any way.

Alberta is blessed with ancient rocks, from the magnificent upthrust of the Rocky Mountains to the deep sedimentary layers that trap rich pools of oil and natural gas. Southern Alberta also contains most of North America's medicine wheels—ceremonial circles of stone built and used by Plains peoples over thousands of years. This trip offers a rare opportunity to visit one of these sacred sites and a chance to tour some fine, overlooked country southeast of Calgary.

The tour begins by heading swiftly south down the twinned Highway 2 to Parkland, where a turn to the east suddenly sheds all traffic. The roughly paved Secondary 529 is initially straight as a rifle shot, bisecting flat prairie that occasionally dips into the Little Bow River Valley. A short detour south on Highway 23 passes the four-elevator village of Champion and soon thereafter the Carmangay tee-pee rings. Aboriginal peoples used such circles of stone to anchor the edges of their hide teepees; in some cases, the circles were expanded to form medicine wheels.

Just beyond is the quiet town of Carmangay, named for C. W. Carman and his wife, Gertrude Gay, who owned a turn-of-the-century wheat farm there. The town was moved to its current location in 1909 to meet the advancing rail line, necessitating the construction two years later of a wooden bridge. The bridge was replaced in 1928 by a striking steel structure that still stands.

This century-old history is a blink of the eye compared to that of the trip's destination a little farther east. As if to advertise something momentous, the landscape soon changes from generally flat and expansive to abruptly undulating, the telltale sign of a stagnating glacier that left behind alternating troughs and hilly deposits. There are other clues that this was an excellent area for a medicine wheel: the prolific scattering of lichen-covered rocks among the short prairie grasses and the magnificent vantage point atop the highest of these hills, where sits Sundial Hill Medicine Wheel.

Upon clambering to the top of the hill, you'll find stupendous views across the fingered gullies of the deeply carved Little Bow Valley. Visible to the north is the upstream Travers Reservoir, created in the early 1950s to provide irrigation water to eventually 73,000 hectares of otherwise parched prairie farms. But attention soon turns to the unique collection of rocks at your feet.

Sundial Hill Medicine Wheel comprises a bushy rock pile, or cairn, and two surrounding circles of rocks connected by a passageway. It fits into one of eight general forms of medicine wheels—some have lines of stones extending away in the four cardinal directions from a central circle—and is the only one of its type in Alberta with a double circle.

Like many of the 43 archaeological sites in Alberta with medicine wheels, Sundial Hill hasn't been scientifically excavated, and its date of construction is thus not known. But excavations 60 kilometres to the northeast reveal that the Majorville Medicine Wheel was first built perhaps 4,500 years ago and, except for a few interludes, continually used and added to thereafter. Southern Alberta's last medicine wheels were constructed by the Blood in the 1940s.

Medicine wheels were built and used for a variety of ceremonial and religious purposes, such as to mark a successful buffalo hunt or to commemorate a great battle or an important chief. In some cases, the chosen location apparently marked the residence, grave, or death site of a warrior chief. While medicine wheels and the meanings of their various forms aren't well understood, they remain important spiritual sites.

Back on the main gravel road, it's worth driving a few kilometres farther east and descending into the Little Bow Valley, which is amazingly deep and wide considering the tiny river that now flows through it. A variety of routes can be taken on the return trip to Calgary, with the distant mountains of the Livingstone Range commanding the western skyline.

## LETHBRIDGE

**Route:** See page 71.

Lethbridge is arguably the most varied and interesting mid-sized city in Alberta. It's blessed with both cultural history and natural history.

The relative flatness of the southern prairie is relieved here by the deep Oldman River Valley. The valley harbours two distinct ecosystems—the cottonwood floodplains and the dry coulees—which can be explored in no less than three splendid city parks. You can also visit a reconstruction of the notorious whisky trading post called Fort Whoop-Up, see the origins of the city's coal-mining history, and tour the site of the last great battle between the Cree and Blackfoot in Alberta. It's easy to spend a whole day in the river valley alone.

The bluff overlooking the valley provides a view of two impressive pieces of architecture: the railway bridge that spans the Oldman Valley and, across the way, the ground-hugging University of Lethbridge, designed by Arthur Erickson. The bluff is also the site of the Sir Alexander Galt Museum, one of Canada's finest small museums, which moved into an expanded building in 2006.

Lethbridge

Jo Alexander Wilderness Park

Jo Fort Macleod

Lethbridge Nature Reserve

Helen Schuler Coulee Centre

High Level Bridge

Scenic Drive N.

3rd Ave E.

Information Centre

Fort Whoop-Up Interpretive Centre

Indian Battle Park

Sir Alexander Galt Museum

University of Lethbridge

Jo Cottonwood Park

Oldman River

Coulees

Mayor MaGrath Drive

Nikka Yuko Japanese Garden

Henderson Lake

Lethbridge is Alberta's fourth-largest city, with a 2012 population of 89,000. It's an important commercial centre for the irrigated farm communities of southern Alberta and is home to several light manufacturing and food processing plants.

Lethbridge is renowned for its strong winds and long hours of sunlight. It also gets my vote as the cleanest city in Canada. Where else can you find such immaculate parks? On an early Sunday morning in Henderson Lake Park, I discovered an attendant with a long broom dusting the eaves of a wooden bathroom. The adjacent Nikka Yuko Japanese Garden is even more carefully groomed.

Although it takes a couple of hours to get to Lethbridge, a visitor can devote several days to sampling its delights. The day tripper is advised to take small bites and digest them well, returning for more helpings at a later date. Check out the city's online presence at www.lethbridge.ca.

---

### EATS & DRINKS

Lethbridge has several fine coffee shops, including **The Penny Coffee House** (331–5th Street S), featuring artisan breads, and the **Round Street Café** (427–5th Street S). Good lunch stops include the **Guesthouse Restaurant** (Highway 3, west of Mayor Magrath Drive S), featuring *spätzli au gratin* and Dutch pancakes, the award-winning **Two Guys and a Pizza Place** (1281–3rd Avenue S), **Coco Pazzo Italian Café** (1264–3rd Avenue S), and **Yo Yo Crepes Panini Gelato** (102–5th Street S). Try the Jamie sandwich at **Backstreet Pub & Pizza** (407 Laval Boulevard W). It's well worth driving 5 kilometres east of Lethbridge and 1 kilometre south of Highway 3 on Broxburn Road to visit **Broxburn Vegetables & Café**, which sells greenhouse vegetables and U-pick fruits. This fresh produce also goes into the lunches and fabulous fruit pies.

---

### En Route to Lethbridge

**Route:** From Macleod Trail/Highway 2, near Calgary's south end, drive 37 kilometres east on Highway 22X. Turn south on Highway 24, which farther south becomes Highway 23. At the junction with Highway 3, turn left for the final 17 kilometres to Lethbridge.

**Driving Distance:** About 200 kilometres one way.

This approach to Lethbridge cuts through the heart of southern Alberta farming country and provides a more scenic alternative to the busier Highway 2 through Fort Macleod.

About half an hour from the city limits, the route crosses the Bow River at the Carseland Dam. The dam supplies water through irrigation canals and storage reservoirs to farmers' fields around Lomond and Vauxhaull. First built in 1910, the dam was needed to raise the river levels sufficiently to divert water down a 67-kilometre canal to McGregor Lake.

An unfortunate side effect of such irrigation dams on the Bow is a decrease in spring flooding, which normally provides the wet mud needed for cottonwood seeds to germinate. Low flows through the summer may also cause these giants to die.

There are still stands of cottonwood and balsam poplar growing in Carseland Provincial Park along the south banks of the placid Bow. The lush growth along the riverbanks provides a rich habitat for a diversity of birds, making this a good birdwatching area, especially during spring and fall migrations. One of the more interesting summer residents along this stretch of river is the white pelican. Other people are attracted by the large brown and rainbow trout that make this stretch of the Bow one of the world's prime angling rivers.

The principal farm centre between Calgary and Lethbridge is Vulcan. The major crop in this area is winter wheat, planted in late summer and harvested the following August. Until a devastating fire struck in 1971, Vulcan's famous "nine-in-a-line" elevators had the largest grain storage capacity in Canada.

Long the dominant architectural feature on the prairies, the wooden elevator is fast disappearing in many small rural towns, the victim of abandoned rail lines. In Alberta, the numbers have dwindled from more than 1,600 in the early 1960s to fewer than 200. Because of their aging condition and liability issues, they continue to be demolished rather than restored. Some have been sold cheaply and moved to area farms; a handful have been preserved as historic buildings. These grand wooden structures are being replaced by huge concrete elevators, which are less dusty and more efficient, but certainly lacking in charm.

Farther south, it's worth stopping at the Carmangay Campground on the banks of the Little Bow River. This scanty stream feeds the dammed

Travers Reservoir downstream. The reservoir is a major cog in the Bow River Irrigation District, which waters more than 73,000 hectares of otherwise parched prairie. Some of the reservoir's irrigation water is also used to create a treed oasis at Little Bow Provincial Park, a short distance to the northeast.

Within a small grassy patch at the Carmangay Campground are nine teepee rings. These circles of stones were once used by Aboriginal peoples to hold down the edges of their hide teepees. When the camp was moved, the stones were left behind. Archaeological discoveries of broken tools and buffalo bone fragments indicate that the site was used sometime between A.D. 200 and A.D. 1700. These early inhabitants were probably attracted here not only by the buffalo but also by the availability of wood and water in a sheltered valley.

South of Carmangay is Nobleford. Here, in the depths of the 1930s Depression, prosperous farmer Charles Noble invented the Noble blade, a landmark in dryland farming. The blade broke the soil and killed weeds but left stubble and other surface debris intact, thus preventing erosion that was blowing many drought-era farms away. For many years, the Lethbridge-made Noble cultivator was sold throughout North America. A small heritage park at Nobleford displays a succession of these blades.

### Henderson Lake Park and Nikka Yuko Japanese Garden

**Route:** From Highway 3 East in Lethbridge, go south on Mayor Magrath Drive S to Parkside Drive S, which provides access to the park and the Japanese Garden.
**Note:** The Nikka Yuko Japanese Garden is open daily from mid-May to mid-October 9:00 a.m. to 5:00 p.m. Admission charged. Phone 403-328-3511; www.nikkayuko .com.

Located just off a major commercial strip, Henderson Lake Park and the attached Nikka Yuko Japanese Garden provide a quiet respite from the bustle of this growing city. Indeed, the Japanese garden is designed as a place of serenity and meditation.

Developed for the International Dry Farming Congress in 1912, Henderson Lake is the city's oldest major park. The 47-hectare park offers a diversity of recreational facilities, such as a lawn bowling green, a golf course, a swimming pool, tennis courts, boat rentals, and a stadium.

Yet this can be a tranquil spot in the early morning or evening for a peaceful amble on the expanse of lawn beneath tall trees or along the water's edge. The lawns, walkways, and buildings are immaculately maintained. You wouldn't dare drop a candy wrapper here.

Immaculate is just the starting point for the 1.6-hectare Japanese garden, an artistic interpretation of nature ranked as one of the top 25 Japanese gardens in North America. It has been precisely designed and constructed, down to the selection and placement of each tree, shrub, and rock. The garden layout encompasses designs developed over a thousand years in Japan and incorporates influences of the Canadian prairie.

A meandering path connects five areas—a dry garden, a mountain and waterfall, a stream, ponds and islands, and a prairie garden—each providing a different viewpoint. All of these elements surround a pavilion, built of rare cypress wood by artisans in Japan and assembled here. The intent is to create a haven where visitors can quietly contemplate the beauty and order of nature and find inner peace.

Built as a symbol of Japanese-Canadian friendship, the garden was officially opened by Prince and Princess Takamatsu of Japan in 1967. The garden also recognizes the considerable contribution of the Japanese Canadian community in this part of southern Alberta. The first Japanese settlers came to the area early in the 20th century to work as farmers and miners. In 1942, after the bombing of Pearl Harbour, some 2,600 Japanese Canadians living on the British Columbia coast were relocated here and put to work in sugar beet fields.

Besides taking a contemplative walk through the garden, visitors can also participate in special events such as traditional tea ceremonies, moonlight tours, and viewing of exhibits by local artists.

## Indian Battle Park

**Route:** From Highway 3 in Lethbridge, head south on Scenic Drive and then west down a hill on 3rd Avenue to Indian Battle Park.

Indian Battle Park lies in the Oldman River Valley, cut here to a depth of nearly 100 metres below the level prairie. This sheltered spot in the heart of Lethbridge harbours coulees, slopes of native prairie grasses and flowers, and floodplains of cottonwood forest.

In fact, nature has outlasted civilization in the river valley. Repeated spring flooding drove residents to the prairie benchlands by 1960. Today, the continued erosion of coulees in Lethbridge is claiming urban backyards and threatening some houses.

The 102-hectare park also harbours history. The valley bottom is the site of the last great Aboriginal battle in North America, the

Walking below High Level Bridge in Indian Battle Park.

first white settlement in Lethbridge, the first coal mines in southern Alberta, and the world's highest/longest viaduct bridge.

The park is named for an 1870 battle between the Cree and Blackfoot that started in a coulee across the river and ended by today's Coal Banks Interpretive Site. The victorious Blackfoot called the area *asinaawa-iitomottaawa*, meaning "where we slaughtered the Cree," in reference to the estimated 350 Cree killed in the battle, compared with some 60 Blackfoot. A year later, a peace treaty was signed between the two nations.

The following attractions—Fort Whoop-Up, the Lethbridge Nature Reserve and Helen Schuler Coulee Centre, and the Coal Banks Interpretive Site—are all within Indian Battle Park.

### Fort Whoop-Up

**Note:** The fort is open daily from 10:00 a.m. to 5:00 p.m. from June 1 to September 30, with reduced hours the rest of the year. Admission charged. Phone 403-329-0444; www.fortwhoopup.com.

Fort Whoop-Up is a replica of the original 1869 post established by American whisky traders at the junction of the Oldman and St. Mary rivers, a short way downstream from this site. The fort's displays and hands-on interpretive programs tell the story of this lucrative, sordid, and short-lived chapter in southern Alberta's history.

No longer able to sell whisky on U.S. Indian reservations, the traders moved north of the 49th parallel in the late 1860s to sell their doctored brew. They found a ready market here: the Blackfoot were too weakened by white diseases to repel such intruders and the Hudson's Bay Company had largely abandoned its trading area in what was then the North-West Territories.

Originally known as Fort Hamilton, Fort Whoop-Up became the centre of a series of whisky trading posts in present-day southern Alberta. Here, traders sold "whisky" and rifles to the natives, primarily in exchange for buffalo hides used to make machinery belts in the burgeoning industrial factories of the eastern United States.

Typically, an 80-cent bottle of pure alcohol was substantially diluted and spiked with such ingredients as red ink, cough medicine, tobacco, gunpowder, and lye soap. A cup of this vile concoction was often sold for a buffalo hide worth six dollars. Through such trade in the 1870s, some 25,000 buffalo hides and 5,000 pelts of kit fox, wolf, coyote, badger, and antelope were shipped by oxen-pulled "bull trains" to Fort Benton, Montana.

This illegal trade prompted the formation of the North West Mounted Police. Arriving at Fort Whoop-Up in 1874, the Mounties found the traders had already fled. While the whisky traders were easily put to rout, it was by no means an end to drinking in the area. By 1885, the rugged coal-mining town of Lethbridge boasted 19 saloons and 3 breweries.

### Lethbridge Nature Reserve and Helen Schuler Nature Centre

**Note:** The Nature Centre is open daily from 10:00 a.m. to 6:00 p.m. from June through August, with reduced hours the rest of the year. Free, one-hour nature walks with an interpreter are also available on Sundays at 2:00 p.m. Phone 403-320-3064.

This 82-hectare nature reserve was set aside in the early 1960s to protect the area's diverse river valley habitats. The centre opened in 1982 to interpret these habitats to visitors. An expansion is doubling the building's size and enhancing its displays.

After an introduction at the centre, the reserve is best explored via its three interpretive walks, which amply demonstrate the valley's contrasting landscapes. On dry coulee slopes, you can find such desert-like species as prickly pear cactus and prairie rattlesnake. On the nearby floodplain are lush forests of tall cottonwoods that attract white-tailed deer, great horned owls, and a variety of songbirds.

Two of the trails, Nature Quest and Oxbow, are 1-kilometre loops that explore the floodplain along the Oldman River. The meandering river has carved this wide valley, its spring floods and deposits of sediment bringing renewed life to the valley bottom. The dominant trees in this riverine habitat are the magnificent stands of tall cottonwoods.

The several species of cottonwood found along southern Alberta's river valleys play an important role on the otherwise dry prairie. Many birds and deer live high in these forests, which offer shelter and food. Beneath the cottonwood canopy are often layers of shrubs, herbs, and grasses that add to the biological diversity. Even a dead cottonwood provides birds with cavities for nesting sites and with burrowing insects for food.

The cottonwood's biggest enemy is upstream dams, such as the Oldman Dam, which restrict spring flooding and thus prevent seeds from germinating. Research by the University of Lethbridge and Alberta Environment has led to altering the operations of such irrigation dams to help preserve these forests.

On the other side of the centre is the Coulee Climb, an interpretive trail into a much different world. The word "coulee" comes from the French *couler*, meaning to flow. In the Lethbridge area, coulees are steep-sided ravines cut primarily by surface runoff that drains from the prairies down into the Oldman River Valley. Most southern Alberta coulees are aligned 70 degrees east of north, suggesting they've also been formed by the strong chinook winds that tend to blow in that direction.

There's a marked difference in vegetation on the north- and south-facing slopes of coulees. The south-facing slopes, exposed to sun and drying winds, support desert-like plants such as cacti and prairie grasses adapted to low moisture levels. By contrast, the sheltered north-facing slopes absorb moisture, allowing shrubs of the valley to proliferate.

### Coal Banks Interpretive Site

Just inside the Lethbridge Nature Reserve is a small open-air kiosk near the entrance of a long-abandoned coal mine. The kiosk's few exhibits relate how coal mining put Lethbridge on the map and made it the first industrial town in Western Canada.

High Level Bridge spanning the Oldman River.

The first miner was Civil War veteran Nicholas Sheran, who arrived in 1874 to operate a ferry and to mine exposed seams of coal along the Oldman River banks. Sheran sold his coal to the whisky traders and later to the North West Mounted Police and to settlements in Fort Macleod and Fort Benton. His second mine was at Coal Banks, a translation of a Blackfoot word meaning "black rocks."

In 1882, a coal company formed by eastern businessman Sir Alexander Galt and his son Elliott began operating drift mines here to feed the steam engines of the new Canadian Pacific Railway (CPR). An inclined railway was built to transport coal from the valley mines up to the railway on the prairie level.

The company then shipped the coal to the CPR main line at Medicine Hat, first by a river steamer and barge operation and then by a narrow-gauge railway. This railway, under lease to the CPR, was later extended west through the Crowsnest Pass to the coal mines of southeastern British Columbia. To improve the crossing of the Oldman River at Lethbridge, the railway completed the High Level Bridge in 1909. At 1,624 metres long and 96 metres high, it's the largest bridge of its kind in the world and an aesthetic delight.

In the mid-1880s, the hamlet of Coalbanks sprang up at the entrance to these mines. Many families moved up to the flats in 1885, when the town of Lethbridge was laid out and named for a coal company president who never visited the town. Under the Galt empire, Lethbridge was a company town in its early years.

The family legacy is commemorated in the 🔥Sir Alexander Galt Museum at the top of the bluff. This splendid, recently expanded museum tells the area's history and provides stunning vistas over the river valley and surrounding prairie. The museum's website is at www.galtmuseum.com.

While coal and the railways launched Lethbridge, it was irrigation agriculture that finally put the town on a solid footing. Again it was Galt, at the urging of Mormon settlers at nearby Cardston, who initiated Alberta's first large-scale irrigation project at the turn of the century. Galt's sugar beet industry at Raymond and his model farm near Lethbridge proved irrigation agriculture could work in the dry south, prompting an influx of settlers until the outbreak of World War I.

### Cottonwood Park and Alexander Wilderness Park

**Route:** To reach Cottonwood Park from Highway 3 in Lethbridge, go south on Scenic Drive, west on Whoop-Up Drive, south on University Drive, and west on 60th Avenue. To get to Alexander Wilderness Park from Highway 3, go north on Stafford Drive.

While Indian Battle Park gets the most attention, and traffic, Lethbridge boasts a number of other fine parks in the Oldman River Valley. Perhaps the two best, and least visited, are Cottonwood Park, in the city's deep southwest, and Alexander Wilderness Park, in the far north. In these two nature reserves, one can take a tranquil morning walk, often with only a browsing deer or feeding white pelicans for company.

The 50-hectare Cottonwood Park contains one of southern Alberta's healthiest stands of floodplain cottonwoods, invigorated by a major flood of the Oldman River in 1995. From a superb viewpoint

Cottonwood Park in the Oldman River Valley of South Lethbridge.

at the parking lot, a walking trail drops sharply into the floodplain and then loops through a cottonwood forest and along the river's edge; a side trail is ringed with bluebird houses. Keep a wary eye out for prairie rattlesnakes, which have been reintroduced here in efforts to reverse their population decline in the area.

At the 42-hectare Alexander Wilderness Park, named for pioneering dairy farmer Lorenzo Alexander, a 2.5-kilometre looping trail descends from the lower of two parking lots and cuts through floodplains, coulees, and cottonwood stands. From the river's edge, watch for American white pelicans feeding in spring and summer.

## ⬥ ALBERTA BIRDS OF PREY CENTRE

**Route:** From Macleod Trail/Highway 2, at Calgary's south end, drive east on Highway 22X for 37 kilometres and then 125 kilometres south on Highway 24, which soon becomes Highway 23. At Nobleford, head east on Secondary 519 for 34 kilometres and then 15 kilometres south on Secondary 845 to Coaldale. The Birds of Prey Centre is located at 2124–16th Avenue.

**Driving Distance:** About 210 kilometres one way.
**Note:** The centre is open daily from 9:30 a.m. to 5:00 p.m. from mid-May to mid-September. Admission charged. Phone 403-345-4262; www.burrowingowl.com.

You wouldn't expect birds at the top of the food chain to need much hospital care. Yet a surprising number of hawks, eagles, falcons, and owls run afoul of barbed wire fences, power lines, vehicles, illegal hunters, and other hazards (including natural hazards). The Alberta Birds of Prey Centre in Coaldale is Canada's largest such facility, specializing in the rehabilitation and release of injured birds of prey. A visit to the centre offers a rare opportunity to see these birds up close and to watch a raptor demonstrate its flying skills.

The approach is a lovely country drive down the twisting Highway 23 towards Lethbridge (see pages 71–72). At Nobleford, the route swings east past a corn maze and close to the Prairie Tractor and Engine Society, which displays more than 100 antique farm machines and pieces of irrigation equipment. Just beyond is the town of Picture Butte, which bills itself as Canada's livestock feeding capital. Close to town is a reservoir with 2 kilometres of walking trails through a wetland that attracts pelicans and Canada geese.

Just east of Picture Butte, the route turns south and crosses the placid Oldman River, set in a valley of beautifully sculpted coulees. Not far beyond is Coaldale, a 6,000-person cattle and grain centre and home of the Alberta Birds of Prey Centre.

Started in 1989, the centre is located along 28 hectares of wetland, dredged from the prairie, which attracts nesting ducks, geese, and shorebirds and visiting ospreys and pelicans. Most of the centre's longer-term residents have, at least temporarily, lost that freedom of flight. Injured birds of prey are brought here to be repaired, rehabilitated, and returned to the wild. Some birds, however, can't safely be released, usually because they've lost their wildness or ability to fly.

Many of these raptors can be seen along the centre's Hawk Walk, sitting on perches with one leg secured by a soft leather strap. Birds on display here include various hawks, a golden eagle, a great horned

A trainer holds a Harris's hawk during a flying demonstration at Alberta Birds of Prey Centre.

owl, a peregrine falcon, and even a turkey vulture—once common when bison roamed the prairies but now rarely seen in Alberta.

Large enclosures nearby house such species as the short-eared owl, ferruginous hawk, and European eagle owl; the latter two are the world's largest species of hawk and owl. An eagle centre allows recovering bald and golden eagles to stretch their wings in a 2,600-square-metre, wire-enclosed exercise aviary. The centre has recently added a new wildlife rescue building and a $600,000 interpretive centre.

Some of the centre's recovering birds are turned loose for daily training and exercise. Trained hawks, falcons, and owls are used in flying demonstrations (every 90 minutes), in which a bird flies to the end of a field and then swoops back to the trainer's protected arm to receive its reward of a dead, day-old chick. Most raptors don't usually drink water, receiving their moisture from the flesh of their victims, which range in size from grasshoppers and mice to rabbits. Visitors can also slip on a leather gauntlet and have a live falcon or owl perch on their arm for a photo.

Despite the presence of some impressive aerial hunters, the Birds of Prey Centre's real star is a pocket-size owl that nests underground, usually in ground squirrel burrows. The burrowing owl is an endangered species on Alberta's prairies, the victim of vehicle collisions, farm pesticide use, and the loss of grasslands to crops. Operation Burrowing Owl attempts to reintroduce these birds to their native habitat and to educate landowners about the importance of their conservation. The Birds of Prey Centre plays its part by hosting a sizable captive breeding program that has released burrowing owl offspring into Canada's four Western provinces.

## EATS & DRINKS

**Coaldale Bakery** (1907–20th Avenue) features sourdough bread, raisin buns, and whipped-cream cakes. It also has a lunch counter and cappuccino bar.

# ♦ VILLAGE OF STIRLING NATIONAL HISTORIC SITE

**Route:** From the southeast outskirts of Lethbridge (see directions to Lethbridge from Calgary on page 71), drive 30 kilometres southeast on Highway 4 to Stirling.
**Driving Distance:** About 225 kilometres from Calgary through Lethbridge, via Highways 2 South and 3 East one way.
**Note:** Andreas Michelsen Farmstead (corner of 2nd Avenue and 6th Street) is open in July and August from 10:00 a.m. to noon and 1:00 p.m. to 5:00 p.m. Tuesday to Saturday. Phone 403-849-2290 • Galt Historic Railway Park (just north of Stirling on 4th Street) is open 11:00 a.m. to 7:00 p.m. Friday to Monday in July and August. Admission charged for both facilities. Phone 403-756-2220; www.stirling.ca.

This trip takes you back more than a century to a unique pioneer community. One of only three Canadian communities designated as National Historic Sites, Stirling is the country's best surviving example of a planned Mormon agricultural village—a unique blend of farm and town life.

A visit to Stirling features a tour of a beautifully preserved and well-furnished pioneer home, now a museum. You can also inspect a historic rail station that once straddled the Canada–U.S. border and stop at one of southern Alberta's best birdwatching sloughs. But the real star of this trip is the town's remarkable layout.

At first glance, Stirling looks like a typical southern Alberta town of 1,000, albeit with remarkably leafy streets considering the surrounding dry prairie. Such greenery and the unusually wide streets are, however, just initial clues that this place is different. What really distinguishes Stirling is the large number of 2.5-acre (1-hectare) residential lots.

They are the legacy of a planned Mormon town, a settlement blueprint arising from the religion's formative years in the eastern United States. The idea was to have large lots, each with a house, sizable vegetable garden, and livestock barn—with nearby fields for crops and grazing. This allowed homesteading families to live in a tightly knit community, instead of the scattered, isolated homes typical of prairie farm settlement. While other southern Alberta Mormon communities—such as Cardston, Raymond, and Magrath—were eventually more prosperous, only Stirling maintained much of its original design, hence the National Historic Site status.

After reading a brief history at a kiosk display near Stirling's entrance, stop at the village office (229–4th Avenue) to pick up a walking tour brochure. It lists more than 30 historical sites, nine of them well-preserved houses with descriptive plaques. These structures include a plainly painted barn and a statelier mansion, with a miniature train track meandering around the ample grounds. Scattered throughout the village are many other oversized lots, where horses and goats can be seen grazing next door to modern houses.

For an inside look at Stirling's pioneer life, head to the village's best-preserved pioneer house, the Andreas Michelsen Farmstead, which has been designated a provincial historic resource. Visitors can inspect the backyard barn and tour the house, being restored to represent the

House on a typical 2.5-acre (1-hectare) lot in Village of Stirling.

early decades of the 20th century, complete with an 1890s stove, tin kitchen countertops, and period furniture.

On the village's northern outskirts is the Galt Historic Railway Park, which houses a restored 1890 international train station filled with period railway artifacts. Relocated from the nearby Canada–U.S. border to Stirling in 2000, the station was once the international customs depot on a narrow-gauge railway that hauled coal and other goods between Lethbridge and Great Falls, Montana.

When the Alberta Railway and Coal Company built that line, it couldn't find buyers for even one of the million dry acres it received in compensation from the Canadian government. After meeting with company officials, the Utah-based Mormon Church agreed in 1898 to build a 50-mile-long (80-kilometre) irrigation canal from the St. Mary River through two prospective settlements, Magrath and Stirling. In exchange, the church received cash, farming land, and an agreement by the federal government to allow rural settlement in communities rather than on individual farms. Less than two gruelling years later, the canal was built and 250 residents were recruited for the brand new town on the unploughed prairie.

A few kilometres northwest of Stirling, it's worth stopping along the south side of Highway 4 at Michelsons' Marsh (road sign), a bird lover's paradise with a viewing platform overlooking the reedy waters. In spring, it's one of the first stopovers in Canada for tens of thousands of migrating ducks and geese. In fall, tundra swans and snow geese pause here on their long journey south. You can also look for nesting waterfowl, shorebirds, muskrats, mink, coyotes, and deer.

## CARDSTON AND REMINGTON CARRIAGE MUSEUM

**Route:** From the Highway 22X overpass, drive 210 kilometres south on Highway 2 to Cardston. The Carriage Museum is located on Main Street.
**Note:** The Remington Carriage Museum is open daily 9:00 a.m. to 5:00 p.m. June through August and 9:00 a.m. to 4:00 p.m. the rest of the year. Admission charged. Phone 403-653-5139; www.history.alberta.ca/remington.

A day trip to Cardston might seem a long haul at two-plus hours of driving. But consider the drivers of oxen-propelled bull trains in the late 19th century, who'd feel fortunate to cover 25 kilometres in a day. If you can't imagine those dark ages, a visit to the $12.4-million Remington Carriage Museum will certainly acquaint you with the long-forgotten era of the horse-drawn carriage. While in Cardston, it's also worth visiting the famed Mormon Alberta Temple and touring the restored historic downtown.

Reach Cardston by driving south on Highway 2 from Fort Macleod. The high, open plains here provide expansive views of Alberta's southern Rocky Mountains to the west and some mini badlands to the east. The most impressive peak is Chief Mountain, just across the U.S. border. This massive chunk of rock, separated by erosion from the surrounding peaks, is a sacred mountain to the Blackfoot. Young Aboriginal males still ascend the peak in search of a spirit to guide their lives.

Driving south on Highway 2 towards Cardston.

The highway soon drops and crosses, in quick succession, the Waterton and Belly rivers, which flow northeast to join the Oldman River. Their ample floodplains are cloaked in tall cottonwoods, poplars, and shrubs, providing a rich habitat for wildlife on these otherwise treeless plains.

Just beyond the rivers, the road passes through the Blood reserve, the largest reserve in Canada. The 7,500-member band operates a sizable farm and ranch, launched at the turn of the 20th century. Historically a nomadic, buffalo-hunting people reputed to be fierce warriors, the Bloods by the mid-19th century were trading with the American Fur Company and the Hudson's Bay Company. In 1872, they burned down Conrad's Post, a new American whiskey-trading fort. Soon after, they signed Treaty No. 7 with the Canadian government and in 1880 moved onto the reserve.

The clean, quiet town of Cardston (www.cardston.ca) is nestled in the foothills of southwestern Alberta, a short drive from Waterton National Park. The provincial Main Street Program has led to the restoration of building facades dating to 1890. Also on Main

Street is the Fay Wray Fountain, honouring the actress born on a nearby ranch who became one of Hollywood's biggest early stars. Another attractive historic building is the Courthouse Museum (89–3rd Avenue W), housed in a 1907 sandstone structure that was one of Alberta's first courthouses.

A less conspicuous but key historic site is the little log house (337 Main Street) built in 1887 by the founder of Cardston, Charles Ora Card. That year, Card led 10 families from Utah by covered wagon to establish a Mormon colony here. Free from religious persecution south of the border, these immigrants settled in mud-chinked log houses and in the late 1890s helped develop Alberta's first major irrigation system.

In 1923, they completed the Alberta Temple (348–3rd Street W), the first such Mormon structure outside the continental United States. One of only two such temples in Canada, it now serves some 70,000 Latter-day Saints in Western Canada and Montana. Recently restored, this massive geometric structure maintains a commanding presence over Cardston from its hilltop perch. While the temple is open only to Mormons in good standing, the general public can tour a visitor centre at its entrance.

The major tourist draw in Cardston is the Remington Carriage Museum, named the best indoor attraction in Canada in 2002. It was the vision of local rancher and businessman Don Remington, who restored 49 carriages, creating the basis for the current collection of more than 240 horse-drawn vehicles, the largest in North America. They range from the crude bull train wagons to elegant carriages that whisked the aristocracy to social functions. At this hands-on facility, you can sink into deep leather seats, learn how to handle buggy reins, discover the etiquette of riding in New York's Central Park, or even go for a real horse-drawn carriage ride along Lee Creek.

Allow at least two hours to tour the museum, which covers the golden era of the horse-drawn carriage in detail. It's hard to believe now that such carriages were an all-purpose means of transportation.

They were used to haul goods, build roads, shelter shepherds, deliver milk, fight fires, and transport passengers.

Fuelled by rapid industrial expansion in the late 19th century, the carriage trade boomed. Several thousand companies built carriages, the largest of them producing 100,000 vehicles per year in a variety of styles. Foreshadowing the development of the automobile, carriage makers introduced such concepts as mass production and showrooms, called repositories.

Those properly worried about car pollution today should consider that in late 19th-century New York City, there were more than 175,000 horses, each producing some 9 litres of urine and 22 kilograms of excrement per day. Imagine wading across those infested streets in a petticoat.

The museum tells this and many other stories through imaginative displays and more audiovisual presentations than you can shake a riding crop at. After touring the exhibit hall, visitors can wander through a livery stable, help harness a fibreglass horse in the tack room, and watch faded carriages restored to shining life by craftsmen in the restoration shop. The highlight for many will be taking an outdoor ride in a Yellowstone coach—once a popular tourist vehicle in U.S. national parks—drawn by two Clydesdale horses.

The introduction of the horseless carriage, at first considered a vulgar and passing fad, all but eliminated the horse-pulled variety by 1920. Some continued to be used until the 1950s, particularly on farms and in the delivery of milk and other goods. In recent years, the horse-drawn carriage has been regaining popularity as a recreational vehicle that harkens back to an era when life was more leisurely.

## EATS & DRINKS

In Cardston, the **Cobblestone Manor** (173–7th Avenue W), built in the late 1880s and later outfitted with river rock cladding, exotic hardwoods, and Tiffany glass lamps, is designated an Alberta historic resource. For day trippers, the manor's restaurant offers breakfast and lunch.

# North

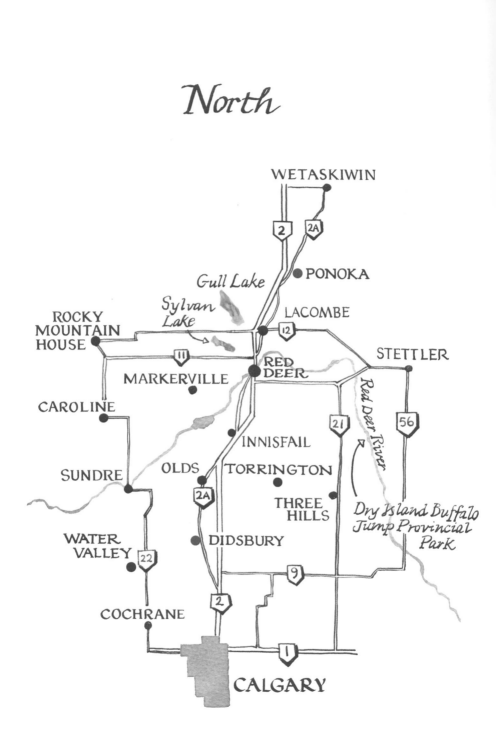

# NORTH OF CALGARY

For many Calgarians, any trips taken north of the city follow the straight and narrow four-lane Highway 2 to Edmonton. While the passing farmland is pleasant enough, this no-nonsense route misses some of the most appealing parts of Alberta.

Perhaps the most pleasant surprise for the adventurous day tripper is the countryside east of Highway 2 and north of Drumheller. Far from being dreary prairie, this is an enchanting land of hummocky hills and intimate valleys. In summer and fall, the surrounding fields are vibrant shades of green and yellow.

So, too, are all the rich farmlands of central Alberta, which seem to be immeasurably enhanced when bisected by a narrow strip of undulating highway. The black soils that reach their productive peak in the Red Deer area yield bumper crops of barley, wheat, canola, and hay, and sustain beef, cattle, and hog operations. One trip journeys to the Markerville area, where immigrants from a diversity of countries arrived to farm.

Much of central Alberta is located in the aspen parkland region, a meeting place of the southern prairies and northern forests. This region also contains several fine recreational lakes, which the day tripper can sample at Sylvan and Gull lakes. Unfortunately, many of the native trees and prairie grasses in the parkland have been removed or ploughed under to take advantage of the fertile soils.

Some remnants of native landscapes, however, have been preserved and can be visited on these northern trips. They include the Rumsey Ecological Reserve, north of Drumheller, and the Red Deer

River Valley, which in places like Dry Island Buffalo Jump Provincial Park provide spectacular examples of badlands terrain. Such sites also preserve the archaeological remains of First Nations camps, ranging from the prehistoric era to the 1800s, when the Cree and Blackfoot ruled this area.

Other northern trips into history can be taken by boarding an old-fashioned steam train in Stettler, viewing the restored antique cars at the Reynolds-Alberta Museum in Wetaskiwin, or travelling through the forested foothills to Rocky Mountain House, the site of several fur-trading posts.

## BALZAC-AIRDRIE LOOP

**Route:** From the Country Hills Boulevard overpass, drive 6 kilometres north on Highway 2 and then west through Balzac on Secondary 566 for 11 kilometres. Head north on Secondary 772 for 32 kilometres to Madden, turning east on Secondary 574 to reach Crossfield in another 18 kilometres. Go south on Highway 2A and then Highway 2 to reach Airdrie. Return to Calgary by going west on Secondary 567 for 12 kilometres and then south on 772 through Simon's Valley to reach the city limits.

**Driving Distance:** About 120 kilometres return.

**Note:** Nose Creek Valley Museum (1701 Main Street SW) in Airdrie is open daily from 10:00 a.m. to 5:00 p.m. weekdays and 1:00 p.m. to 4:30 p.m. weekends from June through August, with reduced hours the rest of the year. Admission charged. Phone 403-948-6685; www.nosecreekvalleymuseum.com.

This trip offers a quick escape from Calgary and a nice drive through the rolling countryside just beyond the city's encroaching and insatiable northern reach. It also includes a stop in the smaller but rapidly growing satellite community of Airdrie. Enjoy this drive while you can, before more of this lovely landscape and productive farmland disappears under the developer's bulldozer.

It's only a few kilometres north along the frenzied Highway 2 before the quiet exit to Balzac, named after 19th-century French novelist Honoré de Balzac. The hamlet is a whistle stop, consisting of a collection of houses, two old churches, a 1929 community hall, a seed-cleaning plant, and the sizable Balzac Garden Centre, its greenhouses overflowing with flowering plants and featuring a carp-filled pool. Behind the greenhouses, a pathway leads around a lovely alpine garden, with sandstone steps descending to a small pond.

Heading west, the road passes through lovely undulating ranchland, home to the nearby livestock research firm Alberta Genetics and the Girletz Rodeo Ranch, which stages rodeos, barbecues, and western barn dances. To the south are occasional glimpses of the big city, inching inexorably north with new subdivisions and outpost acreages.

Between 1986 and 1996, the population in rural areas adjacent to Calgary increased by more than 80 percent, and growth in this so-called exurbia hasn't slowed since. More recently, some 1,870 hectares of farmland in the Municipal District of Rockyview—surrounding Calgary on every side except the south—have been taken out of agricultural production and nearly all converted to residential use.

But as you swing north on Secondary 772, the city recedes in the rearview mirror, replaced by adjacent deep valleys and panoramic views stretching to the mountains. The road passes Colpitts Ranch, established in 1913 and still using three old, low-slung barns, in sharp contrast to an abandoned barn and homestead farther north.

About 17 kilometres north of Colpitts Ranch, a gravel side road drops into a deep valley, passing brightly coloured bluebird houses and the Alberta Institute for Wildlife Conservation. The institute's trauma centre, located in a renovated church and surrounded by outdoor enclosures, treats more than 1,500 injured or orphaned wild birds and animals a year.

Back on Secondary 772, another grand valley is skirted shortly before you enter the hamlet of Madden, which features an old community hall. From here, it's a short drive east to Crossfield (see pages 97–98) and then south to Airdrie, a booming bedroom community of Calgary that grew from 16,000 residents in 1996 to 46,000 in 2012.

Named after a Scottish village, Airdrie is thought to mean "the King's Heights"—an apt name as its mean elevation is 1,089 metres. While Calgary contains some higher hills, its mean elevation is 1,046 metres, leaving Airdrie as officially Canada's second-highest city, behind only the 1,110 metres of Kimberley, B.C., though the latter's population of just 6,500 makes it more of a town.

Established in 1889, Airdrie soon became an important station along the Calgary and Edmonton Railway, as the steam engines could be fed by the year-round, low-alkaline waters from nearby Nose Creek. The arrival of settlers and a post office led to a flurry of construction in the early 1900s, the first of several Airdrie booms. To learn more about the area's history, visit the Nose Creek Valley Museum.

While in the city, stop for a picnic or a walk in the central Nose Creek Park, which includes a pond, natural areas, and nice pathways. Those seeking more adventure can visit one of Canada's largest BMX tracks. In honour of Airdrie's railway past, a 2.4-kilometre miniature railway is being built in Iron Horse Park, complete with a steam locomotive, small-scale towns, and mountain passes. (www.ironhorsepark.net)

Though one can drive straight back to Calgary via Highway 2, a much more scenic alternative is to go west from Airdrie on Secondary 567 and then south on 772, which follows meandering West Nose Creek through the narrow Simon's Valley, flanked by sandstone outcrops and hoodoos. This peaceful drive suddenly gives way to the city's crush at Country Hills Boulevard, just west of Deerfoot Trail.

---

### EATS & DRINKS

In Airdrie, stop at **Paul's Pizza & Steak House** ( 528–2nd Avenue SE) and **Sushi Haru** (400 Main Street W).

# CARSTAIRS-DIDSBURY LOOP

**Route:** From the Country Hills Boulevard overpass, drive 26 kilometres north on Highway 2, taking the Crossfield exit. Continue north on the parallel Highway 2A for 22 kilometres to Carstairs and another 11 kilometres to reach Didsbury. From Didsbury, go 13 kilometres west on Secondary 582 and then about 60 kilometres south on Secondary 766 to reach Highway 1A, just outside Calgary's city limits.
**Driving Distance:** About 140 kilometres return.
**Note:** The Roulston Museum in Carstairs (1138 Nanton Street) is open 1:00 p.m. to 4:00 p.m. Tuesday to Sunday from May to September and 1:00 p.m. to 4:00 p.m. Wednesday to Friday the rest of the year. Admission by donation. Phone 403-337-3710. • The Didsbury Museum (2110–21st Avenue) is open 10:00 a.m. to noon and 1:00 p.m. to 4:00 p.m. Tuesday and Wednesday, and 1:00 p.m. to 4:00 p.m. Saturday. Admission charged. Phone 403-335-9295.

Most motorists heading north of Calgary instinctively join the pedal-to-the-metal throngs on Highway 2. But it's worth slowing down for a leisurely tour along the parallel Highway 2A to the overlooked towns of Carstairs, Crossfield, and Didsbury, which boast a rich history. The return journey is a nice drive through the countryside north of Calgary.

Once stopping points on the old Calgary and Edmonton Railway and its replacement highway, the three towns were left on the relative backwater of Highway 2A when it was superseded by the high-speed Highway 2 in the 1950s. But today these are thriving communities, thanks to agriculture, oil and gas activity, light manufacturing, and housing development for a booming number of commuters to Calgary.

The tour begins in earnest just north of Airdrie, where you leave Highway 2 at the Crossfield exit for the decidedly quieter 2A. The road soon passes the sizable East Crossfield Gas Plant, which processes raw sour natural gas from area wells and stores sweet gas. During sour gas processing, sulphur is recovered and stored as bright yellow blocks until sold, primarily for making phosphate fertilizer. Just beyond is a marsh and then a large concrete granary, one of the modern, utilitarian replacements for the rapidly vanishing and lovely wooden elevators of the Canadian Prairies.

At 1,126 metres, the nearby town of Crossfield is the highest point between Calgary and Edmonton and one of the loftier communities in Canada, offering fine mountain views to the west. It started life as an 1890 stopping house on the old Calgary-Edmonton wagon trail and became a siding station when the replacement railway arrived two years later; it was named for railway survey engineer William Crossfield. A village until 1980, Crossfield is now a burgeoning town of 3,500, with several rapidly filling new subdivisions.

Just south of Carstairs, it's worth taking a short detour east on a signed road to Joe Lucas' West World, offering genuine cowboy tack along with western art and accessories. The store specializes in cowboy ropes, not surprising considering Lucas is a four-time Canadian calf-roping champion. With luck, a calf-roping competition or junior roping clinic might be going on in the ring behind the store.

Carstairs, named for the Scottish town that produced the Clydesdale horse, boasts one of the best small-town museums in central Alberta. Located in a historic Presbyterian church, the Roulston Museum has well-tended collections of such things as old phones, irons, and woodworking tools. Next door is the 1901 McCaig House, restored and furnished and only slightly the worse for wear from a recent fire.

The town's most famous resident was Henry Wise Wood, who in his mid-forties left Missouri to farm in early 20th-century Alberta. A pioneering farm organizer, he became president of the United Farmers of Alberta—which formed the province's second government, in 1921—and helped establish the Alberta Wheat Pool.

A short drive to the north passes through the lovely upper Rosebud Valley and leads to Didsbury—a regional centre with a population of 5,000 and businesses as diverse as a cheese plant and a cubed-hay facility that exports to Japan. The town's first settlers were Dutch Mennonites, who had earlier emigrated from Pennsylvania to Ontario as United Empire Loyalists. In 1894, at the request of Prime Minister

The Didsbury Museum is in a 1907 sandstone and brick school.

John A. Macdonald, Jacob Shantz led a group from Ontario to establish a western Mennonite community in Didsbury. Although development was initially slow and the first railway station wasn't built until 1897, a building boom was well under way by the turn of the century, with other groups and religions becoming predominant.

Like many prairie towns with wooden buildings, Didsbury lost much of its downtown to devastating fires in 1914 and 1924. Many of the replacement structures, built of brick and stone, have been nicely restored through the Alberta Main Street Program. They provide an excellent example of the boom town style of prairie architecture, with adjacent buildings sharing storefront facades. Interesting buildings along the main street include one of Alberta's few remaining "cast stone" buildings, for which concrete blocks were fashioned to resemble sandstone, and a former business that combined furniture sales with an embalming studio.

A walking tour brochure of Didsbury's historic buildings can be picked up at the visitor centre, in the old train station. The nearby Didsbury Museum, located in a 1907 sandstone and brick school that is designated a provincial historic resource, contains many artifacts, including a wreath made of human hair.

Heading west from Didsbury on Secondary 582, rolling, wooded farmland soon replaces civilization. This tranquil drive continues as you turn south on Secondary 766, which follows a branch of the Red Deer River. Closer to Calgary is distinctively humpy knob-and-kettle terrain, formed by stagnating glaciers.

---

**EATS & DRINKS**

In Carstairs, the **Fireside Place** (115–10th Avenue)—incorporating old beams, walls, and floors from the attached Dominion Hotel—has nice lunches. In Didsbury, visit **Mugs Coffee House** (1912–20th Street).

---

## WATER VALLEY LOOP

**Route:** Drive to Cochrane from Calgary via Highway 22 or 1A. From its junction with Highway 1A, drive north on Highway 22 for 25 kilometres, taking a 2-kilometre detour west to reach Bottrel. Returning to Highway 22, go north for 11 kilometres and then west on Secondary 579 for 8 kilometres to reach Water Valley. Continue west on 579 for 41 kilometres and then south on Highway 40 for 6 kilometres to the Waiparous Valley. Go west on a narrow gravel road for 3 kilometres and, taking a right fork across a bridged creek, go another 1 kilometre, parking at the base of the Mockingbird Fire Lookout road. Back on Highway 40, drive 40 kilometres south to reach Highway 1A, 13 kilometres west of Cochrane.

**Driving Distance:** About 150 kilometres return from Cochrane.

**Note:** The hike to the Mockingbird Fire Lookout is 3.2 kilometres one way up a fire road, with an elevation gain of some 350 metres.

This is a fine farm and forest loop through the scenic and lightly travelled foothills northwest of Calgary. The trip features stops at the history-rich hamlets of Bottrel and Water Valley and a hike to a forest fire lookout, providing expansive views of Front Range mountains.

Heading north on Highway 22 from Cochrane—one of Canada's fastest-growing towns—the booming subdivisions soon give way to rolling hills of aspen and small farms, primarily producing forage crops for numerous area ranches. The hillcrest views keep improving as the landscape opens to the north, with mountain glimpses to the west. The side roads in the region are popular among bird watchers, especially in the winter, when several species of owls can be spotted.

A short detour west leads to Bottrel and its 1901 general store, once a cheese factory and now offering everything from snacks to livestock feed (motto: "If we ain't got it, you don't need it"). In the 1890s, Mormons from the south helped pioneer farmers develop irrigation ditches, traces of which are still evident. Drought, though, was seldom a problem in this forested valley and certainly not in June 2005, when heavy rains caused tiny Dogpound Creek to rise more than four metres, devastating the century-old campground and badly damaging the store. A post-flood benefit to help save the store included a chance to win stud services from two stallions.

It's not far north to Water Valley, a hamlet of some 100 residents with an area population of 1,100—thanks largely to a growing number of acreage and vacation property owners. The traffic certainly swells in late June for the annual Traditional Celtic Folk Festival, a one-day event featuring some 60 musicians, dancers, and storytellers performing on a handful of stages. On a similar theme, the Chinook Creative Arts Centre operates in the hamlet's old school, designated a provincial historic resource.

As you head west, Secondary 579 drops steeply into the Little Red Deer River Valley and past William J. Bagnall Wilderness Park, which offers camping and some trails. The gravel road beyond follows the Little Red Deer River as it winds through forests of aspen, spruce, and pine interspersed with ranches, some of which offer horseback riding and overnight stays. There's also good natural grazing along open meadows, and farther west motorists should watch for cattle wandering onto the road. You might also spot people fishing the river for brown trout in deeper pools.

About 23 kilometres west of Water Valley, Secondary 579 enters the Rocky Mountains Forest Reserve, which despite the name does allow logging, oil and gas exploration, and grazing. Although a sign warns that the ensuing road isn't recommended for travel, it usually seems to get no worse. It is, however, more narrow and winding as it descends a long slope just before reaching the gravel Forestry Trunk Road (Highway 40).

Just before you reach the Waiparous Valley, a few kilometres to the south, it's worth the short drive up to a signed viewpoint on the east side of Highway 40. To the west are good views of Black Rock Mountain, the impressive rock face on Devil's Head and, on the distant Banff National Park boundary, Mount Aylmer.

If you'd like closer and more expansive views, plus some exercise, drive another kilometre south and take a side road west, past Mockingbird Camp, to the base of the Mockingbird Fire Lookout. It's about an hour's hike up the fire road through forest, along a ridge, and finally through meadows. The lookout—the second such building on the site—has been active since the early 1950s, when it replaced the lookout on Black Rock, to the southwest. Farther south is another lookout atop the naked brown slopes of Moose Mountain.

In the foreground, Waiparous Creek (*waiparous* is a Stoney word for "crow scalp") winds through the rocky valley. Though it might appear a wilderness from this distance, the valley is a popular spot for off-road vehicles, random camping, and often-boisterous long-weekend parties. The Alberta government has been working with various user groups to draw up a new management plan for the Waiparous and Ghost regions that will perhaps lessen the impact on these landscapes.

The lands in this area have a long history. For evidence, continue 4 kilometres south on Highway 40 to the Ghost Airstrip Provincial Recreation Area, where a roadside interpretive trail follows Waiparous Creek through forest. Across the creek from the parking lot are the remains of an old flood dam, from which water would be released in the spring to flush winter-cut logs down the creek to the Ghost River and eventually the Bow River mill in Calgary. The series of three dams was abandoned when the mill closed in 1945.

Continue south on Highway 40 past the entrance to the Ghost River Valley (see pages 217–21) and onto rough pavement, which winds through the small communities of Waiparous and Benchlands, emerging into a broad grassy valley flanked by hills. Highway 1A is soon reached, just west of Cochrane.

> ═══════ EATS & DRINKS ═══════
>
> In Water Valley, visit the colourful **Water Valley Saloon** and, for snacks, the **Water Valley General Store**.

# ♠ ROCKY MOUNTAIN HOUSE NATIONAL HISTORIC SITE

**Route:** Drive to Cochrane from Calgary via Highway 22 or 1A. From near the west end of Cochrane, head north for 150 kilometres on Highway 22, which takes short jogs west near Sundre and Caroline. The final 7 kilometres to Rocky Mountain House are west on Highway 11. Rocky Mountain House National Historic Site is 7 kilometres west of town via Highway 11A.
**Driving Distance:** About 190 kilometres one way.
**Note:** Rocky Mountain House National Historic Site is open 10:00 a.m. to 5:00 p.m. from July to Labour Day, with reduced hours till early October. Admission charged. Phone 403-845-2412; www.pc.gc.ca/rockymountainhouse.

Rocky Mountain House National Historic Site is the scene of a fascinating chapter in the fur-trading history of Western Canada. Beginning in 1799, a series of forts operated here as a base for trading with Aboriginal peoples and exploring farther west. Despite limited success in either endeavour, the forts persisted until 1875.

Today, the area is preserved as a National Historic Site. Visitors can tour a recently renovated interpretive centre and take short walks along the North Saskatchewan River past the sites of four forts, fur-trading artifacts, and a buffalo paddock. Interpretive displays and programs are offered throughout the park in summer.

The route from Calgary to Rocky Mountain House follows the edge of the lower foothills into the boreal forest of west-central Alberta. North of Cochrane, there are impressive views of the mountains, which soon angle away to the northwest. The rolling terrain is dotted with farms and ranches cut from a cover of aspen that progressively gives way to spruce. North of the Red Deer River, the boggy lowlands support extensive stands of American larch, which have deciduous needles that turn a stunning gold in the fall.

Not surprisingly, logging is an economic staple in this heavily forested region. So, too, is oil and gas, particularly the removal of large quantities of sour gas, so-called because of its high concentrations of poisonous hydrogen sulphide. North of Sundre is the $1-billion Caroline gas plant, completed in 1992 to exploit a deep field containing some 2 trillion cubic feet (30 billion cubic metres) of sour gas.

The sparkling foothill rivers also attract whitewater boaters and anglers. The nearby town of Caroline is famous for two things: the wary brown trout in nearby streams and multiple world figure skating champion Kurt Browning.

Rocky Mountain House is the economic hub of this region with a population of 7,000. It also serves as central Alberta's gateway to the mountains. The scenic David Thompson Highway, which intersects the Icefields Parkway north of Lake Louise, is well worth taking as an alternative return to Calgary if time permits.

The major attraction here is Rocky Mountain House National Historic Site, located along the north shore of the North Saskatchewan River. The 228-hectare site protects the remains of four historic forts, a burial ground, archaeological sites, and the surrounding natural landscape of forest, meadows, and riverfront. Recently renovated, the visitor centre tells the area's fur-trading history through exhibits of Aboriginal artifacts, archaeological discoveries, a replica trading room, several videos, and a puppet show. A children's play fort is nearby.

An interpreter in period costume at Rocky Mountain House National Historic Site.

You can learn much more by taking two interpretive walks, on your own or with a guide. The longer, 3.2-kilometre David Thompson Trail loop takes visitors to the sites of the first two forts, built in 1799 by fur-trading rivals, the North West Company and the Hudson's Bay Company. The two merged under the latter's name in 1821 and continued operating its fort here until 1835. The original intention of trading with the Kootenai on the west side of the Rocky Mountains never materialized. Instead, Rocky Mountain House served the rival northern Plains peoples, principally the Blackfoot Nation, which consisted of the Peigan, Blood, and Blackfoot tribes. But other than a brief period during the 1820s, the trade for beaver pelts and, later, buffalo hides never prospered.

David Thompson, arguably the greatest map-maker in western Canadian history, used the North West Company fort as a base for his explorations through the mountains. Thompson's plans to forge a route from Rocky Mountain House through Howse Pass to the West Coast were thwarted in 1810 by the Peigan, who wanted to prevent trade with the Kootenai. Thompson was forced to develop a more northerly route through Athabasca Pass near Jasper.

Near the 1799 fort sites are replicas of the large York boats, used by the Hudson's Bay Company to transport goods, and the birch-bark canoes of the North West Company. Each year, voyageurs would make the round trip on the rivers between Rocky Mountain House and Lake Superior.

The food staple for these gruelling trips can be found in the nearby buffalo paddock. The Nor'Westers learned from native people to dry buffalo meat into pemmican, a highly concentrated source of protein that saved the voyageurs from having to hunt for fresh meat during their paddling expeditions.

The shorter, 900-metre Chimney Trail loops past the sites of the 1835–61 and 1864–75 forts. The former was abandoned, and then burned to the ground by a band of Blackfoot. Two chimneys from the latter are the only visible structural remains of the fur-trading era here.

The last fort closed in 1875, when the Hudson's Bay Company was convinced it was safe to build a post on the plains south of Rocky Mountain House. By then, the North West Mounted Police had arrived, and the once-feared Blackfoot had been decimated by smallpox and the disappearance of the buffalo.

---

## ═══ EATS & DRINKS ═══

Eight kilometres west of Caroline on Highway 22, **Clearwater Trading** advertises the largest ice cream cones in the West, while **Little Country Cappuccino** (105 Centre Street N) in Sundre has good soups and sandwiches.

# WOOL TOUR

**Route:** From the Country Hills Boulevard overpass, drive 6.4 kilometres north on Highway 2, 22 kilometres east on Secondary 566, and 26 kilometres north on Highway 9. From Beiseker, continue north on Secondary 806 to Linden and then 15 kilometres west to reach Custom Woolen Mills. From the mill, drive south on a gravel road to Secondary 581, which is followed west across Highway 2 to Carstairs. Follow the signs west and south to PaSu Farm.

**Driving Distance:** About 140 kilometres one way.

**Note:** Custom Woolen Mills (www.customwoolenmills.com) is open for self-guided tours 9:00 a.m. to 3:00 p.m. Monday to Friday. Phone 403-337-2221. • PaSu Farm (www.pasu.com) is open 10:00 a.m. to 5:00 p.m. Tuesday through Saturday and noon to 5:00 p.m. Sunday. Phone toll free 1-800-679-7999.

Alberta is cattle country. The pre-eminence of the barons of beef is obvious to anyone touring the ranchlands or passing the feedlots of southern and central Alberta. Yet there's a small but growing sheep industry in the province. More people are eating tender farm-raised lamb and buying woollen garments with a "Made in Alberta" stamp.

This outing tours the farmland of south-central Alberta en route to two unique sheep-based establishments. The first destination is Custom Woolen Mills, where raw wool is processed into various pro-ducts using machinery normally found in a museum. The second stop is to the west at PaSu Farm, a working sheep farm with the added comfort of a retail gallery and a high-ceilinged dining room.

Early on, the odds were stacked against sheep on the prairies. In 1881, much of the arable land in southwest Alberta was carved into 100,000-acre (40,470-hectare) ranching leases and stocked with grazing cattle. One of these giant spreads, at Cochrane, briefly replaced cows with 8,000 sheep, herded north from Montana. A spring snowstorm, a prairie fire, and low prices spelled the end of the sheep operation within three years. Farther east, entrepreneurial Englishman Sir John Lister-Kaye brought an even larger sheep herd north, but this, too, failed.

These experiments were the exception. While this area was spared the range wars waged between U.S. cattle ranchers and sheep farmers, federal legislation restricted sheep grazing leases in Western Canada until 1903.

The route to Custom Woolen Mills is a pleasant drive through farmland northeast of Calgary. The urban sprawl is quickly replaced by rural solitude on narrow highways bordered by fields of grain, sloughs, and roadside grasses.

Highway 9 passes through Irricana, settled in the early 1900s when both Canadian Pacific and Canadian Northern built railways through the village. The name comes from the irrigation canals that flowed through this productive farmland. Just outside Irricana is Pioneer Acres (www.pioneeracres.ab.ca), home of a plowmen's and threshermen's club and an impressive collection of vintage farm machinery. In early August, the club hosts a show and reunion that one year attracted 8,000 people.

Just beyond Irricana is Beiseker (town mascot is a 4-metre-high skunk), where a restored 1910 CPR station is now home to a museum, library, and village office. Farther north, the road drops into a valley near the junction of Kneehill and Lonepine creeks, which eventually empty into the Red Deer River near Drumheller.

Nearby is Linden, a village of 700 people situated in a lovely coulee. Settled in 1902 by Mennonite farmers, it has overcome the lack of a railway and grain elevators by building an agriculture-based manufacturing industry that includes a feed mill and truck parts manufacturer.

On farmland west of Linden is Custom Woolen Mills, the only complete wool-processing plant still operating in Western Canada. This is a virtual working museum because its wool is produced on carding machines, spinning mules, and other machinery dating back to 1868. The small plant, owned by Fenn Roessingh and husband Bill Purves-Smith, is open during operating hours to curious visitors who can watch the smoothly clicking and whirring antiquities at work.

All the mill's products are made from virgin wool sheared off western Canadian sheep. Because these sheep live in a cold climate,

Custom Woolen Mills and its historic wool-processing machinery.

their wool has more loft and is often of better quality than imported wools. The raw wool is turned into natural-fibre comforters, mattress pads, sleeping bags, and socks, as well as carded wools and yarns for knitting. These and other products are sold in a small gift shop and by mail order to customers across Canada.

From Custom Woolen Mills, it's a half-hour's drive west on gravel highways to PaSu Farm. Along the way, the road passes through Carstairs, established as a ranching community and now also serving dairy and grain industries.

PaSu, named for owners Pat and Sue deRosemond, is a working ranch that features some 12 breeds of sheep, many of which spend their summers grazing in hills to the west. The meat is sold to retail markets, and the wool is processed at Custom Woolen Mills to produce such items as wool blankets. These and other products—including moccasins, fine wool fashions, sheepskin coats, and hides—are sold in an extensive gift shop. Attached to the shop is an airy restaurant that opens onto a yard, where visitors can pet the sheep and admire the view of distant mountains.

**≡ EATS & DRINKS ≡**

In Linden, stop at **Global Grounds** (107 Central Avenue E) for coffee and muffins. **Country Cousins Bistro** (101–1st Street NE) offers a fine and very popular Mennonite lunch buffet, featuring sausage, new potatoes, and broccoli and cauliflower salads. Be sure to try the famous peanut butter pie. **PaSu Farm**'s restaurant offers fine lunches and dinners and, on Sundays, a brunch and an afternoon tea. The feature, of course, is fresh lamb.

# ◆ TORRINGTON GOPHER HOLE MUSEUM AND OLDS

**Route:** From the Country Hills Boulevard overpass, drive 71 kilometres north on Highway 2. To reach Torrington, go 30 kilometres east on Highway 27. To reach Olds, drive 5 kilometres west on Highway 27. Olds College is on the eastern outskirts of town, along Highway 2A.

**Driving Distance:** About 135 kilometres one way.

**Note:** The Torrington Gopher Hole Museum is open 10:00 a.m. to 5:00 p.m. daily from June 1 to September 30. Admission charged. Phone 403-631-2133.

• Walking tour maps of the botanic gardens at Olds College are available in the Administration Building, near the college's main entrance off Highway 2A. Phone 403-556-8281 or toll free 1-800-661-6537; www.oldscollege.ca.

The museum is scarcely bigger than a trailer, located along a secondary highway few would normally bother to investigate. And it's entirely dedicated to a rodent most farm folk consider a pest and most motorists view as roadkill.

Yet the Torrington Gopher Hole Museum is a magnet for curious tourists and media coverage from around the world, putting this central Alberta village on the map. It's worth a visit or at least a detour of an hour or two off Highway 2 between Calgary and Red Deer. You can finish the trip by visiting the town of Olds and touring the grounds and gardens of Olds College.

After exiting frenetic Highway 2, it's a pleasant drive east on Highway 27 through rolling farmland to Torrington. From its elevated perch, the village offers expansive views north and west, with the Rocky Mountains visible on the far horizon. The gopher theme is immediately apparent, with a statue of Clem T. GoFur at the village entrance and a dozen fire hydrants colourfully painted to resemble members of Clem's extended clan.

But the real shrine is the Gopher Hole Museum. Its 40-plus miniature displays, with nicely painted backdrops, feature gophers mounted using taxidermy and dressed in costumes. They whimsically and quite comically depict various aspects of village life, real and fictional—from a wedding and a church service to a hunting scene and a bank holdup.

Some people might find the use of stuffed critters distasteful, and at least one environmental group has complained, though apparently no gophers were killed specifically for museum display. The museum operators seem quite happy to endure the ongoing controversy, which has attracted considerable media attention and healthy numbers of visitors. Souvenir hunters can peruse the requisite merchandise, while listening to the "Gopher Call Song" playing endlessly in the background.

The animals at the heart of the exhibit aren't true gophers but instead Richardson's ground squirrels, along with a couple of thirteen-lined ground squirrels. Widespread throughout central and southern Alberta's prairies and foothills, Richardson's ground squirrels are commonly seen sitting quizzically alongside roadways or scampering jerkily and dangerously across the hardtop. These suicidal individuals are primarily youngsters, exploring the world outside their burrows in late spring and early summer and providing easy pickings for hawks, crows, magpies, and coyotes. The ground squirrels start going into hibernation in mid-August, with adults heading underground first.

As you return west on Highway 27, cross Highway 2 and drop into Olds College, on the eastern outskirts of Olds, for a short walking tour of this relaxed, friendly campus. Since it opened as the Olds

Clem T. GoFur at the entrance to Torrington.

School of Agriculture and Home Economics in 1913, the college has provided education and training for farm managers, agronomists, nursery operators, golf course greenskeepers, blacksmiths, veterinary assistants, and grain inspectors, to name a few occupations. The college is also a leader in agricultural research, conducting experiments in such areas as developing improved grasses for athletic fields, recycling swine and dairy waste, and investigating goat genetics.

The 600-hectare campus features a natural arboretum and buildings that range from modern glass structures to those built by early settlers. The Olds College Farm, which opened in 1911, is the largest teaching and demonstration farm in Western Canada. It contains cereal, hay, and pasture land, and houses nearly 3,000 animals in its horse, beef, swine, sheep, and dairy barns.

Visitors can take a self-guided walking tour through the college's Botanic Garden, a living classroom for horticultural students. It features prairie-hardy plants set in several specialty gardens, including ones dedicated to roses, herbs, irises, alpine plants, and dwarf conifers.

While in Olds, visit its historic downtown. Many of the buildings, dating back to the turn of the 20th century, feature tall oak and brass doors (a tour brochure is available at the town's tourist information office). The area's first settler was David Shannon, who arrived in 1890 in an open handcar and applied for squatter's rights. In its early years, Olds was known as the Hay City for its abundant hay crops, particularly of timothy grass, much of it shipped to B.C. lumber camps as feed for horses. Olds overcame devastating fires in 1922 and 1978 to become a prosperous agriculture- and energy-based town.

For a more scenic return to Calgary, drive south on the two-lane Highway 2A, once the main highway between Calgary and Edmonton. In summer, the roadside fields of canola are a brilliant yellow. It rejoins the freeway north of Airdrie.

**EATS & DRINKS**

In Torrington, drop by **Barrie and Bernie's Diner** (119 Centre Street). Popular dining spots in Olds include **Olympia Restaurant & Lounge** (5018–50th Street; Greek food) and **Stonewood Grill** (5012–52nd Avenue). For fresh-roasted coffee and warm blueberry muffins, head to **Bean Brokers** (5104–46th Avenue) or try **Granny Jacks** (5303–50th Avenue) for coffee or lunch.

## RCMP POLICE DOG SERVICE TRAINING CENTRE AND INNISFAIL

**Route:** From the Country Hills Boulevard Road overpass, drive about 95 kilometres north on Highway 2, taking exit 365 east (the southernmost of two overpass accesses to Innisfail) and then following the signs south to the RCMP Police Dog Service Training Centre. To reach Innisfail, return north, entering the town by one of the two exits off Highway 2.

**Driving Distance:** About 110 kilometres one way.

**Note:** Free demonstrations at the dog-training school (about 1 hour) are offered every Wednesday at 2:00 p.m. from late May until early September. Admission is free. Phone 403-227-3346. • The Innisfail and District Historical Village (52nd Avenue and 42nd Street) is open in summer 10 a.m. to 5:30 p.m. Monday to Saturday and noon to 5:00 p.m on Sunday. Admission charged. Phone 403-227-2906.

If it's true that the Mounties always get their man or woman, it's often their dogs that do the legwork leading to the arrest. Here, at the only Royal Canadian Mounted Police (RCMP) dog-training centre in Canada, visitors can watch young German shepherds (and their trainers) go through an obstacle course and chase down a "suspect." The day can be rounded out in nearby Innisfail by visiting historical sites and taking a nature walk.

The RCMP began formally training its police dogs in 1937 and has based its canine training facilities near Innisfail since 1965. At any time, about six teams of dogs and their handlers—RCMP officers from across Canada—attend this rigorous, five-month boot camp.

During 80 training days, the dogs learn to track, search, attack and hold, and detect bombs and drugs. To graduate, they must be able to perform these tasks while, say, on slippery floors, in heavy crowds, or under gunfire—at all times remaining under the firm control of their handlers.

During the public demonstrations, visitors can watch these dogs jump over barriers, climb through open windows, and scramble up and down steep stairs. The highlight of the show comes when one dog chases a trainer (playing a villain), seizes a padded arm, and detains the suspect until released by its handler. While the dogs are trained to hold—not savagely attack—a culprit, their bites can be considerable; several handlers have needed stitches when a dog's teeth found a thin spot in the padding during these exercises.

The RCMP uses only German shepherds (usually young males) because of their versatility, strength, courage, and ability to work in cold climates. Several young trainees have been imported from the Czech Republic, where German shepherds are used as border guard dogs and haven't been bred for show. The Innisfail training centre has started raising its own puppies, not only to hasten the learning

A German shepherd collars a "suspect" during a demonstration at the RCMP Police Dog Service Training Centre.

curve but also to forestall the rising price of buying a dog. Still, it costs some $60,000 to train a dog-handler team, and fewer than 20 percent of the dogs make the grade.

Just north of the dog-training centre, in the heart of Alberta's most productive farmland, is the town of Innisfail. In 1754, Anthony Henday passed near here in a vain attempt to convince the Blackfoot people to trade with the Hudson's Bay Company. His trip, however, helped persuade his employers to establish a string of fur-trading posts along major rivers west of Hudson Bay. Henday is also thought to be the first white man to see the Rocky Mountains.

The area's more recent history is celebrated at the Innisfail and District Historical Village, which features restored buildings, artifacts, pioneer farm machinery, and several gardens. One highlight is The Spruces, an 1880s stopping house that once stood 7 kilometres north along the old Edmonton-Calgary Trail, on the site of a winter supply cache used by the Palliser Expedition in the late 1850s.

The nearby Dr. George/Kemp House, built in 1893, housed the first museum in what was then the North-West Territories; Mrs. George later designed Alberta's original provincial crest. On the western outskirts of Innisfail is the Napolean Lake Natural Area, which contains a 1.4-kilometre self-guided nature trail through an aspen parkland forest filled with late spring and summer flowers.

## RED DEER

**Route:** See page 119.
**Note:** Red Deer's Visitor Information Centre—along Highway 2 North, just north of the 32nd Street overpass—is open 9:00 a.m. to 5:00 p.m. weekdays and 10:00 a.m. to 5:00 p.m. weekends, with extended summer hours. Phone 403-346-0180; www.tourismreddeer.com.

Like many Calgarians, I used to consider Red Deer a strip of highway gas stations halfway to Edmonton. No longer. Red Deer, I've discovered, is a great place for nature and history buffs.

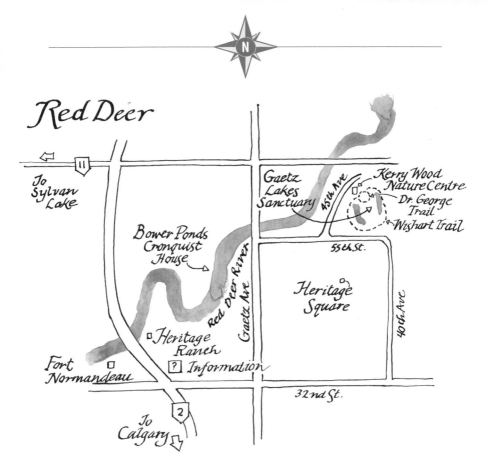

**Red Deer**

To Sylvan Lake

Gaetz Lakes Sanctuary

45th Ave

Kerry Wood Nature Centre

Dr. George Trail

Wishart Trail

Bower Ponds Cronquist House

Red Deer River

Gaetz Ave

55th St.

Heritage Square

40th Ave

Heritage Ranch

Information

Fort Normandeau

32nd St.

To Calgary

The city has one of the best urban river park systems in Alberta and an excellent nature centre. Even if you have only an hour or two, you can take a walk in the woods or embark on a quick family bike ride along the Red Deer River. The park system can be quickly accessed from the Visitor Information Centre, which also houses the Alberta Sports Hall of Fame and Museum.

Across the highway is the historic Fort Normandeau, site of the first Red Deer settlement and home to a reconstructed North West Mounted Police post. Visitors can also explore Red Deer's past by touring a downtown square of heritage buildings or going on their choice of five historic walking tours.

Not all the interesting architecture is historic. Scattered throughout downtown are 10-plus life-size bronze sculptures and two murals. Not far away is the semicircular St. Mary's Church (1968), one of

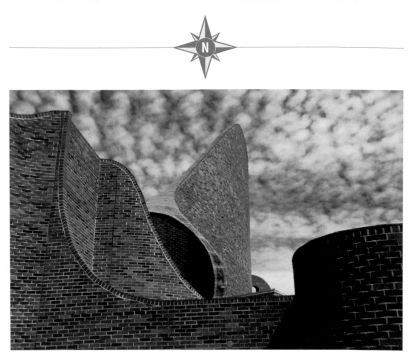

St. Mary's Church, designed by architect Douglas Cardinal.

the first signature buildings of architect Douglas Cardinal, who was inspired by a spider's web. At Red Deer College, the innovative Arts Theatre was designed by Arthur Erickson.

The name Red Deer is actually a misnomer. Early settlers mistook the area's elk for a type of European red deer. Thus, they called the river and the first village Red Deer, and the name stuck. The more accurate Cree name was Waskasoo Seepee, which means "elk river." Today, the city's river valley park system is called Waskasoo, helping alleviate a historical error.

Red Deer is now Alberta's third-largest city, recently surpassing Lethbridge, with a 2011 population of 92,000. Its petroleum, agriculture, food processing, and manufacturing sectors have all been growing, thanks in large part to its location smack in the middle of the Calgary-Edmonton corridor. With a record number of Alberta oil and gas wells drilled in recent years, for example, Red Deer's oilfield service industry is thriving, while the nearby, expanded Joffre complex is now Canada's third-largest cluster of petrochemical plants.

**═══ EATS & DRINKS ═══**

**City Roast Coffee** (4940 Ross Street) roasts its own beans and has fresh-baked goods and lunches, while the nearby **Quenched Coffee House** (5005–50th Avenue) also has good coffee. Local favourites include **Burger Boy** (6005–54th Avenue), **Las Palmeras Mexican Restaurant** (3630–50th Avenue), **It's All Greek to Me** (3701–50th Avenue), and **Glenn's Restaurant** (Highway 2 South, teapot on the roof), which offers breakfast, lunch, and more than 40 varieties of loose tea.

## En Route to Red Deer

**Route:** From the Country Hills Boulevard overpass, drive 130 kilometres north on Highway 2.
**Driving Distance:** 130 kilometres one way.

Judging by the steady stream of traffic at any time of day between Calgary and Edmonton, you'd think this route through Red Deer had a long and glorious past. But it wasn't until the relatively recent date of 1875 that wagon wheels carved the Calgary-Edmonton Trail onto the land. Until then, Aboriginal groups and later explorers and missionaries had taken various other routes north to reach the Fort Edmonton area.

The establishment of Fort Calgary by the North West Mounted Police in 1875 created a need for a more direct line. This was accomplished by opening a fork of Reverend John McDougall's trail between Fort Edmonton and his mission at Morley, to the west of Calgary. The fork branched south from near present-day Bowden to Fort Calgary.

In the early days, the wagon track extended south to Fort Benton, Montana, where eastern goods were unloaded from steamboats on the Missouri River. The goods were then transported north on bull trains—strings of heavy wagons pulled by teams of oxen. North of Calgary, however, the bull trains bogged down in the soft black soils.

To solve this problem, the bull trains were replaced on this stretch by Red River carts. These all-wood carts with ungreased axles produced a horrible, squealing sound. But they were lightweight and manoeuvrable, easy to repair on the trail, and could be floated across rivers. The principal river crossing on the Calgary-Edmonton Trail was the Red Deer River near today's Red Deer.

The arrival of the railway in Calgary in 1883 brought settlers to the west and greatly increased traffic on the Calgary-Edmonton Trail. Within a few years, passengers could ride between the two towns on open stagecoaches for the princely sum of $25. A five-day trip in good weather, it often took much longer when rain, snow, or fog moved in. In winter, the snow often disappeared south of Olds, forcing the coaches to switch from runners to wheels.

To serve these passengers, stopping houses were strategically placed along the route. Between Calgary and Red Deer, they included Dickson's (near today's Airdrie), Scarlett's (northeast of Carstairs), Lone Pine (near Bowden), Content's (near Innisfail), and Miller's (near Penhold). The accommodations at these early "motels" ranged from the luxury of a bed with cotton sheets to sleeping on the floor.

The trail quickly fell into disuse upon the completion in 1891 of the Calgary and Edmonton Railway, which roughly followed the trail's route. The railway, however, did lead to the creation of towns at sidings and stations along the way. The stations were spaced about every 30 kilometres, with the sidings halfway between. Between Calgary and Red Deer, these towns are Airdrie, Crossfield, Carstairs, Didsbury, Olds, Bowden, Innisfail, and Penhold. Many were named for towns in England and Scotland or after employees of the Canadian Pacific Railway.

The trail was back in business in 1906 when G. Corriveau and his son made the first recorded automobile trip from Edmonton to Calgary, covering the distance in less than 12 hours. After 1910, car traffic increased steadily and the dirt trail was upgraded to gravel and finally to pavement.

The present-day Highway 2A followed much of the original highway. In the 1950s, the high-speed Highway 2 was built to bypass the towns created by the railway. Ironically, much of the four-lane, divided freeway between Calgary and Red Deer closely follows the original wagon route. In 2005, Highway 2 was renamed Queen Elizabeth II Highway.

Recently, the province has begun investigating the feasibility of building a high-speed, Calgary-to-Edmonton rail link. It could cost as much as $20 billion, if a 480-kilometre-per-hour train technology is chosen. That could put a significant dent in the 10 million passenger vehicle trips per year now taken along this overcrowded Edmonton-Calgary highway.

As you approach Red Deer, notice the bountiful crops in roadside fields. The black soils in central Alberta are the most fertile in the province, producing grains that have won championship awards as early as the 1893 World's Fair in Chicago. In the Red Deer area, the farms are one-third smaller than the provincial average, with no loss in production.

Nearly half the cultivated land here is devoted to barley, primarily used for feeding livestock and producing malt in beer. Another major use of farmland is to produce the hay and forage crops used to feed more than 100,000 beef cattle in the area. There are also several dairy farms, where black-and-white Holsteins produce milk.

## Fort Normandeau

**Route:** From the 32nd Street interchange on Highway 2 in Red Deer, follow the Fort Normandeau signs west and north for 5 kilometres.
**Note:** Fort Normandeau is open daily, 10:00 a.m. to 5:00 p.m. from mid-May to early September. Phone 403-347-7550.

Fort Normandeau, a reconstruction of an old military post, is located on the banks of the Red Deer River near a natural crossing of the river. The shallow water, slow current, and low banks made this the best place to ford the river for 80 kilometres in either direction.

Used for perhaps thousands of years by Aboriginal peoples, the crossing was also favoured in the late 19th century by Metis buffalo hunters and by commercial wagon-drawn freighters travelling between Edmonton and Calgary. To serve this traffic, McClellan's Hotel and a ferry began operating in 1884. A small community also sprang up at the crossing, where settlers could graze cattle and horses.

During the North-West Rebellion of 1885, Louis Riel and others led an armed uprising of Metis and Aboriginals angry about federal indifference to their grievances over land and self-government. While the few battles of the Northwest Rebellion occurred to the east, settlers at the Red Deer River crossing were evacuated. Led by Lieutenant J. E. Bedard Normandeau, a group of soldiers fortified McClellan's two-storey stopping house to protect the settlement and keep communication lines open.

The fort never saw action during the rebellion. For several years, it was used as a North West Mounted Police detachment before being dismantled and rebuilt as a nearby farmhouse in 1899. The present replica of the fort was built in 1974, using some of the original logs. An interpretive centre now tells the story of the fort and the river crossing. Live interpretive programs, where visitors can make bannock, dance to native music, or toss the caber, are performed throughout the summer.

The crossing fell into disuse with the arrival of the Calgary and Edmonton Railway in 1891. Reverend Leonard Gaetz, who earlier owned a store at the crossing, offered the railway an interest in his land to the east in exchange for routing the line through his property, which soared in value. Thus, the town of Red Deer was located several kilometres downstream.

Across the river from the fort is the site of a federal industrial school for Aboriginal children. They were compelled to leave the reserve and board at the school, where they were taught skills such as farming, carpentry, and domestic work. This sorry chapter in native relations ended at the conclusion of World War I, when the school was converted to a training farm for returning soldiers.

## Waskasoo Park

**Route:** The park can be reached from Heritage Ranch in Red Deer, near the Visitor Information Centre, on the east side of Highway 2, just north of the 32nd Street overpass. To access other parts of the park, ask for directions and maps at the information centre.

**Note:** Kerry Wood Nature Centre is open daily from 10:00 a.m. to 5:00 p.m. Phone 403-346-2010; www.waskasoopark.ca.

Red Deer is blessed with an excellent parkway system that snakes through the city along the Red Deer River. Named Waskasoo, the park boasts more than 50 kilometres of paved trails on which to cycle, walk, and gain access to riverside picnic areas, recreational facilities, and trout ponds.

The park can be quickly sampled by taking a short walk or cycle through a riverside forest below Heritage Ranch. Another favourite spot is Bower Ponds, overlooked by Cronquist House, a 1911 Victorian farmhouse fully restored as a municipal historic resource. If time permits only one destination, I recommend the excellent Kerry Wood Nature Centre and the adjoining ▲Gaetz Lakes Sanctuary, where some 160 species of birds and mammals have been spotted.

The river valley through Red Deer is much different than farther downstream, where the bedrock has been severely eroded into wondrous badland formations. Here, a historically moister climate produced more vegetation, which provided a protective cover against intense erosion. Over thousands of years, the decay of this vegetation has created the black soils for which central Alberta is famous.

The rich soils around Red Deer have been both a blessing and a naturalist's curse. They produce Alberta's most bountiful crops and sustain a large livestock industry. But good farming has meant most of the native prairie and woodlands have disappeared under the plough. The remnant tracts of native vegetation are found mainly on steep slopes and in river valley bottoms, such as along the Red Deer River.

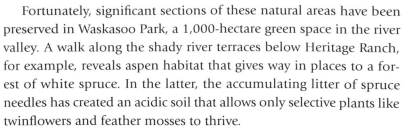

Fortunately, significant sections of these natural areas have been preserved in Waskasoo Park, a 1,000-hectare green space in the river valley. A walk along the shady river terraces below Heritage Ranch, for example, reveals aspen habitat that gives way in places to a forest of white spruce. In the latter, the accumulating litter of spruce needles has created an acidic soil that allows only selective plants like twinflowers and feather mosses to thrive.

The Red Deer River that placidly flows through the city originates in the Drummond Glacier area north of Lake Louise. As it tumbles out of the mountains and foothills, the river angles north toward Red Deer. A short distance before the city, it's slowed by the fairly recent Dickson Dam, which, by restricting spring flooding, has adversely affected downstream cottonwood trees.

Yet this isn't the first time the river has been dammed. At the end of the last ice age, glacial meltwaters from the mountains were backed up by the stagnating continental ice sheet, creating the immense Glacial Lake Red Deer. Eventually the lake overflowed the ice dam, cutting a new route southeast and abandoning a previous channel to the east, now followed by the Battle River.

Visitors can learn more about the Red Deer River and other area habitats through the exhibits and interpretive programs at the Kerry Wood Nature Centre. The centre, named after a local naturalist, also has a good natural history gift shop.

The nature centre is at the entrance to the Gaetz Lakes Sanctuary, a federal migratory bird sanctuary since 1924. The sanctuary protects 118 hectares of spruce, poplar, and mixed wood forest along with meadows, marshes, and two oxbow lakes—bow-shaped lakes formed in an abandoned channel of the river.

The shorter of two walks within the sanctuary is the Dr. George Trail, a 1-kilometre paved loop (wheelchair accessible) through poplar forest. A branch of the trail leads to a bird blind and viewing deck, where visitors can spot a diversity of waterfowl and songbirds through a telescope. The Wishart Trail is a more strenuous 4-kilometre walk that circles the West and East lakes, passing through meadows and deciduous and spruce forests and climbing to several lookouts.

## MARKERVILLE-DICKSON

**Route:** From the Country Hills Boulevard overpass, drive 118 kilometres north on Highway 2. Take Highway 42/Secondary 592 west through Penhold for 19.5 kilometres to its junction with Secondary 781. Continue west on a gravel road for 6.5 kilometres to Markerville. Stephansson House Provincial Historic Site is 9 kilometres to the north. From Markerville, drive 6 kilometres south on gravel Range Road 22, 8 kilometres west on Highway 54 to Spruce View, and 3.2 kilometres south to Dickson.

**Driving Distance:** About 175 kilometres one way.

**Note:** Stephansson House is open daily 10:00 a.m. to 5:00 p.m. from mid-May to Labour Day. Admission charged. Phone 403-728-3929; www.history.alberta .ca/stephansson. • During the same season, the Historic Markerville Creamery Museum (403-728-3006 or 1-877-728-3007) is open 10:00 a.m. to 5:30 p.m. Monday to Saturday and noon to 5:30 p.m. Sunday. Admission charged. See www .historicmarkerville.com. • The Dickson Store Museum (403-728-3355) and the Danish Canadian National Museum and Gardens (403-728-0019) are open mid-May to Labour Day from 10:00 a.m. to 5:30 p.m., except for Sunday, when they open at 11:30 p.m. Admission charged at the latter.

The lovingly restored buildings of Markerville and Dickson provide a fascinating trip back to the pioneer days of central Alberta. A century ago, settlers from the distant countries of Iceland and Denmark cleared and drained homestead land to create farms and unique communities. The trip's highlight is a tour of the restored house of Stephan Stephansson, a pioneer farmer by day and one of the Western world's great poets by kerosene light at night.

En route to Markerville, Highway 592 west passes through the rich farmland of central Alberta that usually produces bumper crops. The flatlands near Penhold were created by Glacial Lake Red Deer, a huge buildup of glacial meltwater at the end of the last ice age.

Located on the banks of the placid Medicine River, Markerville is a unique community in its origins and in the preservation of its pioneering past. The area was first settled in 1888 by a group of Icelanders escaping the droughts of the U.S. Dakotas. They were captivated by the lush, isolated parkland here, where they could maintain their customs and language.

The early struggles of homestead farming were greatly relieved by the creation in 1899 of a federal government–sponsored creamery, which became the community's economic lifeblood. Not surprisingly, the town's name was changed from Tindistoll to Markerville in honour of C. P. Marker, dairy commissioner for what was then the North-West Territories. Under the stewardship of Daniel Morkeberg and later his son Carl, the creamery operated until 1972, producing some of Alberta's finest butter from area farmers' cream.

Now designated a provincial historic resource, the ▲Historic Markerville Creamery Museum has been restored to its 1932 condition, complete with all the butter-making equipment of the period. Tours are conducted during the summer months.

The quiet hamlet of Markerville has several other historical buildings, including a 1903 community hall, a 1907 Lutheran church, and a general store (walking tour brochures are available at the creamery). For several decades, Markerville maintained its rich Icelandic culture, expressed in traditional dishes and woollen clothing, an Icelandic library, and even a men's debating society.

As you take the short drive north to ▲Stephansson House, consider the mix of nationalities that settled this area. The Icelanders were followed in 1903 by Danes, who homesteaded near Dickson, and later by Swedes, who farmed near Sylvan Lake. The area west of Markerville became known as Yankee Flats for the numerous American settlers. Despite this diversity, English-language schools, new roads, and increased communication with the outside world eroded the distinctiveness of these communities. By the 1930s, this area was much like any rural Alberta community. Today, perhaps 10 percent of the people in the Markerville area are of Icelandic descent.

Pioneer home of Icelandic poet Stephan Stephansson.

Stephan Stephansson (1853–1927) arrived in the Markerville area in 1889. He was a community leader and hard-working pioneer farmer. But he was best known for his prolific, stirring, and often controversial poetry, all written in Icelandic after the day's work was done. Although little known in Canada, he's considered Iceland's greatest poet since the 13th century. Many Icelanders today make the pilgrimage to Markerville to visit Stephansson's house.

A costumed guide greets visitors to this historic site, provides tours of the restored house, and serves Icelandic cookies fresh from the oven. Stephansson built the house himself, originally a log structure that was expanded and refurbished to accommodate his family of eight children. He even built the desk where at night he wrote his poetry.

To the south of Markerville is Dickson, the oldest Danish settlement in Western Canada. It was first settled in 1903 by 17 Danes, who had earlier immigrated to the United States. Though inexperienced as farmers, they drained the boggy land around Dickson and helped establish dairy farming in central Alberta.

In 1991, Queen Margrethe II of Denmark opened the Dickson Store Museum. The store, beautifully restored to appear as it did during the 1930s, is stocked with groceries, hardware, and dry goods typical of the period. Just to the south is the Danish Canadian National Museum and Gardens. The museum, located in a 1933 dormitory school, is surrounded by traditional Danish flower and vegetable gardens, along with a children's garden of imagination.

===== EATS & DRINKS =====

At the Historic Markerville Creamery Museum, the **Kaffistofa** coffee shop offers Icelandic dishes typical of a century ago. The **Dickson Store National Museum** sells ice cream and old-fashioned candies; the nearby **Danish Canadian National Museum** has a coffee shop with Danish open-faced sandwiches.

# SYLVAN LAKE

**Route:** From the Country Hills Boulevard overpass, at Calgary's northern outskirts, drive 137 kilometres north on Highway 2 to just past the Red Deer gas strip. Go 16 kilometres west on Highway 11 and then 3 kilometres north to reach the beach in the heart of Sylvan Lake.

**Driving Distance:** About 155 kilometres one way.

For those who don't mind a crowded tourist setting, Sylvan Lake is a pleasant place to spend a day at the beach. It's one of the few lakes within two hours of Calgary that offer a sandy beach and reasonably warm and clean water to swim or play in. You can also canoe, windsurf, waterslide, water-ski, jet ski, fish, or just take a long walk along the waterfront. It's the perfect place for active young families and teenagers.

Best of all, the town's beach is within Sylvan Lake Provincial Park, established in 1932. The park is essentially a 1.6-kilometre stretch of sandy waterfront backed by a thin strip of grass dotted with picnic

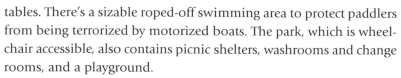

tables. There's a sizable roped-off swimming area to protect paddlers from being terrorized by motorized boats. The park, which is wheelchair accessible, also contains picnic shelters, washrooms and change rooms, and a playground.

On sunny summer weekends, it can be hard to find a parking spot, let alone a private space to build sandcastles. But at other times, the pace is less frenzied, and you can turn your back to the lakefront shops and gaze placidly across this sizable lake to the distant horizon.

Sylvan Lake has been attracting recreational visitors to its shores since the turn of the 20th century, when it was known as Snake Lake. Early visitors were often nearby farm families, a number of whom were immigrant homesteaders from Scandinavia. In 1912, a Red Deer auto club made the first recorded motorized excursion to Sylvan Lake. To remove one broken-down car from the road, the women passengers pulled and the men pushed.

Better highways brought more tourists from central Alberta and beyond. Today, Sylvan Lake is one of the busiest lake resort towns in Alberta, attracting nearly 1.5 million visitors a year. It offers the

Wading into Sylvan Lake.

amenities of motels, campgrounds, shops, restaurants, a huge water-slide, and Alberta's second-largest marina. Besides the cottages that ring the lake, an increasing number of people, including Red Deer commuters, are living in the town year-round, making Sylvan Lake one of Canada's fastest-growing communities, with a permanent population of 11,000.

Another provincial park, Jarvis Bay, is 3 kilometres north of the town of Sylvan Lake on Highway 20. Though principally a campground, the park has several short trails through aspen and balsam poplar forest and down to the lakeshore. These can be accessed from a parking lot near the park entrance. Ask at the entrance booth for a park newspaper, which contains an area map showing the trails.

A more pristine spot is the Sylvan Lake Natural Area, an 11-hectare site that protects forested and shoreline habitats on the northwest edge of the lake. It's the only public land on the lakeshore still in a natural state. This moist transition zone between parkland and boreal forest harbours a variety of marsh plants, ferns, and at least 30 species of breeding birds, including pileated woodpeckers.

Unfortunately, trails and signs are minimal, and it can be very wet underfoot. At such times, only the most persistent nature lovers and birders will enjoy the experience. To reach the natural area from the eastern edge of Sylvan Lake town, drive 9.7 kilometres north on Highway 20, 11.6 kilometres west on Rainy Creek Road, and 1.5 kilometres south on a narrow gravel road to a dead end. The scenic drive en route offers several magnificent views of forested hills and farmland.

For more prolonged views of this rolling topography, return to Calgary via Secondary 781, which heads south from the town of Sylvan Lake. The road passes through some of Alberta's finest farmland, where the black soils produce bumper crops of barley, wheat, hay, and canola.

At a T-junction, head east on Highway 54 to regain Highway 2 south at Innisfail. The town was once called Poplar Grove because of the area's abundant aspen forests. In the 1880s, it was a popular overnight stopping place for wagons carrying freight and passengers between Edmonton and Calgary.

---

═══════════ **EATS & DRINKS** ═══════════

**Pete's at the Beach** (4711 Lakeshore Drive) is a popular spot for eggs Benedict, burgers, and pizzas. Choose from 100 flavours of ice cream at the **Big Moo Ice Cream Parlor** (4603 Lakeshore Drive).

---

# 🔥 LACOMBE AND GULL LAKE

**Route:** From the Country Hills Boulevard overpass, drive 153 kilometres north on Highway 2. Gull Lake is 13 kilometres west on Highway 12, while Lacombe is 3 kilometres east on the same highway. The Ellis Bird Farm is 8 kilometres east of Lacombe on Highway 12 and then 8 kilometres south on Prentiss Road.

**Driving Distance:** About 155 kilometres one way to Lacombe.

**Note:** Michener House Museum (5036–51st Street) is open 9:00 a.m. to 5:00 p.m. Tuesday to Saturday from Victoria Day to Labour Day and reduced hours the rest of the year. Admission free. Brochures for the self-guided tour of historical downtown Lacombe can be obtained there or at the interpretive centre in the Flatiron Building. Phone 403-782-3933. • This number can also be used to book tours of the Blacksmith Shop Museum (5020–49th Street); www.lacombe.ca.

• The Ellis Bird Farm is open 11:00 a.m. to 5:00 p.m. Tuesday to Sunday and holiday Mondays from Victoria Day to Labour Day. Phone 403-885-4477 or 403-346-2211 (off-season); www.ellisbirdfarm.ca.

Alberta has had an unfortunate tendency to bulldoze its all-too-brief history. So it's well worth taking a 90-minute drive north to Lacombe to see a rare prairie town that has preserved and restored many of its early 20th-century buildings and maintained one of Alberta's finest Edwardian streetscapes. Indeed, *Harrowsmith Country Life* magazine named Lacombe one of Canada's 10 prettiest towns. The Lacombe area offers day trippers other diversions, such as an exquisite bird farm and the sandy shores of nearby Gull Lake in Alberta's oldest provincial park.

If you intend to visit all three locations, it makes the most sense to start the tour at Gull Lake and Aspen Beach Provincial Park, established in 1932 as Alberta's first provincial park. The park's waterfront offers a wide public beach and relatively warm waters for swimming. A boat launch provides access to the lake's deeper waters, where anglers can troll or cast for northern pike, yellow perch, walleye, and lake whitefish.

Beyond the beach's west end, an interpretive trail crosses a bird-rich marsh on an elevated boardwalk. Fifty years ago, this marsh was covered in water, but soon thereafter the lake's level mysteriously dropped, leaving some cottage owners stranded far from the waterfront. To ensure more predictable water levels, Alberta Environment has since periodically pumped water from the Blindman River into Gull Lake.

From Gull Lake, it's a short drive east to Lacombe, entered along its long and wide main street (50th Avenue), lined with stately two- and three-storey houses with high-pitched roofs. Fiftieth Avenue also crosses the old Calgary-Edmonton Trail, which in the 1880s was a pathway for wagons and Red River carts.

Lacombe is named after Father Albert Lacombe, an Oblate missionary who helped forge peace—first between the Blackfoot and Cree in the mid-1800s and later between these nations and white settlers. Some of those settlers flocked here in 1881 with the arrival of the railway connecting Edmonton and Calgary. By the turn of the century, Lacombe was bigger than Red Deer and soon had a federal agricultural research station that developed the world-renowned Lacombe hog. Still in operation, the station is now noted for its meat-packing research. While Red Deer quickly eclipsed Lacombe as a major centre, the latter retains its small-town charm with a population of some 12,000 people.

On the outskirts of downtown is Lacombe's oldest building, the Michener House Museum. Built in 1894, this Queen Anne–style house

The Michener House Museum in Lacombe is the birthplace of former governer general Roland Michener.

was originally the manse for the Lacombe Grace Methodist Church. In 1900, it became the birthplace of former Canadian Governor General Roland Michener; his father, Edward, was the church minister. Restored by the local Maski-Pitoon Historical Society, the house was declared a provincial historic resource and in 1984 became a museum, housing community archives and Michener family artifacts.

A few blocks away is the Blacksmith Shop Museum, built in 1902 and one of only two Alberta blacksmith shops on their original sites. Today, the restored historic structure is a working museum where blacksmiths use turn-of-the-century tools and forging techniques to mould hot metal on anvils.

In the late 1980s, Lacombe became one of the first participants in Alberta's Main Street Program, using government monies to help restore its historic downtown buildings. Highlights include a brick-and-sandstone 1904 flatiron building (the oldest of only three such structures in Western Canada and now home to the town's

Touring the grounds of Ellis Bird Farm.

interpretive centre); a building with a pressed tin ceiling; and an old billiard hall that once hosted upstairs dances and gambling parties. A turn-of-the-century Chinese restaurant and laundry offered all-you-can-eat meals for 25 cents. The owner's wife was one of Alberta's first Chinese women: with the help of his partner, the owner paid a $500-per-head tax to bring her and their children to Canada.

Three kilometres north of Lacombe is Canadian University College, a Christian educational institution dating back to 1909 and run by the Seventh-day Adventist Church. A church on the college grounds has a membership of 1,100 and thus boasts one of Canada's largest Adventist congregations. Also just north of town is the First Baptist Church, located in two new, unique monolithic domes.

The ⬥Ellis Bird Farm, 16 kilometres southeast of town, is an immaculately maintained oasis dedicated to the conservation of mountain bluebirds, tree swallows, and other native cavity-nesting birds. A short, delightful trail leads past ponds, an old farm-sized grain elevator, a water garden, a native wildflower garden, and a butterfly/hummingbird garden. Nailed to old fences and walls are bluebird nest boxes donated from throughout North America, billed as the world's largest collection.

The bluebirds, being shy creatures, are unlikely to nest at this fairly busy site. But up to 100 pairs a year nest in boxes that farm staff monitor and maintain in a surrounding 100-kilometre-square area.

The bird farm is the legacy of Charlie and Winnie Ellis, who on their parents' pioneer farm in the mid-1950s started erecting nesting boxes for bluebirds and tree swallows and houses for black-capped chickadees, purple martins, and flickers. They also transformed the backyard into a wildlife haven by dredging ponds and planting orchards and flower gardens.

When the Ellises retired from active farming in 1980, they sold part of the larger farm to Union Carbide as a site for a petrochemical plant. In return, the company agreed to help establish and fund a non-profit organization to keep the bird farm and its programs running in perpetuity.

For a shorter return to Calgary, continue south from the bird farm on Prentiss Road then go west on Secondary 597 to Blackfalds. A short drive south on Highway 2 leads to Red Deer's northern outskirts.

---

### EATS & DRINKS

In Lacombe, **Kavaccino's** (5028–51st Street) is a friendly café with lunch specials such as German potato bake, Japanese cabbage salad, and Italian meatball soup, while the nearby **Leto's Steak and Seafood House** (4944 Highway 2A) is worth visiting for lunch or Sunday brunch. The **Ellis Bird Farm** has a charming tea house that serves lunch and afternoon tea; try the saskatoon pie or fresh-squeezed lemonade.

---

## PONOKA

**Route:** From the Country Hills Boulevard overpass, drive 168 kilometres north on Highway 2 and, taking the Ponoka/Wetaskiwin exit, continue north on Highway 2A for 15 kilometres.

**Driving Distance:** About 185 kilometres one way.

**Note:** For Ponoka Stampede information or to order tickets, phone 403-783-0100; www.ponokastampede.com • Vold, Jones & Vold cattle auctions are held every Wednesday on the western edge of Ponoka. Phone 403-783-5561. • Fort Ostell Museum (5320–54th Street) is open Tuesday to Friday 10:00 a.m. to 5:00 p.m. and Sunday 1:00 p.m. to 5:00 p.m. from Victoria Day to Labour Day. Admission charged. Phone 403-783-5224; www.fortostellmuseum.com.

Ponoka proudly proclaims itself the cattle capital of Canada—with good reason. There are considerably more cattle than people in and around this central Alberta town of 6,800, which boasts Canada's biggest cattle auction market and its third-largest rodeo. This bovine legacy is the by-product of rich farming and grazing lands and a hard-working population whose jeans, cowboy hats, and pickup trucks are staples of daily living. Ironically, *ponoka* is the Blackfoot word for "elk."

It's well worth timing your visit to coincide with the Ponoka Stampede, a week-long event running over the July 1 weekend. A trip to the weekly, Vold, Jones & Vold cattle auction also offers colourful insight into Alberta's rural culture. Beyond cattle, Ponoka features interesting historical landmarks and a lovely pathway, with good birdwatching along the meandering Battle River.

For a vivid introduction to the area's aspen parkland landscape, stop en route at the J. J. Collett Natural Area, just east of Highway 2A, about 10 kilometres before Ponoka and just south of Morningside. This natural area has 257 hectares of rolling meadows and aspen stands intersected by a wetland-fed stream. Observant strollers along the network of trails might spot deer, coyotes, and a variety of songbirds.

The Ponoka region has some of the richest farmland in Alberta, with black soils and usually ample rain producing excellent yields of barley and forage crops such as hay, alfalfa, and various grasses. Much of this output is used to raise Angus, Hereford, and Charolais cattle on area pastures and then in feedlots.

In the midst of this cattle country is the Vold, Jones & Vold auction market and its 7,500-head handling capacity. Interested visitors

can experience the cacophony of the weekly Wednesday auction, with cattle sold in three rings simultaneously, as well as through Internet bidding; the 2004 world champion livestock auctioneer worked here. The auction is operated by the fourth generation of the Vold family, who also built the Scottish links–style Wolf Creek Golf Resort—consistently ranked one of the finest courses in Canada—on nearby sandy lands. Not surprisingly, Ralph Vold traded some cattle to help buy the land and build the large log clubhouse.

The town's western showpiece is the Ponoka Stampede. Now running for more than 75 years, the six-day rodeo draws more than 60,000 spectators, some arriving a week early to claim a prime site in a sea of white trailers and campers beside the stampede grounds. They come for the professional rodeo and chuckwagon races, the pancake breakfasts, the country concerts, the massive beer gardens and dance, the singing pastor, and the chance to win a raffle; one year, the winner's choice was 40 heifers or $40,000.

Bronc rider hangs on at Ponoka Stampede, Canada's third-largest rodeo.

It seems every town and village in central and southern Alberta has an annual rodeo, a living vestige of a cowboy life that has all but disappeared from working ranches. In Canada, the Ponoka Stampede, with its purse of more than $400,000, is eclipsed in size only by the Calgary Stampede and Edmonton's Canadian Finals Rodeo. Ponoka attracts competitors from across North America, some driving to and from overlapping rodeos as far away as central British Columbia and Colorado. Despite its considerable prize money, the Ponoka Stampede retains a feeling of intimacy, and it's possible to wander along the fences, close to the thundering horses and bulls.

While you're in Ponoka, it's worth taking a stroll along the tranquil Battle River pathway and viewing several restored historic downtown buildings. The community dates back to the 1870s, when the Battle River Crossing was a supply point on the wagon trail between Forts Edmonton and Calgary. The town got started with the 1891 completion of the Calgary and Edmonton Railway, and some of the first businesses served the subsequent wave of settlers. An early merchant was Frederic Algar, who eventually built the brick building on the corner of Railway Street, which still has its original tin ceiling.

Just south of town is Alberta Hospital, Ponoka. It opened in 1911—under the decidedly less tactful name Provincial Hospital for the Insane—with the idea that a rural setting with spacious, landscaped grounds was therapeutic for psychiatric patients. The original brick main building, designated a provincial historic resource in 1977, now houses administrative offices, with many of the psychiatric and brain injury programs operating in attractive new buildings. The Fort Ostell Museum, in Ponoka's Centennial Park, has a unique display depicting the hospital's history.

The museum also tells the story of Ponoka's pioneering and Aboriginal past and that of the short-lived Fort Ostell, a fur trade building hastily converted to a fort in 1885 to help quell the anticipated spread of the Riel Rebellion west of Manitoba. The Metis-led rebellion soon dissipated, in large part because local native chiefs swore allegiance to Canada.

# REYNOLDS-ALBERTA MUSEUM

**Route:** From the Country Hills Boulevard overpass at Calgary's northern outskirts, drive 220 kilometres north on Highway 2. Take the Wetaskiwin exit and drive 17 kilometres east on Highway 13 to the Reynolds-Alberta Museum.
**Driving Distance:** About 235 kilometres one way.
**Note:** The Reynolds-Alberta Museum (www.machinemuseum.net) is open daily 10:00 a.m. to 6:00 p.m. from July 1 to Labour Day, with slightly reduced hours the rest of the year. Admission charged. Phone 780-361-1351 or toll free 1-800-661-4726. • The Alberta Central Railway Museum (www.abcentralrailway.com) is open 10:00 a.m. to 4:00 p.m. Wednesday to Sunday and holiday Mondays from Victoria Day to Labour Day. Admission charged. Phone 780-352-2257.

The Reynolds-Alberta Museum is a major tourist attraction in central Alberta and a shiny tribute to the machine age. Built around the collection of Wetaskiwin businessman Stan Reynolds, the $22.5-million facility features hundreds of historic vehicles ranging from ancient fire engines to vintage automobiles, many in working condition. Opened in 1992, the museum uses glossy exhibits, hands-on displays, videos, and interactive computers to tell Alberta's history of mechanization in three areas: transportation, agriculture, and industry. But above all, it's a monument to the car in Alberta.

You might think a two-and-a-half-hour drive on the immaculate pavement of Highway 2 constitutes an onerous day trip. But as you drive, consider what motorists endured at the beginning of the century, when the automobile was introduced to Alberta. Back then, roads followed old trails, railway allowances, ruts in farmers' fields, and even creek beds. By the 1920s, the roads were usually good when dry but boggy or treacherously slippery when wet.

One solution, tried near Edmonton in 1923, was to apply a layer of bitumen to the road. The experiment worked, but the cost of transporting the bitumen from distant oil sands near Fort McMurray was prohibitive. Instead, a gravel surface, graded and crowned to shed water, continued to be the easiest way to improve dirt roads. Many of these improvements resulted from the lobbying of early auto clubs such as the Alberta Motor Association, which also published the first road maps.

Despite such difficulties, the car provided unprecedented personal freedom and changed the way people lived and especially the way they played. The car opened the way for people to go to Banff or Sylvan Lake for weekend outings. It also led to the introduction in the 1920s of summer villages and campgrounds, in which motorists slept in bungalow tents attached to the sides of their cars. These were hardly primitive outings. Campers often came equipped with folding chairs, tables, camp stoves, and even portable phonographs. A later convenience was the bungalow camp, a forerunner of the motel, which featured a cluster of modest cabins around a central lodge.

These and other stories in the annals of the automobile industry are told at the Reynolds-Alberta Museum. Did you know that in the early years of the 20th century, there was a race for supremacy between three means of powering motorized vehicles: steam, electricity, and, the ultimate winner, the internal combustion engine? In fact, Alberta's first recorded car was a steam-powered Locomobile brought to the Calgary area by William Cochrane around 1901.

There was also a battle for supremacy between the car and the horse. In Alberta, early automobiles were held responsible for all accidents with carriages. Later, they were still compelled to slow down or stop when passing horses. The first provincial motor vehicles act of 1906 restricted speeds to 10 miles per hour in settled areas and 20 elsewhere. And it wasn't until 1915 that cars were allowed into Banff National Park.

Historic vehicle at Reynolds-Alberta Museum in Wetaskiwin.

The real automotive boom came after World War II, when affluence descended to the middle classes and the province began a major road-building program. By 1955, there was one car for every five Albertans.

The Reynolds-Alberta Museum—boasting more than 350 historic vehicles—relives that era by recreating period service stations, car dealerships, and drive-in theatres. It also tells the parallel story of how agriculture was revolutionized by the gasoline-powered tractor and motorized truck.

Museum admission covers a visit to the adjacent Canada's Aviation Hall of Fame and an aviation hangar. Founded in 1973, the hall recognizes Canadians who made a significant contribution to our aviation history. The hangar displays 70 vintage aircraft—Canada's second-largest collection—including transport, sport, military, and northern bush planes. On summer weekends, visitors can book rides in an open cockpit biplane.

While in Wetaskiwin, you may wish to tour the historic downtown buildings, including a fine 1907 courthouse (now part of city hall), and admire Canada's oldest working water tower, built in 1906 and recently refurbished. At nearby By-the-Lake Park, you can picnic or stroll on walking trails.

The word *Wetaskiwin* means "the place where peace was made." It refers to the legend of two braves from the warring Blackfoot and Cree nations who fought and then shared a peace pipe. Today, Wetaskiwin prides itself on being a city of 12,500 people in motion, with the highest per capita car sales in Canada.

If time permits, consider visiting Alberta Central Railway Museum— 6.6 kilometres east of Wetaskiwin on Secondary 613 and then 10 kilometres south on Secondary 822. Named after the railway that served central Alberta from 1913 to 1981, the museum features a train station, a collection of old locomotives, freight cars, and cabooses, and a 1906 grain elevator. Visitors can take a short ride in an observation car or try the working telegraph.

To return to Calgary, continue south on Secondary 822 for 6.5 kilometres, go west on Secondary 611 for 11 kilometres to Hobbema, and then follow Highway 2A south to Ponoka, just east of Highway 2.

---

### EATS & DRINKS

In Wetaskiwin, have lunch at the **Blacktop Diner** at the Reynolds-Alberta Museum, try the warm huckleberry pie or dill pickle soup at **Huckleberry's Café** (103, 3840–56th Street), or sample some smoked ribs or chili cheese fries at **Terracotta Café** (4808–50th Avenue).

---

## DRY ISLAND BUFFALO JUMP PROVINCIAL PARK

**Route:** From the intersection of 16th Avenue and 68th Street NE, drive 50 kilometres east on the Trans-Canada Highway. Turn left on Highway 21 and drive 102 kilometres north, to just past Huxley, and then 19 kilometres east on a good gravel road to Dry Island Buffalo Jump Provincial Park.

**Driving Distance:** About 170 kilometres one way.
**Note:** Dry Island Buffalo Jump Provincial Park is a day-use area open 7:00 a.m. to 11:00 p.m. from May through September. The park may be closed during rainy periods when the steep entrance road becomes impassable. Phone 403-823-1749.

Arriving at the bluff overlooking Dry Island Buffalo Jump is one of the most dramatic moments a motorist can experience in Alberta. Suddenly the grassy plateau drops away to reveal fantastically eroded badlands and their primary sculptor, the placidly winding Red Deer River. While any such perch over the Red Deer River Valley inspires awe, this is one of the most magnificent. Certainly, this approach provides the steepest descent through the geological ages to the valley bottom.

Dry Island Buffalo Jump Provincial Park (now there's a mouthful) has no campgrounds and only a few scanty trails. The idea is to marvel at the scenery without contributing to its rapid erosion. It's worth packing a picnic lunch, which can be eaten at tables near the Red Deer River. The rest of the day can be profitably spent visiting the nearby towns of Trochu and Three Hills.

The drive north on Highway 21 is one of the loveliest in central Alberta. Along the way, the road dips through several green valleys of considerable size. You might wonder how they were formed, considering the creeks that flow through them—including Kneehills, Threehills, and Ghostpine—are scarcely noticeable. At the end of the last ice age, melting glacial waters and mountain runoff formed the huge Glacial Lake Drumheller behind the retreating continental ice sheet. The fingers of this lake reached up into the drainages you're crossing. When they drained, broad valleys were left behind.

From the viewpoint overlooking Dry Island Buffalo Jump Provincial Park, the Red Deer River Valley drops through 200 metres of badland terrain. It was created over the past 13,000 post-glacial years as the forces of water, wind, and frost cut through the soft layers of exposed bedrock, which were laid down as marine sediments between 63 million and 68 million years ago.

In front of you is a large flat hill, or mesa, severed from the surrounding prairie by the eroding power of side streams. Because it was never

Badlands of Red Deer River Valley from Dry Island Buffalo Jump Provincial Park.

surrounded by water, it's called Dry Island. The prairie grasses atop the island have also never been disturbed by grazing or cultivation.

The Buffalo Jump portion of the park name refers to a large cliff to the south, used several times by early Aboriginal hunters to drive buffalo to their death. Tools, bits of pottery, firepits, and other evidence of processing camps unearthed near the base of the cliff indicate the jump was used at least four times between 700 and 2,800 years ago. This 45-metre buffalo jump is unusually high compared to others, such as Head-Smashed-In near Fort Macleod, which in its prime had a mere 10-metre drop (see pages 48–52).

Dry Island was one of the more northerly buffalo jumps. Farther north, increased tree cover and different topography favoured other means of hunting, such as stalking and herding the animals into corrals. Later the horse and gun allowed native peoples to chase buffalo more directly.

Archaeologists weren't the first whites to scour this landscape for buried treasures. Famed American palaeontologist Charles Sternberg rafted down the river here in search of fossils during the Great Cana-

dian Dinosaur Rush, which reached its peak just before World War I. More recently, the bones and teeth of *Tyrannosaurus* and *Dromaeosaurus* were discovered here, along with the fossilized remains of clams, fish, turtles, and birds dating back some 65 million years.

You can find refuge from the heat trapped in these arid badlands by descending steeply to picnic sites along the Red Deer River. Here, the moist valley floor supports cottonwood and aspen trees and an understorey of saskatoons and wild roses. This greenery provides shelter and food for a variety of birds and animals. Early morning and evening are good times to see deer and coyotes along the river's edge.

A walk down to the river reveals slow-moving water that cuts into the soft banks and carries deposits of mud, silt, and sand downstream. Across the river, tall stands of white spruce thrive in the cool, moist conditions of the steep and sheltered slope. From the river's edge, rough trails lead northeast up to the mesa and west to the base of the buffalo jump. Route-finding skills are needed and care must be taken to not further erode the area's fragile soils.

On the return trip south on Highway 21, it's worth stopping in Trochu, an exceptionally tidy prairie town that features a museum and

The historic St. Ann Ranch Country Inn, near Trochu.

an arboretum with some 200 varieties of trees and shrubs. On the outskirts of town is the St. Ann Ranch Country Inn, a provincial historic site that now boasts a bed and breakfast and a museum featuring several pioneer buildings. A group of aristocratic cavalrymen from the Brittany area of France formed the ranch in 1905. While many left to defend their homeland during World War I, a few returned, including Ernest Frère. His grandson's family now owns the ranch.

A short drive south of Trochu is Three Hills, a strong Christian community with nine churches and the Prairie Bible Institute. It's one of the largest bible schools in North America, preparing missionaries for work around the world. Guided tours of the institute's campus and its 4,500-seat auditorium can be arranged by phoning toll free 1-800-661-2425.

---

### EATS & DRINKS

In Three Hills, the **Floral & Gift** coffee shop (507 Main Street) has good coffee and ice cream, while **Harvest House** (126–4th Avenue N) offers nice, reasonably priced lunches.

---

# RUMSEY ECOLOGICAL RESERVE

**Route:** From the Country Hills Boulevard overpass at Calgary's northern outskirts, drive 125 kilometres to Drumheller via Highway 2 north and Highway 72/9 east. From Drumheller, drive about 53 kilometres north on Highway 56 and turn east onto a small, unmarked road (if you miss the turn, it's about 3 kilometres south of the Byemoor/Endiang Road).
**Driving Distance:** About 180 kilometres one way.
**Note:** Though the ecological reserve is on crown land, it's part of a grazing lease. Please take care to tread lightly on the land and not disturb any cattle. • The Morrin Sod House and Historical Park is open 9:30 a.m. to 5:30 p.m. Wednesday to Sunday in summer. Phone 403-772-3870 to arrange a tour.

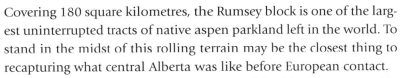

Covering 180 square kilometres, the Rumsey block is one of the largest uninterrupted tracts of native aspen parkland left in the world. To stand in the midst of this rolling terrain may be the closest thing to recapturing what central Alberta was like before European contact.

In 1990, about 34 square kilometres of this block were set aside as the Rumsey Ecological Reserve. It has thus been protected from the fate of more than 80 percent of Canada's aspen parkland, lost to farming and other development.

En route, it's worth stopping at Morrin (20 kilometres north of Drumheller) to visit the Morrin Sod House and Historical Park, built to honour the area's early pioneers and reconstructed in 2009. Such buildings weren't uncommon on prairie homesteads, especially where wood was in short supply. Sod strips for the walls were often dug from sloughs, and poles covered with grass or hay fashioned a rather porous roof. Yet the thick walls of these crude shelters provided surprisingly good insulation from cold and heat.

Another nearby relic is the ghost town of Rowley, with a population of about a dozen. Despite its abandonment by people and the railway, the remaining locals have restored several pioneer buildings, including a saloon, and purchased the local grain elevators. A couple of movies, including *Bye Bye Blues*, have also been shot in Rowley.

North of Morrin, the terrain suddenly becomes hilly. This is classic knob-and-kettle topography, created when large ice sheets stagnated and disintegrated some 10,000 years ago. As the ice melted, it deposited large mounds of glacial debris separated by hollows. The result today is closely spaced hills with soils, wetlands, and topography generally unsuited for cultivation. As a result, much of this area was untouched by the farmer's plough, which destroys native grasslands.

Aspen parkland is a transition zone between boreal forest to the north and prairie to the south. Rumsey is near its southern boundary on the plains. Aspen parkland is characterized by aspen forest in moist, sheltered areas and by fescue grasslands on drier, exposed areas such as hilltops and south-facing slopes.

The Rumsey Ecological Reserve preserves native aspen parkland.

The zone between grass and trees is a constant battleground for supremacy. In the Rumsey area, where some 70 percent of the landscape is covered in grass, fires are believed to have helped limit the spread of aspen. In the past, Aboriginal peoples set fires to keep aspen and willow in check and to regenerate the grasses on which their main source of food, the bison, grazed. Where fire is suppressed, aspen will eventually reclaim lost territory.

The trees within an aspen grove are often remarkably similar, both in size and in the timing of the greening and yellowing of their leaves. They are, in fact, clones. The roots of mature aspen produce suckers, which shoot out of the ground to become trees. Thus a considerable grove can arise from one parent root system.

The aspen in the Rumsey Ecological Reserve are relatively short and grow in dense thickets, as anyone attempting to walk through will discover. The groves provide excellent cover for sizable populations of mule and white-tailed deer and some sharp-tailed grouse. The reserve harbours several animal and plant species not commonly found in the area or the province. These include Baird's sparrow, upland sandpiper, sharp-tailed sparrow, the rare prairie vole, and plants such as alkali bluegrass, American winter cress, and spangletop grass.

At the north end of the reserve, several uncommon flat-topped hills rise above the hummocky moraine. In the southwest area is a glacial spillway and eskers—serpentine ridges of gravel left by streams that once flowed under glacial ice. Other noteworthy habitats within the reserve are numerous wetlands, moist alkaline meadows, and an ungrazed quarter-section in the southeast corner.

In the winter of 1793, Hudson's Bay Company explorer Peter Fidler passed through or near the area. This was an important wintering area, as the rolling terrain provided shelter for both the buffalo that roamed the plains and their Blackfoot pursuers. With the disappearance of the buffalo and the signing of treaties, this area became open rangeland in the early 1900s. The grazing rights were acquired in 1911 by the Calgary-based Burns empire, which relinquished its lease to Jim Walters and Tom Usher six years later.

The Usher family was an excellent steward for many decades. In 1990, more than 13 sections of their lease became the Rumsey Ecological Reserve, with the reserve lands still grazed in a carefully managed fashion to ensure that the native grasslands would be perpetuated (the grazing lease was taken over by another local family in 2001). Please show the same respect when visiting the reserve to ensure the preservation of this small piece of a vanishing habitat.

In 1996, a 150-square-kilometre natural area, just south of the ecological reserve, was created by the province. Unfortunately, this much larger chunk of fescue grassland doesn't enjoy the same level of protection, as oil and gas leases have been sold on these lands, with plans to produce coalbed methane.

## STETTLER STEAM TRAIN

**Route:** From the Country Hills Boulevard/Delacour Road overpass, drive 126 kilometres north on Highway 2 to the south end of Red Deer. Take Secondary 595 east for 45 kilometres, Highway 21 north, and Highway 12 east to Stettler. Alberta Prairie Railway Excursions is located in the train station on the east side of Stettler.

**Driving Distance:** About 210 kilometres one way.

**Note:** Alberta Prairie Railway Excursions (www.absteamtrain.com) operates old-fashioned steam train trips from Stettler from spring through the fall, with a couple of Christmas specials. Ticket purchases include a country dinner. For information and schedules, phone toll free 1-800-282-3994 or 403-290-0980 in Calgary.

• The Stettler Town and Country Museum (6304–44th Avenue) is open daily 10:00 a.m. to 5:30 p.m. from early May to early September. Phone 403-742-4534.

In the 1920s and '30s, the train was the way to travel through rural Alberta. It carried passengers to the city, mail and freight to distant destinations, and even hockey fans to a rival town for a Saturday night game. With all the stops to pick up passengers and freight, a rural run of only 80 kilometres might take nearly all day.

Today's frenzied urban dwellers can now experience that era of leisurely travel. Since 1990, Alberta Prairie Railway Excursions of Stettler has been offering day trips through central Alberta farmland, complete with country meals. Passengers can once again watch engine smoke billowing past the window, stick their head out between cars, and feel the swaying, clickety ride as they head to the concession or bar car. The trips travel south from Stettler to Big Valley and return five to six hours later.

A steam train is a great way to see rural Alberta. Instead of focusing on a blurred white line, you're riding high on the rails as you pass close by open fields, aspen groves, sloughs, and farmyards at a leisurely pace of about 35 kilometres per hour. On a country train, wildlife is just outside the window. You're likely to see ducks, geese, and perhaps tundra swans winging by, deer grazing, and hawks circling overhead. On one trip, I saw a coyote chasing a red fox across a field.

An Alberta Prairie train is also a vehicle for a moving entertainment show. A couple dressed in cabaret finery passes through the cars, singing popular songs from early in the century. Train host "Gabriel Dumont"—with his long hair, scraggly beard, and Sharps rifle—provides commentary on the passing countryside and a history of the great

Historic steam train pulls into restored station in Big Valley.

Metis leader he portrays. Dumont is usually called upon to apprehend masked and mounted bandits who halt the train and extract from passengers loose change, given to children's hospitals. Alberta Prairie also offers special murder mystery and live theatre trips.

The train is an eclectic connection of a steam locomotive, two cabooses, and passenger, lounge, and observation cars. Many were built around 1920 and served for decades on a variety of lines, including the southern United States, before being bought and restored for Alberta Prairie's use. On a full run, the string of coaches can extend more than 300 metres, making it one of the longest passenger trains in Canada.

The rail line on which these trips run was built in 1911 by Canadian Northern Railway as part of a branch line from Calgary to Vegreville, where it joined the Edmonton-Winnipeg main line. When Canadian Northern merged with the rival Grand Trunk Pacific Railway to form Canadian National Railway around 1920, most north-south traffic shifted to the nearby Grand Trunk line to the east, though this line still carried passengers and freight.

Part of this money-losing stretch through Stettler was finally bought in the mid-1980s by Central Western Railway, a small company that still hauls grain and other commodities. Alberta Prairie was formed in 1990 to take over Central Western's passenger service, thus keeping this important tourist attraction alive.

While Stettler is enjoying the fruits of this fledgling railway, its vibrant economy still revolves around agriculture and, to a lesser extent, petroleum. It's a key commercial centre in east-central Alberta, with a population of some 6,000 providing business services to rural areas as distant as the Saskatchewan border. While in Stettler, it's worth visiting the Town and Country Museum—which houses more than two dozen early buildings—or taking a walking tour of a dozen historic downtown buildings (pick up a brochure in the town office).

The production end of the area's agricultural economy can be seen as the train chugs south past fields of wheat, barley, canola, and hay. One reason for Stettler's long-standing success is that the valley's farmland has never experienced a crop failure. Much of the acreage is devoted to hay, which fuels a strong cattle industry. The Stettler area is known for its purebred strains, such as Charolais and Simmental, which are raised as seed stock and then crossbred by beef producers elsewhere in Alberta.

Signs of the petroleum industry are soon visible as the train approaches Big Valley. A major oil field was discovered here in 1950, producing large quantities of oil and gas that are now largely depleted. The petroleum discovery replaced an earlier coal boom that once saw seven mines producing coal, primarily for heating homes.

Big Valley, a pretty community of 300 residents nestled in a broad valley, is no stranger to booms and busts. At one time, it was a major divisional point on this rail line, supporting a population of more than 1,000. Locomotives were serviced and repaired here in a roundhouse, so-called because of its circular layout around a turntable. Today, the roundhouse is a concrete skeleton, with interpretive signs relating its glory days. Across the tracks, Big Valley's 1912 railway station has been lovingly restored to serve the new passenger train and to house a collection of historical photographs and community artifacts. Up the hill is the 1916 St. Edmund's Anglican Church, which retains its original pews and some 30 years ago was painted a vibrant blue.

---

### EATS & DRINKS

In Stettler, stop at **Coffee Tree** (4816–50th Street; try the paninis at lunch) and **Bloke's Bakery** (5009–50th Avenue). The Stettler steam train trips include a roast beef buffet meal, usually served in Big Valley. Five-course fine dining trips run on selected winter weekends. On Big Valley's Jimmy Jock Boardwalk, **Hulley's Hideaway Café** offers coffee, tea, cinnamon buns, and light meals, while **Granny's Fudge Factory** sells homemade fudge.

# East

# EAST OF CALGARY

The popular impression of the land east of Calgary is flat-as-a-pancake prairie. That impression no doubt dissuades many people from contemplating day trips east of the city.

Yet the prairies east of Calgary are surprisingly diverse and by no means flat. Anyone travelling east on the Trans-Canada Highway will soon realize these high plains are rolling. In many places, they provide panoramic views over a landscape that gradually becomes lower and flatter to the east and south. Even relatively flat stretches are periodically cut by draws and small drainages.

The most impressive landscape east of Calgary is the dramatic badlands of the lower Red Deer River Valley. The forces of erosion have cut deeply through the exposed bedrock, creating a fantastic array of sculpted shapes. In sharp contrast to these desert-like lands are the nearby valley bottoms, which provide an oasis in the dry prairie for a diversity of plants and wildlife.

The two best places to see the badlands east of Calgary are in the Drumheller Valley and at Dinosaur Provincial Park, the latter a UNESCO World Heritage Site. Both contain rich deposits of dinosaur and other fossils. Many of these fossils are on display near Drumheller at the Royal Tyrrell Museum, one of the best museums of its kind in the world. Drumheller also offers the day visitor two of Alberta's finest short driving loops, both packed with scenery and coal-mining history.

The other major destination east of Calgary is the Brooks area. Irrigation has transformed much of the shortgrass prairie here into productive farmland and created wetland habitats for many species of birds. Visitors to Brooks can visit a historic aqueduct or watch white pelicans and other birds at Lake Newell.

Despite the impact of irrigation agriculture, there are still tracts of native mixed-grass and rough fescue prairie on the eastern plains. One of the best places to visit these is the Hand Hills Ecological Reserve, east of Drumheller.

Halfway between Brooks and Calgary is the recently opened, $25-million Blackfoot Crossing Historical Park. With its superb design, wealth of artifacts, and spectacular setting, it rivals Head-Smashed-In Buffalo Jump as one of the finest Plains Aboriginal interpretive centres in the world.

# IRRIGATION CANAL CYCLE

**Route:** Follow Southland Drive east to its terminus at an off-leash parking lot. Cycle across the Bow River Bridge, turn right along the pathway and, in a few hundred metres, go left on a path that skirts a large quartzite boulder. At its intersection with 18th Street SE, follow Riverglen Drive east, then go left on Riverstone Road and left again on 24th Street. After two blocks, go right on 83rd Avenue and then left on 26th Street to reach the Glenmore Trail/Shepard Road intersection. Cross Shepard Road to intercept the Western Headworks Canal pathway along the south side of Glenmore Trail. Turn right and follow the pathway (along the left side of the canal) south, then east and finally northeast to Chestermere Lake. (For a more visual sense of this description, consult a *City of Calgary Bike & Pathway Map*, available at many cycling shops.) Return the same way, or have a pickup vehicle at Chestermere, reached off the Trans-Canada Highway east of Calgary.
**Cycling Distance:** About 40 kilometres return, to and from Chestermere Lake.

Here's a pleasant half-day trip from Calgary where you leave your car in the city. Instead, you cycle along the Western Irrigation District canal pathway from southeast Calgary to Chestermere Lake. Along the way, you'll see a diversity of birdlife, pass two wetlands, and traverse farmland.

Cycling along the Western Headworks Canal near Chestermere Lake.

The pavement is wide, smooth, and level, which also makes it attractive for athletes training on in-line skates and rollerblades. The pathway is generally uncrowded, though you may have to dodge droppings from young families of Canada geese nesting along the irrigation canal. Unless you're fighting a headwind or dawdling, the cycling time should be less than two hours each way.

The path follows an old service road alongside the Western Headworks Canal. When the canal underwent a major overhaul and expansion in the early 1990s, trail promoters and various government agencies convinced reluctant adjacent landowners to convert the service road into a recreational path. Completed in 1994—and running from the diversion weir on the Bow River, just downstream of the Calgary Zoo, to Chestermere Lake—the pathway earned Alberta Environment a heritage award.

Those interested in cycling the full 27-kilometre path (54 kilometres return) can start from Max Bell Arena and cross the Deerfoot pedestrian bridge; a start at the Bow Waters Canoe Club (just east of Deerfoot Trail and 17th Avenue SE) cuts a few kilometres off. The

route described here trims another 10 kilometres by starting at the Southland Drive off-leash parking lot and intersecting the canal pathway closer to the eastern city limits.

Once on the pathway, cyclists initially pass industrial warehouses and rail yards, with the din of heavy truck traffic nearby. But soon enough, the city falls behind, with the route following the left side of the irrigation canal past fields of canola, grain, and hay, occasionally crossing quiet roads.

The Western Headworks Canal was built between 1903 and 1906 by Canadian Pacific Railway (CPR), which had earlier received federal lands east of Calgary for completing the railway and wanted to develop irrigation to attract settlers to these generally dry farmlands. The timber headworks (later replaced by concrete) were built on the Bow River in Calgary, diverting water into a 26-kilometre canal that flowed into a reservoir, now known as Chestermere Lake. From there, a system of secondary canals, flumes, and ditches delivered the irrigation water to farmers near Strathmore and beyond. At the time, the diversion project was the world's second largest, behind only that of the Nile River in Egypt.

Although the irrigation project was initially successful in attracting farmers, the CPR was ready to abandon the money-losing system by the early 1940s. The system was saved by the 1944 formation of the Western Irrigation District (WID), which now provides water for some 400 member farmers on 39,000 hectares of land, as well as to 12,000 people in four neighbouring communities. Currently, WID canals are increasingly being contaminated by stormwater runoff from booming housing development just northeast of Calgary, with the resulting weed and algae growth affecting irrigation water quality and pumping efficiency.

Beyond the city limits, the pathway passes a golf course and two wetlands that provide important habitat for geese, ducks, snipe, killdeer, blackbirds, marsh wrens, and blue herons. In the fall, early-morning and evening cyclists can often pass beneath skies black with waterfowl preparing for their long migration south.

In early October, the canals are allowed to run dry for the approaching winter. At such times, trout and other fish that have migrated into the canal from the Bow River can become stranded in deeper pools. To protect them from near-certain death, Trout Unlimited Canada has since 1996 undertaken a fish rescue program on this and other southern Alberta irrigation canal systems; the fish are temporarily shocked, netted, and returned to the river. The overall program, which has thus far saved hundreds of thousands of fish lives, would be unnecessary if an admittedly more expensive solution was implemented: installing sturdy screens to prevent fish from entering such canals in the first place.

Just beyond an old steel bridge, you reach the town of Chestermere. Long a summer village that attracted visitors who came to sail, paddle, or picnic, Chestermere has become a booming bedroom community of Calgary, its population growing from 700 in 1989 to 15,000 in 2012. Cyclists who wish to add about 5 kilometres to their journey can pedal around the 300-hectare lake through neighbourhoods of large houses.

---

### EATS & DRINKS

The fast-food restaurants and gas station convenience stores clustered towards the north end of Chestermere Lake may well meet the quick-fix needs of sweaty cyclists. For more substantial refuelling, try the Vietnamese subs to go at **Pho Lan Restaurant**, farther southwest at 402 Merganser Drive West.

---

# BIRDWATCHING TOUR

**Route:** From Barlow Trail SE, take Glenmore Trail/Secondary 560 east for 41.5 kilometres. Go south on Secondary 817 and then east on Township Road 232 for 3.2 kilometres, turning north on Range Road 250 to reach the southwest corner of Eagle Lake. To reach Namaka Lake, return to Township Road 232 and drive about 12 kilometres east, turning south just past the northeast end of Namaka Lake and following a short gravel road to a dead end, where a parking area provides foot access to the lake.

**Driving Distance:** About 70 kilometres one way.

The Calgary area is a bird lover's paradise. The overlapping of three distinct ecosystems—fescue grassland, aspen parkland, and foothills forest—provides a diversity of habitat for nesting and migrating birds. Add sloughs, alpine meadows, and boreal forest within an hour's drive, and it's easy to see why some 350 feathered species have been recorded in the greater Calgary area.

This tour of Eagle and Namaka lakes covers two of the area's best birdwatching sites. Because of their proximity to the city, both can be comfortably visited in a half-day's outing. Plan this trip for spring or late summer to mid-fall, when the influx of migratory birds fills the skies and wetlands. Try to be at the lakes in the early morning or evening, when birds are most active.

Carry a bird identification book, if you have one, and binoculars or a spotting scope. While any type of binoculars will do, a pair with a magnification of about 7 × 35 is recommended, especially for the distant viewing often required on lakes.

Heading east of Calgary, the city bustle quickly vanishes in the vast prairie landscape. These lands are part of the Western Irrigation District (WID), as is evident from irrigation canals and pivot sprinklers along the way. Water diverted from the Bow River within Calgary is fed east through a system of canals and reservoirs, including Eagle and Namaka lakes, to more than 400 farms (covering 39,000 hectares) and to 12,000 people in four communities. Unlike on the dry prairie farther east, irrigation in the WID is more of an insurance policy than a necessity.

En route, a variety of winged predators can often be seen preening on fence posts, resting in treetops, or circling high overhead in pursuit of unwary rodents or other small animals. The most common of these are Swainson's and red-tailed hawks, although the odd bald eagle or snowy owl might be spotted in winter.

A hawk vacates a fence post near Eagle Lake.

From a hilltop 40 kilometres east of the starting point, ◗Eagle Lake suddenly comes into view. It's one of the largest lakes in the Calgary vicinity and a prairie oasis.

Eagle Lake holds little allure for swimmers. The shallow water is murky brown and weedy. But it contains lots of nutrients for a variety of waterfowl and shorebirds. From the south end of the lake, those with persistence and a trained eye might also spot great blue herons, eared grebes, soras, and terns. A marshy roadside slough near Eagle Lake Park along the east shore is also a good place to see numerous songbirds up close.

In fall, mallard and pintail ducks and Canada and white-fronted geese use the lake as a base for morning and evening forays into nearby fields of wheat, barley, oats and, surprisingly, peas. Essentially, they're carbo-loading for the long flight south. Geese prefer to land in summerfallow or ploughed fields and then walk into adjoining fields of harvested grain.

Although smaller than Eagle Lake, nearby ◗Namaka Lake is one of the best places in the Calgary region to see waterfowl and shore-birds, especially during the spring and fall migrations. An astounding 175 species of birds have been spotted here, including such treats as tundra swans, snow geese, sandhill cranes, common loons, white pelicans, and American bitterns.

Nature has been aided by humans. Originally a smaller lake, Namaka increased in size early last century when the Canadian Pacific Railway started the irrigation system to lure settlers to lands east of Calgary. The pioneer conservation group Ducks Unlimited helped the cause in 1949 by building control structures and canals that resulted in more consistent water levels. More recently, the bird habitat has been improved by the planting of trees and shrubs and the creation of nesting islands.

From the parking lot, a grassy track leads down to the water on a neck of land that almost cuts the lake in two. Some of the best bird-watching is farther south, along the reedy shoreline.

For more excellent birdwatching, head to Frank Lake, just east of High River (see page 29).

## MARKET GARDEN TOUR

**Route:** This is a design-your-own trip. The Alberta Farm Fresh Producers Association (AFFPA) publishes a brochure, *Come to Our Farms*, which lists member growers in Alberta. The brochure is available at many travel information offices. Or you can call the AFFPA at 1-800-661-2642, or check out its site at www.alberta farmfresh.com. Alternatively, simply drive east of Calgary a short distance on the Trans-Canada Highway and watch for U-pick road signs.

Not all fruits and vegetables come from grocery stores or farmers' markets. And the freshest produce one can find, outside a backyard plot, is within easy driving distance of the city. These are market gardens, where a variety of fruits and vegetables can be picked or bought straight off the vine. A tomato, strawberry, or cob of corn never tasted sweeter than when eaten in its prime, rather than at the transportation convenience of a foreign agribusiness.

Purchasing produce at the farm gate is cheaper than at the supermarket, with all the proceeds going into the farmer's pocket. It's also an opportunity to see how the product is grown and what chemicals, if any, have been used. If nothing else, it's an excuse for a family outing into the countryside and a chance to chat with rural residents.

A trip to a market garden is also a means of replacing the losses from your own city garden. Despite its warm chinook winds in winter, Calgary has one of the worst climates in Alberta for growing vegetables, as anyone who has tried raising corn or tomatoes can attest. The reason is Calgary's high elevation (1,049 metres), which results in cool nights and frosts in late spring and early fall. I've lost more than one bean crop to an August snowstorm.

Many of the nearby market gardens are on small farms or acreages east of the city, though their numbers are increasing north of Calgary. The rolling farmland to the east is lower and slightly warmer than in Calgary, extending the growing season somewhat. True, these market gardeners don't benefit from the heat as do Taber's corn growers to the south, or from rich soils as do Red Deer–area growers to the north. Most years, however, they produce abundant and diverse crops of vegetables and fruits.

The most common crop is strawberries, which I guarantee are sweeter than anything imported from California or Mexico. Other fruits are saskatoons, raspberries, and tomatoes. Vegetables include peas, beans, carrots, potatoes, parsnips, lettuce, spinach, cucumbers, asparagus, and onions.

U-pick market gardens in the Calgary area include Serviceberry Farms (403-934-2412, Strathmore nearest community), Buckler Farms (403-932-6097, Cochrane), Freshfield Berry Farm (403-226-0056, Balzac), Purple Ridge Farm (403-948-7735, Airdrie), and Solstice Berry Farm (403-946-4759, Crossfield). A few other area market gardens only sell their produce at the farm gate. Note: All the phone numbers in this and the following paragraph are local calls from Calgary.

The Saskatoon Farm (403-938-6245), east of Okotoks, resembles an old prairie town. Its café features saskatoon pie, scones, and ice cream as well as breakfast burritos and home-raised-buffalo dishes. Just south of Strathmore, Bumbleberry Orchards (403-934-2749) offers the usual U-pick for its berries. In 2005, it also opened Alberta's first cottage fruit winery, Fieldstone Fruit Wines, which produces fruit and dessert wines with crops of its raspberries, strawberries, wild cherries, and saskatoons.

Although it's always possible to drop in on market gardens, it's best to phone ahead. That ensures the owners will be home and the crop is ready and hasn't temporarily been picked clean. The U-pick season is generally from early July until early September. If you can't make it to a market garden, you can often find the growers selling their produce at area farmers' markets.

# ROSEBUD

**Route:** From the intersection of 16th Avenue and 68th Street NE at the eastern outskirts of Calgary, drive 61 kilometres east on the Trans-Canada Highway. At the big bend in the highway, angle left onto Secondary 561 and follow it east for 7 kilometres. Turn north on Secondary 840, which leads to Rosebud in 31 kilometres.
**Driving Distance:** About 100 kilometres one way.
**Note:** The Rosebud Theatre operates from spring until Christmas. All tickets are by reservation only. Phone 403-667-2001 or toll free 1-800-267-7553; www.rose budtheatre.com.

This is a delightful trip through rolling countryside to the small town of Rosebud. Many Calgarians make this a full day's outing by attending the well-known Rosebud Theatre. But just getting there is at least half the fun.

The approach is on a quiet secondary highway northeast of Calgary. The road rises over hills etched with small draws and descends into intimate valleys with slow-moving streams. Famed Canadian artists A. Y. Jackson and H. G. Glyde came to Rosebud in 1944 to sketch and paint the area's farms and ranches.

The lower valleys of the Rosebud River and its tributary, Serviceberry Creek, once contained fingers of Glacial Lake Drumheller. This huge lake formed at the end of the last ice age, when glacial runoff was backed up by the retreating continental ice sheet. When the lake drained, it left broader, flatter valleys behind.

The Blackfoot called the river Akokiniskway, the "river of many rosebuds." The name refers to the profusion of wild roses, Alberta's provincial flower, that appear along the river's banks in June. Serviceberry Creek, which joins the river just west of Rosebud town, is named for the wild, delicious saskatoon berries, also called serviceberries, which ripen in summer in the river valleys.

Aboriginal peoples came to these valleys to pick berries, fish, and seek shelter from winter storms. In the surrounding hills, they hunted the buffalo that once covered the mixed-grass prairie in vast numbers. In 1792, Hudson's Bay Company surveyor Peter Fidler witnessed native people stampeding buffalo to their death over a steep cliff along the Rosebud River.

This area was long the domain of the Blackfoot. When a hunting party of Cree entered this Blackfoot territory around 1860, they were decisively beaten in a bloody combat at Battle Hill, south of Rosebud near Severn Creek. In the early 1950s, Severn Creek was dammed to control flooding and erosion and to provide water for downstream cattle. The resulting reservoir, 10 kilometres south of Rosebud, is now a popular place for picnicking and fishing for stocked trout.

In the winter of 1875, Methodist missionary John McDougall travelled east from his mission at Morleyville to the open country around Rosebud in search of buffalo. But by then the vast herds of buffalo had been nearly wiped out. Two years later, the Blackfoot, deprived of this life support and decimated by white diseases, signed Treaty No. 7 and thus relinquished their claim to these lands.

That paved the way for settlers. The first was the Wishart family, who camped here in 1885 en route to a new home in Montana. Captivated by the area's beauty, they never left, building a log house on a homestead along the Rosebud River.

In the ensuing years, Rosebud (www.rosebud.ca) became a thriving community of farmers and ranchers, reaching a population of 300 in the 1920s. The big boost was the completion of the Canadian

The Rosebud Opera House is one of many restored buildings in charming Rosebud.

Northern Railway's line between Drumheller and Calgary. This so-called Goose Lake Line stopped at Rosebud, where several elevators were erected to transport grain to distant markets. A number of coal mines also operated in the area, the last closing in the mid-1960s.

Today, tourism and the arts supplement the area's agricultural economy, with more than 40,000 visitors a year flocking to this hamlet of fewer than 100 residents; many visitors stay at one of the charming bed-and-breakfast establishments. A handful of Rosebud's early 20th-century buildings have been restored and converted to new uses. Rosebud Centennial Museum is housed in an old Chinese laundry, Akokiniskway Art Gallery is in a historic United church, Rosebud School of the Arts is in a hotel, and Rosebud Theatre is in a converted grain bin (now called the Opera House), with its dining room in an old mercantile building. It's a lovely, short stroll around the hamlet to view and read about these historic buildings.

The School of the Arts is a post-secondary Christian school that focuses on theatre arts. Since 1983, it has operated a popular non-denominational dinner theatre, attracting audiences from a wide area. In the early 1990s, it helped spawn a sister organization on Vancouver Island, the equally successful Chemainus Theatre Festival.

### EATS & DRINKS

In Rosebud, stop for afternoon pie at the **Rosebud Country Inn**. In summer, Field of Dreams Bed and Breakfast offers U-pick saskatoon berries.

# DRUMHELLER

**Route:** From the Country Hills Boulevard overpass, drive north on Highway 2 for 26 kilometres. Take the exit and follow Highway 72 east, which beyond Beiseker becomes Highway 9 leading to Drumheller. It's well worth stopping at Horseshoe Canyon, 8 kilometres before Drumheller, for a good introduction to the badlands landscape.
**Driving Distance:** About 125 kilometres one way.
**Note:** Drumheller can also be reached by driving east of Calgary on the Trans-Canada Highway and then heading north up a choice of Highway 9, Highway 21, or Secondary 840, with the last two offering perhaps the most scenic approaches. For a description of the Secondary 840 approach, see pages 164–65. The website is www.traveldrumheller.com.

The dinosaurs are long gone. So, too, more recently, are the coal mines. But their stories are told in the museums, relics, and even soft rocks of the Red Deer River Valley that cuts deeply through the area. It's the combination of natural features and history that makes the Drumheller Valley one of the most compelling destinations in Alberta, attracting more than 500,000 visitors a year. Though the valley is increasingly busy, especially on weekends from spring to early fall, it's still refreshingly uncrowded most weekdays. Arrive in the early morning and you'll be assured mostly empty roads.

The big draw, of course, is the Royal Tyrrell Museum, which opened in 1985. But the museum is only a lure to the other worthy

# Drumheller

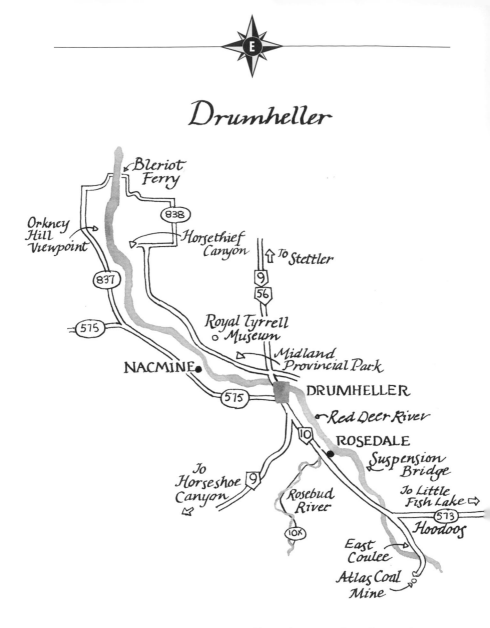

attractions of the Drumheller Valley. There are hoodoos, old coal mines, a stretch of 11 narrow bridges, a cable ferry, and native prairie grasslands. The most compelling feature of all is the deeply sculpted badlands of the Red Deer River Valley.

It's easy to get overwhelmed or overscheduled on a day trip to the Drumheller area. The best bet for the day tripper is to visit the

Visting the Hoodoos Recreation Area along the Hoodoo Trail.

museum and take one of the two superb short driving tours described here. The alternative is to stay overnight in one of the numerous area campgrounds, bed and breakfasts, or motels. If you have many visiting relatives and friends, chances are you'll be making more than one trip to Drumheller anyway, so you can divide the attractions into manageable pieces.

Drumheller is named after Samuel Drumheller, an American entrepreneur who, in the early 20th century, registered the sixth of 138 coal mines that once operated in the valley. Actually, the town could easily have carried the name of an earlier homesteader, Thomas Greentree. He lost a coin toss with Drumheller to see what the town should be called when the first post office opened in 1911.

Once well known for its jail, Drumheller has now awakened to its tourist opportunities. It boasts a growing number of small private museums, rock and fossil shops, and even a living Reptile World. Recent additions include a huge *Tyrannosaurus rex* replica—which at 26 metres high is billed as the world's largest dinosaur—a popular

The "world's largest dinosaur" in Drumheller.

spray park for overheated children, and a collection of whimsical, colourfully painted "cementosauruses" scattered around downtown. This town of 8,000, nestled in the floodplain of a deep valley, is also supported by the bread-and-butter industries of agriculture and oil and gas services.

## EATS & DRINKS

For breakfast, stop at **Whif's Flap Jack House** (in the Badlands Motel, 801 Dinosaur Trail). Elsewhere, try the grilled paninis at **Café Italiano** (35–3rd Avenue W) the mammoth burgers and fries at **Bernie & the Boys Bistro** (305–4th Street W), or the baked brie at **Sublime Food and Wine** (109 Centre Street).

### 🔥 Royal Tyrrell Museum

**Route:** The museum, located within Midland Provincial Park, is 7 kilometres west from downtown Drumheller on Secondary 838, also known as the Dinosaur Trail.
**Note:** The museum is open daily 9:00 a.m. to 9:00 p.m. from mid-May to the end of August, with reduced hours the rest of the year (closed Mondays winter and spring). Admission charged. Phone toll free 1-888-440-4240 or 403-823-7707; www.tyrrellmuseum.com.

The Royal Tyrrell Museum is arguably the finest dinosaur museum in the world. The $30-million-plus facility, which opened in 1985, contains dozens of complete dinosaur skeletons, as well as many audiovisual presentations and hands-on displays.

The Tyrrell is more than just a celebration of dinosaurs. Befitting a museum devoted to palaeontology—the study of ancient life through fossils—it chronicles 3.5 billion years of the earth's history, of which the dinosaur era was a significant snapshot. It's also a major research facility, where excavated fossils are studied, preserved, and, in many cases, prepared for display. Visitors can often watch this process up close.

As one of Alberta's most popular attractions, the Royal Tyrrell Museum is crowded with "dinophiles" throughout the summer. The best bet is to arrive at 9:00 a.m. sharp or in late afternoon or early evening, when the crowds have thinned somewhat. Expect to spend three or more hours touring the exhibits. Those with young children might consider limiting the time spent in the introductory sections to concentrate on the dinosaur displays.

The museum's name honours Joseph Burr Tyrrell, a renowned geologist with the Geological Survey of Canada, who, in 1884, discovered the first dinosaur remains, an *Albertosaurus* skull, in the Drumheller area. On the same trip, Tyrrell also noted the coal deposits in the Drumheller Valley. His discoveries eventually provoked rushes for both coal and dinosaur bones. The "Royal" in the name commemorates a British royal visit after the museum opened.

The Royal Tyrrell Museum houses one of the world's great dinosaur collections.

A tour of the museum includes meticulous reconstructions of the region's ancient underwater worlds, such as the 375-million-year-old Devonian Reef and the 500-million-year-old Burgess Shale, the latter complete with a glass floor. The highlight, of course, is the 150-million-year-old age of dinosaurs. In the Dinosaur Hall, one can gaze in wonder at fossilized footprints, dinosaur eggs, and magnificent skeletons of such creatures as the carnivorous *Albertosaurus* and the duck-billed *Edmontosaurus*.

The showstopper is still the immense and toothy *Tyrannosaurus rex*, the largest of the meat eaters and one of the last dinosaurs in this area. Scattered throughout the museum are special exhibits that feature recent finds such as a juvenile *Gorgosaurus*, one of the most complete specimens of its kind in the world.

Many of these skeletons were unearthed from ancient rock formations in the Red Deer River Valley, particularly around Drumheller and in Dinosaur Provincial Park, 140 kilometres downriver (see pages 199–202). The park's dinosaur beds are rivalled only by sites in China's Gobi Desert.

The dinosaur's world was closer to today's Florida coast than to the dry, rocky Red Deer Valley we now see. Seventy million years ago, this was a warm, lush environment on the edge of an inland sea. Dinosaurs roamed through swamps and marshes, eating the abundant vegetation or, if carnivorous, other creatures. An approximation of this environment can be experienced by visiting the museum's palaeoconservatory. It contains many prehistoric plants, including some that trace their ancestry back 350 million years.

What led to the sudden demise of the dinosaurs some 65 million years ago? There's still no conclusive answer. Some scientists believe it was caused by a gradual change in climate, while others lean to the catastrophic consequences of a huge meteorite impact. It's instructive to realize there was a much larger extinction of species prior to the dinosaur era. In fact, some 99 percent of all species that have ever lived on the earth are thought to be extinct.

Prehistoric exhibit at Royal Tyrrell Museum.

While the museum provides a gripping account of the dinosaur era, the surrounding valley also reveals millions of years of history to the observant. It's a good idea to escape the glassy-eyed indoor crowds and venture up to a viewpoint overlooking the badlands.

Better yet, take a short, self-guided interpretive walk into the badlands from near the museum's entrance. This trail provides a close-up look at the various layers of ancient silts, sands, muds, and plants compressed over the millennia into stratified rocks and coal deposits. These rock layers erode rapidly, occasionally exposing their long-buried treasures of dinosaur bones. Note: Don't disturb or remove any fossils you may encounter.

Those wishing to delve even deeper into this landscape or the dinosaur remains it contains can register for guided fossil prospecting hikes, badlands tours, or even a class in casting fossils. A fee is charged for these and other special services.

## Dinosaur Trail

**Route:** The route is well marked throughout as the Dinosaur Trail. From downtown Drumheller, cross the Red Deer River on Highway 9. Turn west on Secondary 838, which follows the river's north side. The route crosses the river at the Bleriot Ferry and loops back along the south side of the valley to Drumheller.
**Driving Distance:** About 47 kilometres return.

The Dinosaur Trail packs a lot of history and natural features into 47 kilometres as it follows a looping course along both sides of the Red Deer River. It's one of the best short driving tours in Alberta; to do it justice, allow at least two hours.

The tour begins by passing the Homestead Antique Museum, open May to October (403-823-2600; admission charged). Its 10,000-plus artifacts and antiques include a stuffed two-headed calf and a 1919 house purchased from an Eaton's catalogue.

Just beyond is Midland Provincial Park, a combination of riverside greenery and coal-mining history. Most of the park's lands were donated by Sidney McMullen, president of the Midland Mining

The Red River Valley from Orkney Hill Viewpoint, along the Dinosaur Trail.

Company, the last of four major coal mines that once operated in the boom-bust community of Midlandville. Within the park, you can follow interpretive trails to displays at grassed-over remains of old coal-mining sites. A 1912 mine office building contains a thick-walled safe, which held payrolls delivered by armed guards.

Across the road is McMullen Island, an oasis in the otherwise parched badlands. On a hot day, it's a good spot for a picnic, particularly if you've spent the morning hours in the nearby Royal Tyrrell Museum. As you drive into this day-use area, notice the sharp transition from desert-like to riverine vegetation. The dry sagebrush gives way to poplars, tall cottonwoods, and, finally, thick clumps of sandbar willows along the banks of the Red Deer River. The luxuriant growth here is made possible by deposited silts in the broad, flat part of a river valley that elsewhere is eroded into steep banks. This island of vegetation attracts deer, rabbits, and several songbirds.

A short distance past the Tyrrell Museum is the roadside Little Church, a non-denominational place of worship and meditation that seats six. Built by a local contractor in the late 1960s, it was reconstructed by inmates of the Drumheller federal penitentiary in 1991. For a closer look, duck into the church and squeeze into one of the single-person pews.

Not far beyond are views of the stratified layers of sandstones, mudstones, ironstones, and coal seams that make up the badlands; the nearby golf course features a spectacular back nine weaving through these deeply sculpted formations. Small rocks scattered alongside the road were carried here thousands of years ago by glaciers from as far away as the Precambrian Shield of the Northwest Territories. Some of these rocks—particularly those of granite, gneiss, or schist—could be more than 2 billion years old.

The road now climbs to a plateau overlooking the Red Deer River. In surrounding fields, pumpjacks are rhythmically lifting a mixture of oil, gas, and water from rock formations some 1.5 kilometres below the surface. The gas in this field is sour, meaning it contains deadly hydrogen sulphide gases. With several thousand oil and gas wells within a 50-kilometre radius of Drumheller, it's not surprising that

Gazing into the maze of badland gullies of Horsethief Canyon, along Dinosaur Trail.

energy servicing, along with agriculture, is a critical component of the area's economy.

The importance of ranching is evident in the name of a spectacular viewpoint, ◆Horsethief Canyon, just off the main road. In the past, horses apparently lost in the maze of badland gullies below would often reappear with different brands. While horses and cattle now graze in nearby fields, the prairie grasses that once flourished here were home to vast herds of bison as well as the now extinct plains grizzly bears and wolves. The wildest creatures one might see now are the more adaptable deer and coyotes.

An ancient form of life, oysters are preserved in a large fossilized rock at the Horsethief Canyon lookout. They are a 67-million-year-old legacy of a vast sea that once covered this now arid landscape.

The road soon drops steeply to the Red Deer River, which you cross on the Bleriot Ferry, one of the last remaining cable-operated ferries in Alberta. The small ferry, now gas-powered, previously made the short voyage by pointing its nose upstream and, with the aid of channel boards, allowing the current to carry it across. The ferry is named after Andre Bleriot, who homesteaded near here in 1902. He built and for many years operated the ferry. He was overshadowed, however, by brother Louis Bleriot, who in 1909 became the first person to fly a plane across a much bigger body of water, the English Channel.

Along the far side of the river is the Bleriot Ferry Campground. Cottonwoods and willows grow by the river; farther inland are native prairie grasses and wildflowers. Some of the area's first dinosaur bones were discovered nearby in the 1880s. That sparked the Great Canadian Dinosaur Rush of the early 20th century, during which internationally renowned scientists scoured the Red Deer Valley for fossilized dinosaur remains.

As the route leaves the river flats, the prairie grasses give way to stands of white spruce, which grow on the cooler and wetter north-facing slopes of the valley. Back on top of the plateau, it's a short drive to yet another magnificent lookout, ◆Orkney Hill Viewpoint. This high perch provides a clear view of how the river has cut its ever-shifting channel out of the soft banks. The higher terraces above the current floodplain are former riverbeds, abandoned when periods of high water flow cut a new and deeper channel.

Like a roller coaster, the road drops again to the floodplain and crosses several brackish streams. Despite their diminutive size, these streams have travelled many kilometres from the northwest to empty into the Red Deer River. The final stretch of road passes Nacmine (short for North American Collieries Mine) and Newcastle, two early coal-mining towns on the outskirts of Drumheller.

## Hoodoo Trail

**Route:** From the junction of Highways 9 and 10 in southeast Drumheller, follow Highway 10 (the Hoodoo Trail) east for 22 kilometres to the Atlas Coal Mine National Historic Site. Return the same way, taking a 7-kilometre detour from Rosedale to Wayne via Highway 10X.
**Driving Distance:** About 60 kilometres return.
**Note:** The East Coulee School Museum is open daily 10:00 a.m. to 5:00 p.m. in the summer, with reduced hours on weekdays the rest of the year. Phone 403-822-3970; www.ecsmuseum.ca. • The Atlas Coal Mine National Historic Site is open daily 9:30 a.m. to 8:30 p.m. from early May to mid-October, with reduced hours in spring and fall. Phone 403-822-2220; www.atlascoalmine.ab.ca. Admission charged for both facilities.

The Hoodoo Trail is another outstanding short driving tour in the Drumheller area. It's primarily a journey into the rich coal-mining history of the Drumheller Valley, including visits to a coal-mining National Historic Site and a Great Depression–era schoolhouse museum. Along the way are opportunities to stretch your legs on a long suspension bridge and stroll up to hoodoos sculpted by wind and water.

As you drive along this route, it's easy to see why coal mining was the dominant industry in this valley for the first half of the 20th century. The dark, narrow layers in the badland rocks are seams of coal, formed by the compression and transformation of swamp-like vegetation that grew here along the coast of an inland sea some 70 million years ago. Of the 11 identifiable coal seams in the valley, only four were commercially viable.

Peter Fidler noted these exposed coal strata while leading a Hudson's Bay Company expedition through the area in 1793. Nearly a century later, geologist Joseph Burr Tyrrell (for whom the nearby museum of palaeontology is named) rediscovered the valley's abundant coal deposits. Early settlers burned lumps of the coal in their stoves. But it wasn't until the Canadian National Railway arrived in 1911, providing access to Canadian markets, that a coal boom erupted.

Within a few years, more than 40 mines were operating in the Drumheller Valley, creating instant towns and prosperity. The coal was used to heat homes and the coal dust compressed into briquets to power steam railway locomotives. With the big oil discovery at Leduc, near Edmonton, in 1947, the demand for coal slumped, and most of the valley's remaining mines closed soon thereafter. The Atlas Coal Mine was the last to go, ceasing operations in 1979.

Relics of old mines and still-smouldering heaps of coal slag are evident along this drive. Just past Rosedale, you can walk on a 117-metre suspension bridge across the Red Deer River to the abandoned Star Mine, which operated from the mid-1910s to 1957.

If you think this swaying walk is exciting, consider the early miners who crossed the river first in rowboats, then in aerial cable cars. The suspension bridge was constructed in 1931 and rebuilt and upgraded by the Alberta government—after the mine closed—to allow the safe passage of visitors.

The next stop, 7.5 kilometres beyond the bridge, is the Hoodoos Provincial Recreation Area, where you can inspect the forces of nature on the rock pillars across the road. Hoodoo, a variation of the word *voodoo*, was the European term for these fantastically shaped formations. The Blackfoot and Cree had a more vivid sense of the pillars, believing them to be petrified giants who came alive at night to hurl rocks at intruders.

The Red Deer River Valley badlands from above Atlas Coal Mine National Historic Site.

Hoodoos are formed when a cap of hard sandstone protects the softer underlying rock from eroding as rapidly as the surrounding rock. The result is a free-standing pillar of sandstone on a thick base of shale. Once exposed to wind and water, hoodoos will erode away in a few thousand years. Geologists believe these particular pillars could be gone in a hundred years, a process perhaps accelerated by thoughtless people clambering all over the site.

It's another 5.4 kilometres to the entrance to East Coulee. This hamlet was, in the 1930s and '40s, a boom town of 3,500 people, many of them immigrants from Hungary and the Ukraine who worked in six area coal mines. The East Coulee School Museum, still heated with coal, has preserved that era through exhibits, a 1930s school classroom, and a reconstructed miner's shack and house.

Beyond East Coulee, the Atlas Coal Mine National Historic Site is reached by crossing a narrow trestle bridge, which once served cars and trains. The mine contains the last standing wooden tipple of its kind in Canada. This large wooden structure sorted and stored coal in bins for loading into boxcars and trucks bound for distant markets.

The mine closed in 1979 and is continually being restored as a coal museum, complete with an interpretive centre and several mining buildings. Various tours allow visitors to ride in an authentic mine locomotive, climb to the tipple's top, venture into a re-timbered mining tunnel, hear mining ghost stories, and hike up the hillside to a superb vantage point overlooking the badlands of the Drumheller Valley.

Return on Highway 10 to the small town of Rosedale, once the site of the largest coal mine in the Drumheller field, and drive south on Highway 10X. Over the next 7 kilometres, the road crosses 11 single-lane bridges over the meandering Rosebud River, called Misaskatoo-mina Sipisis by the Cree for the abundant saskatoon bushes in the narrow valley. Many of the original timbers for these bridges were floated downstream from Red Deer on the Red Deer River.

During its heyday, the Rosebud Valley near Wayne boasted six operating coal mines and a population of 2,000 people, more than Drumheller. Today, Wayne is a ghost town whose claim to fame is as a location for such films as *2001: A Space Odyssey* and *Shanghai Noon*. At the end of the road, The Last Chance Saloon in the century-old Rosedeer Hotel is a colourful place with historical black-and-white photos on the walls, a unique electronic bandbox, and bullet holes in the walls.

## EATS & DRINKS

The **East Coulee School Museum** has a tea room (open daily 11 a.m. to 4 p.m. in summer) offering lunches and tea; reservations are recommended for groups of more than three. The **Last Chance Saloon** in Wayne serves soups, stews, and thick steaks.

## Hand Hills

**Route:** From Highway 9 in Drumheller, drive 15.5 kilometres east on Highway 10. Turn left on Secondary 573, a good gravel road that leads in 25 kilometres to Little

Fish Lake Provincial Park. There are two ways to access the Hand Hills Ecological Reserve. One is to head about 1 kilometre north of Secondary 573 from west of Little Fish Lake. The other is to drive north of Little Fish Lake Provincial Park on Secondary 851, west for 5 kilometres on Secondary 576, and then south on Range Road 170 to the reserve boundary, marked with signs.

**Driving Distance:** About 45 kilometres one way from Drumheller.

**Note:** Although the Hand Hills Ecological Reserve is on crown land, leaseholders graze cattle on the site. Please respect these operations as well as the fragile natural habitat.

Little known or advertised, the Hand Hills contain one of the largest intact tracts of fescue grassland in the world. Since native prairie grasslands are among the most threatened habitats in the world, a visit to the Hand Hills Ecological Reserve is a rare opportunity. A picnic lunch at Little Fish Lake Provincial Park and a short drive north into the heart of the Hand Hills makes a nice half-day outing from Drumheller.

Most people imagine the terrain east of Drumheller to be flat and low-lying, so it's surprising to encounter the Hand Hills, the second-highest point in Canada between the Rocky Mountains and the east coast. A thick gravel cap has protected these hills of sandstone and shale from repeated glacial erosion, leaving them standing up to 185 metres above the surrounding prairie.

The Hand Hills cover a circular area extending north from Little Fish Lake to near Delia. The topography is undulating and cut by numerous steep-sided drainage valleys. The views of the rolling prairie and deep Red Deer River Valley are superb from these heights.

Established by the province in 1988, the Hand Hills Ecological Reserve protects 2,229 hectares of land near Little Fish Lake. The reserve lies in the northern fescue zone, a prairie grasslands subregion unique to Canada's Prairie provinces. Its ecosystems include rough fescue grasslands, alkaline seepage areas, seasonal sloughs, moist meadows, and aspen groves.

Much of Canada's fescue grasslands has been lost to agriculture. Once the fragile soils are turned by the plough, the native grasses are

Walking near the edge of Little Fish Lake.

lost forever. Intensive cattle grazing can also disturb this native prairie beyond repair.

The ecological reserve's native prairie is still largely intact because it has been neither ploughed nor intensively grazed. A management plan was devised for the Hand Hills reserve to allow for some continued grazing while preserving the natural habitats. But this area is still vulnerable to further damage.

As you stand amid the reserve's swaying grasses, try to imagine this landscape as early explorers would have seen it 200 years ago. Back then, the native prairie stretched to the horizon on rolling hills. Aboriginal hunters frequently set up teepees in these high hills, gaining extensive views over the surrounding prairie. According to legend, the Hand Hills are named for a Blackfoot warrior with a withered hand who died during a battle here with the Cree.

Today, perhaps the most immediate sensation for visitors is felt through the feet. Unlike a planted field or an urban lawn, the native prairie ground is uneven, crunching underfoot as you gingerly walk over it. It's a bit like tramping around the hummocky edge of a slough. If you get down on your hands and knees, you'll discover the layer above the dark brown soil consists of tiny plants such as clubmosses, mosses, and lichens.

Arising from these humps is a variety of grasses, principally rough fescues, which grow in large clumps up to 50 centimetres tall. Because these fescues are fairly sensitive to grazing, secondary grasses such as porcupine, June, and wheat grasses become more dominant in disturbed areas. Blue grama grasses and low sedges are found on more heavily grazed sites.

Among the reserve's profusion of summer wildflowers are rare and uncommon plants, including crowfoot violet, stiff yellow paintbrush, mountain shooting star, and, along the lakeshore, small-flowered evening primrose. Aspen groves and shrubs are found in sheltered draws.

The reserve's wildlife includes sharp-tailed grouse, thirteen-lined ground squirrels, long-tailed weasels, badgers, coyotes, mule deer, and such threatened or endangered species as Baird's sparrow, ferruginous hawk, and peregrine falcon. The 10,000-year-old fossilized bones of prairie dogs have also been found in the Hand Hills. During the last interglacial period, they created extensive networks of tunnels beside rivers. A species of gregarious burrowing rodent, prairie dogs are no longer found in Alberta.

Little Fish Lake, which cuts into the eastern boundary of the ecological reserve, was once a popular destination for fishing and boating. Though the lake has receded considerably in recent years and is now usually dry, the provincial park at its southeast corner still attracts some campers. The park contains several archaeological sites, where teepee rings and campsites have been discovered.

Piping plovers, an endangered species in Canada, often nest along the lake's gravelly shores. Fewer than 150 piping plovers have been recorded in recent surveys in all of Alberta, prompting the creation of a provincial recovery plan for these small shorebirds. Controlled grazing and restricted pedestrian access, particularly during critical nesting periods, are among the measures being used to protect piping plovers at Little Fish Lake. Please keep a respectful distance at all times.

To reach the height of the Hand Hills, take the scenic drive north of Little Fish Lake on Secondary 851. Just south of Delia is Mother Mountain, which offers a panoramic view over the prairies. Return to Drumheller via Highways 9 west and 56 south.

# DOROTHY-HANNA LOOP

**Route:** From the intersection of 16th Avenue and 68th Street NE, drive east on the Trans-Canada Highway for 61 kilometres and then continue east on Secondary 561 for 29 kilometres to Hussar. Go north on Highway 56 for 17 kilometres, east on Secondary 564 for 15 kilometres and then north on gravel, bearing right after 7 kilometres onto Secondary 848, which soon leads to Dorothy. Head east on Secondary 570 for 35 kilometres to reach Highway 36, which is followed north for 40 kilometres to Highway 9, just east of Hanna. Returning from Hanna, drive 145 kilometres due west on Highways 9, 27, and 582 (only the numbers change, not the direction) to Highway 2, which is followed south to Calgary.

**Driving Distance:** About 425 kilometres return.

**Note:** The Hanna Museum and Pioneer Village (Pioneer Trail and 3rd Avenue E) is open 10:00 a.m. to 6:00 p.m. daily from June through August and in May and September by appointment. Phone 403-854-4244; www.hanna.ca.

This is a big, meandering drive through gorgeous, rolling country to the charming semi–ghost town of Dorothy and then across flatter prairie to Hanna, a farming centre in east-central Alberta. Along the way, you'll see badlands, bluebirds, perhaps pronghorn, and, in early fall, swarms of migrating geese. On the return, a short detour to the elevated community of Delia rounds out the grand tour. The drive to Dorothy also makes a lovely alternative access to the Drumheller area.

The trip starts on the four-lane Trans-Canada Highway, but where the freeway bends south beyond Strathmore, continues east to Hussar on yet another impeccable, lightly travelled Alberta secondary highway. The views are expansive across undulating farmland dotted with clusters of farm buildings and their encircling shelter belts.

Just past Hussar—which like many small Alberta towns has an annual rodeo—the route heads north past hillocky terrain that soon gives way to beautiful, rolling countryside with long ridgelines and intersecting broad valleys and small coulees. A short stretch of gravel roads leads to an overview of yet another superb landscape, the deeply incised badlands of the Red Deer River Valley. As the road descends steeply past hoodoos, watch for mountain bluebirds perched on fence lines or peering out from little nest boxes made especially for them.

Shortly after crossing the Red Deer River on an old steel bridge, you reach the hamlet of Dorothy on the broad valley floor. Dorothy is an odd mix of scattered small houses interspersed with long-abandoned buildings surrounded by prairie grasses. Still standing are two lovely historic churches and a soaring wooden grain elevator, evidence of a once-thriving community. With this spectacular setting, it's not surprising Dorothy has been featured in television commercials and many photographers' portfolios.

Beyond Dorothy, the prairie gets progressively flatter and drier, especially as you head north on Highway 36. With luck, you might spot the magnificent ungulate of the treeless plains—the pronghorn, or antelope as it's commonly called. Almost wiped out at the turn of the 20th century by agriculture and hunting, the pronghorn's numbers have rebounded to some 15,000 in Alberta. On the open prairie, they can reach speeds of 95 kilometres per hour. But unlike deer, they're not jumpers. Indeed, they usually crawl under barbed wire fences, an exercise made easier where landowners have removed or raised the bottom strand.

Not far away is a herd of somewhat untamed animals. Some 500 horses and 80 bulls are housed on the 880 hectares of the Stampede Ranch, providing rodeo stock for the Calgary Stampede and other high-profile rodeos. At the ranch's entrance is a graveyard for its superstar rodeo broncs and bulls. Visits to the ranch are by appointment only (403-566-2206).

Further north, Highway 36 passes the Sheerness Generating Station, where coal from nearby strip mines is turned into electricity. The plant's cooling ponds provide water for irrigation, the town of Hanna, and migrating waterfowl.

In fall, bird hunters from afar flock to Hanna to shoot the plentiful Canada geese and ducks that feed on the area's ripened grain before migrating south. The town of 3,000 residents is well known

Red Deer River badlands south of Dorothy.

for the large goose statue at the town's east end, as well as being the home of mega rock group Nickelback.

Make sure you visit the Hanna Museum and Pioneer Village. It features a full block of beautifully restored, well-stocked buildings—including a church, general store, blacksmith shop, train station, ranch house, and Hanna's first hospital. Downtown Hanna also contains a few large murals and some historic buildings, particularly the structures clustered around the "Four Corners" intersection of 2nd Avenue and 1st Street West.

Not far west of Hanna and just off Highway 9 is Craigmyle, which boasts the 1915 Craigmyle United Church and some other historic buildings. About 5 kilometres farther west, it's worth taking a short detour south on a gravel road that winds to near the top of Mother Mountain, in the Hand Hills. This lofty, 1,070-metre perch offers superb views over the surrounding plains. From this height, it's a short drive west to Secondary 851, which soon leads north to Delia, a lovely village featuring an old, wind-powered gristmill on the lawn of the local museum.

Abandoned grain elevator near Dorothy.

Due west on Highways 9 and 27 and then Secondary 582 (don't be confused by the changing numbers; you keep following a straight line) the route again crosses the spectacular Red Deer River Valley and a couple of other broad valleys, with extensive views west and north from the intervening highlands. After a short jog north, Secondary 582 empties onto Highway 2 near Didsbury.

---

**≡ EATS & DRINKS ≡**

Besides housing a collection of more than 4,000 dolls, the **Doll Palace & Tea Room** (400 Pioneer Trail) in Hanna offers tea, homemade soups, and cream and fruit pies Wednesday to Sunday. Similarly, **Willow Creek Bistro & Gifts** (217–2nd Avenue W) operates a cappuccino bar amidst its gift items, while **Lazy "J" Cafe** (209B–2nd Avenue W) features homemade soups. In Delia, **Mother Mountain Tea House & Restaurant** (102–1st Avenue, open Friday through Sunday) is in a delightfully restored 1912 lumber building and offers day trippers good coffee and tea, fresh breads and soups, and a Sunday brunch. It's also worth visiting Friday evenings for baby back ribs and on Sundays for the roast beef dinner.

---

# BLACKFOOT CROSSING HISTORICAL PARK

**Route:** From the intersection of 16th Avenue and 68th Street NE, drive 92 kilometres east on the Trans-Canada Highway. Go south on Secondary 842, through Cluny, for 7 kilometres to the Blackfoot Crossing Interpretive Centre parking lot.
**Driving Distance:** About 100 kilometres one way.
**Note:** The Blackfoot Crossing Interpretive Centre is open 9:00 a.m. to 5:00 p.m. daily from mid-May to early September, with reduced hours the rest of the year. Admission charged. Phone toll free 1-888-654-6274 or 403-734-5171; www.black footcrossing.ca.

Blackfoot Crossing Historical Park is a world-class Aboriginal interpretive facility.

Until recently, Alberta's only world-class Aboriginal interpretive facility was Head-Smashed-In Buffalo Jump. Now there's a second: Blackfoot Crossing Historical Park, a $25-million project that officially opened in 2007. Indeed, it may well eclipse the former in the splendour of its interpretive centre and location—perched on the rim of the broad, winding Bow River Valley.

A National Historic Site, the 800-hectare Blackfoot Crossing park celebrates the rich cultural heritage of the Blackfoot Confederacy, which long ruled the plains of what became south-central Alberta and much of Montana. The park includes the archaeological remains of an ancient and rare earth lodge village; the gravesite of the great Blackfoot chief Crowfoot; and one of the largest intact prairie river ecosystems in North America.

The showpiece of the site is its interpretive centre. Designed by Calgary architect Ron Goodfellow with guidance from native elders, the centre is an inspired reinterpretation of Blackfoot culture. The front incorporates symbolic buffalo drive lanes and a glass eagle feather fan that casts colourful shadows across the entryway. Around the back is a magnificent amphitheatre, with high glass walls of gold (representing the earth) and blue (the sky) topped by crisscrossing steel poles that represent those used in the sun dance ceremony.

From inside the 62,000-square-foot building, the glass wall provides an enormous window overlooking the river valley. But most visitors will be engrossed in the story of the Blackfoot, told in displays located in and around five lofty teepees.

Historically, the Blackfoot Confederacy was an alliance of three Plains peoples sharing a common language and culture—today's Blood, Peigan, and Blackfoot nations. (The latter is properly known as the Siksika Nation, and Blackfoot Crossing is located on its reserve.) The confederacy fiercely ruled the southern plains for centuries, first using dogs to haul nomadic possessions and then switching to horseback, in the 1700s, to hunt and wage war against outside tribes.

Though the Blackfoot tribes later traded for European goods, they refused to allow fur-trading posts on their lands and effectively blocked the passage of explorers and traders. But with the disappearance of the massive buffalo herds and the introduction of two deadly white poisons—liquor and diseases such as smallpox—their numbers by 1870 had shrunk to some 6,150 people living in 760 teepees. Led by Crowfoot, they thus reluctantly signed Treaty No. 7 in 1877, ceding their traditional territories in exchange for the three reserves they now live on. (While visiting on the 100th anniversary of the treaty signing, Prince Charles suggested a cultural centre be developed on this historic site; three decades later, the largest First Nations–owned and –operated interpretive facility in Canada was completed.)

Although the interpretive displays acknowledge this dark chapter and that of the residential schools that followed, the overall mood is celebratory and proud. Alongside recordings of elders' voices and interactive displays on the Blackfoot language are exquisite artifacts from the late 1900s, including bows and arrows and powwow dance costumes.

After exploring these exhibits, leave sufficient time to visit at least one of the outdoor sites, on your own or with a Siksika guide (guided tours of the interpretive centre are also available). One gravel trail leads north, passing monuments to the visionary Cree chief Poundmaker and to the Treaty No. 7 signing, and ending at Crowfoot's gravesite.

Another trail descends steeply from the interpretive centre into the broad Bow River flats. It's well worth the approximately 15-minute walk, for those willing to make the equally steep ascent on the return. Just after passing a modern assembly of teepees and accompanying interpretive signage, the trail levels off in a cool, dense poplar forest, still a long way from the river. Even on a hot summer afternoon, when I visited, there was an amazing chorus of birds—including the drilling of two downy woodpeckers.

The large clearing just beyond is where Blackfoot for centuries set up large winter teepee camps, close to shelter, water, and game. The nearby river offered one of the few area crossings of the Bow River, hence the name Blackfoot Crossing.

The trail ends at the site of a rare Aboriginal earth lodge village, which once featured a fortified palisade wall, a moat-like trench, and half-moon dwellings of logs and mounded earth. Though its exact origins are a mystery, it is believed to have been built around 1740 by a native group from the U.S. Dakotas that migrated northwest and briefly lived here. The abandoned site was seen by several white visitors in the mid-1870s and later excavated by archaeologists, who found animal bones and fragments of pottery and beads.

# BROOKS

**Route:** See page 194. Page 198 describes an alternate route for getting back to Calgary.
**Note:** The Brooks & District Museum is open 9:00 a.m. to 5:00 p.m. daily from the May long weekend to Labour Day. Phone 403-362-5073; www.brooksmuseum.ca.

For a prairie community of 14,000 people—it became a city in 2005—Brooks (www.brooks.ca) has a surprising diversity of attractions. The area's variety of things to see and do may well be unmatched outside Alberta's major cities.

# Brooks

The biggest draw is nearby Dinosaur Provincial Park, a World Heritage Site and one of the finest depositories of fossilized dinosaur bones in the world. It's just one of three provincial parks near Brooks, the others being Tillebrook and Kinbrook Island. The latter is a fine place to watch birds, particularly the graceful white pelican. Brooks also boasts a historic aqueduct and a horticultural research centre.

Given its distance from Calgary, it's best to pick a couple of attractions for a day trip. The best bets are Dinosaur and Kinbrook provincial parks and the Brooks Aqueduct. The alternative is to stay overnight at a motel or one of the fine provincial park campgrounds and explore the area at your leisure.

The Brooks & District Museum (568 Sutherland Drive East) houses an impressive 20,000 artifacts in 17 buildings on its three-hectare site. The collection is organized so visitors "walk" through the early days of ranching, the arrival of the North West Mounted Police and the Canadian Pacific Railway, and the ongoing era of irrigation farming.

---

### EATS & DRINKS

In Brooks, stop at **Koffee Bean Kafé** (403–2nd Avenue W) or **Dingwall's Café** (328–7th Street E) for coffee, **Wasana Restaurant** (4 Pine Avenue W) for Thai food or the **Brooks Hotel** (111–1st Street W) for its famously thick, inexpensive sandwiches. At 101–1st Avenue E, **Garth's Restaurant & Lounge** (get the pun?) serves good steak sandwiches and prime rib dinners.

---

### En Route to Brooks

**Route:** From the intersection of 16th Avenue and 68th Street NE, drive 176 kilometres east on the Trans-Canada Highway to Brooks.

The route from Calgary to Brooks and Medicine Hat is on the heavily travelled Trans-Canada Highway and follows the Canadian Pacific Railway (CPR) main line. Yet it's perhaps the most recent of the major transportation corridors in Alberta.

While fur traders, explorers, and whisky traders established a network of trails elsewhere, an east-west route across the southern prairies was ignored until the late 19th century. The major reason for this was the Blackfoot Confederacy's control over these lands for many years.

The arrival of the North West Mounted Police in 1874 ended the illegal whisky trade with Plains tribes, or nations. But already hard hit by white diseases and the decimation of the buffalo, the Blackfoot, led by Chief Crowfoot, signed Treaty No. 7 at nearby Blackfoot Crossing

Overlooking the Bow River Valley near Cluny, east of Calgary.

in 1877. Several years later the Blackfoot, or Siksika, Nation—who along with the Blood (Kainaiwa) and Peigan (Piikani) comprised the Blackfoot Confederacy—moved onto their reserve near Gleichen, just south of the Trans-Canada Highway.

Despite the completion of the Canadian Pacific Railway (CPR) in the early 1880s, this route remained largely undeveloped for the next two decades. Only the periodic railway sidings and the odd store disturbed the prairie skyline between Calgary and Medicine Hat. All of that changed when irrigation was introduced to this dry landscape, attracting settlers and encouraging the growth of small communities.

The impact of irrigation is visible all along the Trans-Canada Highway from Calgary to Brooks. Just beyond the city limits, the highway passes the burgeoning community of Chestermere Lake. In 1910, the lake became a reservoir for storing water diverted from the Bow River at Calgary. Eagle Lake, just east of Strathmore, is also part of this network of canals and built reservoirs in the Western Irrigation District, east of Calgary.

Verdant field east of Strathmore.

Strathmore is a prosperous, 12,000-person satellite community of Calgary, but its economy is still closely tied to cattle production and grain farming. Strathmore was the home of an 800-hectare demonstration farm established in 1908 to teach newly arrived settlers the basics of farming in this dry landscape. The farm raised cows, horses, pigs, and chickens and had a large garden and greenhouses that produced vegetables, flowers, and berries for CPR dining cars and hotels in Western Canada. The CPR also had a colonization office, transporting settlers to new lands that included ready-made 32-hectare farms, complete with a small house and barn.

The rolling farmland east of Calgary has been largely shaped by glaciers that periodically covered southern Alberta for much of the past 2 million years. The road crosses an end moraine, a ridge of rock deposited by melting glaciers, at a rise of land just before the turnoff to Cluny.

From such panoramic high points, the eastern horizon begins to expand and flatten. But this is by no means the bald prairie of popular belief. The landscape continues to roll, albeit more gradually, and is cut by many small valleys. At about 110 kilometres, the deep Bow River Valley becomes visible as it parallels the highway before swinging south to join the South Saskatchewan River.

Seven kilometres south of Cluny, on Secondary 842, the Siksika Nation has completed a major tourist destination—Blackfoot Crossing Historical Park—that includes Cree Chief Crowfoot's gravesite and an ancient native earth lodge village. The park's highlight is a $25-million interpretive centre, located on a spectacular escarpment overlooking the Bow River Valley (see pages 189–92).

When Captain John Palliser passed through the area east of Cluny during his prairie reconnaissance of the late 1850s, he described desert-like conditions unfit for farming. In all, these arid lands became known as Palliser's Triangle, an area containing much of southwest Saskatchewan and southeast Alberta. Yet a look at today's County of Newell map reveals a prairie oasis dotted with lakes, sloughs, and other wetlands. Virtually all these bodies of water have been created by irrigation.

Scanning the fenceless prairie near Majorville Medicine Wheel.

The source of this transformation can be viewed by taking a 10-kilometre detour south at Bassano to the Bassano Dam on the Bow River. Completed in 1914, the dam created a reservoir that now provides water, through a network of canals, to some 110,000 hectares of irrigated farmland and six communities.

This system is a legacy of the CPR, which was granted vast tracts of land in the 1880s as part of its agreement to build the national railway. The CPR introduced irrigation to these semi-arid grasslands around 1910 as a means of attracting settlers and building a viable farm economy. But the railway lost money operating the system and in 1935 turned its lands and irrigation infrastructure in this area over to a farmer-owned co-operative, the Eastern Irrigation District (EID).

Today, the EID is the largest irrigation district in Canada, encompassing more than 600,000 hectares, an area bigger than Prince Edward Island. Of that total, the district owns some 245,000 hectares of rangeland, making it the largest private landowner in Alberta. Large numbers of cattle are grazed on these lands and also raised in feedlots. Given the abundant supply of land and easy access to Canadian and international markets, via the CPR main line and Trans-Canada Highway, it's not surprising that the cattle industry is king here.

But the Bow River's water supply, upon which much of this prosperity has been built, is now oversubscribed by irrigation farming and other uses. In 2007, the river was closed to all new water licenses.

### Optional Return

For those with sufficient time and wanderlust, a nice meandering return involves going south from Brooks on Highway 36 and then west on Secondary 539, which briefly passes above the deeply cut Bow River Valley; you might spot pelicans flying along the river. Not far north, across the dry prairie, is the Majorville Medicine Wheel, built perhaps 4,500 years ago and used for many years thereafter as a native spiritual site. Continue west of Lomond on Secondary 531 through fine, rolling terrain, and then go north on the gravel Secondary 842 alongside McGregor Lake to Milo and west to High River.

McGregor Lake is a long, narrow irrigation reservoir completed in 1920 and situated in a valley once used as an important travel corridor by the Blackfoot Confederacy. Today, the lake is popular for boating, fishing, and swimming, with a growing number of cottages overlooking its clear waters.

## Dinosaur Provincial Park

**Route:** From the Trans-Canada Highway on the western edge of Brooks, follow the Dinosaur Provincial Park signs for 48 kilometres north and east on paved secondary highways.
**Note:** The park visitor centre is open daily 8:30 a.m. to 7:00 p.m. from mid-May to the end of August and on a shorter schedule the rest of the year. Park tours and programs (fee charged) are offered from May until October. Phone 403-378-4342, ext. 235 for more information. www.albertaparks.ca/dinosaur.

Dinosaur Provincial Park contains one of Alberta's most fascinating and diverse landscapes—the severely eroded badlands. Here, one can find fantastic rock shapes, stands of plains cottonwood trees, cacti, and prairie rattlesnakes. Perhaps most importantly, it boasts one of the most abundant sources of fossils in the world. Not surprisingly, this unique park is a UNESCO World Heritage Site.

Much of the park is closed to individual exploration, so the best way to see its treasures is to take a tour or a self-guided interpretive walk near the visitor centre. Bus tours and interpretive hikes are extremely popular in summer, and reservations are recommended. There are also five short interpretive trails that explore badland, coulee, prairie, and river flats environments.

Dinosaur Provincial Park contains the largest tract of badlands in Canada. A pull-off near the park entrance provides an excellent overview of this landscape. The term "badlands" is a translation of *mauvaises terres,* a description early French traders applied to a similar landscape in North Dakota. Badlands are largely barren areas in which soft rock strata have been rapidly eroded by water and wind into steep slopes and varied, fantastic forms.

About 14,000 years ago, torrential meltwaters from retreating glaciers began to deeply carve this stretch of the Red Deer River Valley. Today, about 100 metres of sedimentary bedrock have been exposed from the level prairie to the valley bottom, revealing a geological timeline. As the river's murky colour shows, this rapid erosion continues today, washing away sand, silt, and mud deposited millions of years ago.

The harsh badlands are a far cry from the flat, semi-tropical world that existed here 75 million years ago. This was a coastal plain near the eastern edge of an inland sea. Ferns, mosses, and other lush vegetation grew here, supporting diverse plant- and meat-eating dinosaurs.

The dinosaurs disappeared about 65 million years ago, but their legacy was preserved. During the dinosaur era, rivers from young mountains to the west deposited thick layers of sand, silt, mud, and clay that encased and eventually preserved many bones as fossils. Over time, these deposits were compressed into horizontal layers of sandstone, mudstone, shale, and ironstone.

These are the layers of the badlands, which are eroding away at a rate of about 4 millimetres per year. The badlands' loss is the paleontologist's gain. The rapid erosion has unearthed many fossilized remains of dinosaurs and other animals and plants, making Dinosaur Provincial Park the world's most abundant source of fossils from the late Cretaceous period. To date, more than 35 species of dinosaurs have been discovered here.

The Drumheller-based Royal Tyrrell Museum maintains a field station here, where scientists continue to make exciting discoveries. Recent excavations include skeletons of the huge, carnivorous *Albertosaurus*, the duck-billed hadrosaur, and the rarely found pterosaur, a flying reptile with a wingspan exceeding 6 metres. These fragile specimens are painstakingly removed and preserved. Many are prepared for display at the Tyrrell Museum or in Dinosaur Provincial Park's

Walking the Badlands Trail in Dinosaur Provincial Park.

new, energy-efficient visitor centre, which features hands-on natural history displays and an enlarged theatre.

A number of outdoor tours and programs venture into the park's natural preserve, which is otherwise off limits to visitors. These include a badlands bus tour—offering up-close views of dinosaur bones preserved in rock—hikes through coulees and bone beds, and fossil safaris. More adventurous explorers can participate in one- or two-day fossil digs or go on half- or full-day hikes into some of the most beautiful, rugged parts of the park. Those wishing a shorter jaunt, particularly on scorching days, might consider the 1.3-kilometre Badlands Trail, which loops through hoodoos off a main public road.

Incidentally, scientists can accurately date dinosaur remains, but not from the fossils themselves. Instead, they examine the volcanic ash in the rock layers containing the fossils. The ash, deposited during the dinosaur era, is preserved in thin green bentonite clay beds.

Anyone driving these roads after a rainstorm will soon be acquainted with the slippery properties of bentonite clays.

While the badlands are themselves largely sterile, the valley is by no means devoid of life. In fact, it contains rich ecosystems of sharp contrast. The Red Deer River is a natural oasis in the dry, mixed-grass prairie of southeast Alberta. This stretch of the river is home to one of the greatest concentrations in Alberta of plains cottonwoods. These giants, some more than 200 years old, provide nesting sites, shelter, and insect food for a variety of birds. Unfortunately, the annual spring flooding needed to establish new generations of cottonwoods has been affected by an upstream dam. You can view this habitat by following the short, self-guided Cottonwood Flats Trail along the river.

The river bottom and shaded tributary valleys also support dogwood, willows, saskatoon bushes, and small birch trees. In the morning and evening, thirsty deer and coyotes might be seen along the river's edge and cottontail rabbits along park roads. During the day, predators such as ferruginous hawks, golden eagles, and prairie falcons can be spotted riding thermal air currents high above. With some 165 recorded species visiting or nesting within its 80-square-kilometre boundaries, Dinosaur Provincial Park boasts the second-highest density of breeding birds in Canada.

Away from the river, the environment is desert-like. Here, among the sagebrush and cactus, the inhabitants include prairie rattlesnakes, scorpions, and black widow spiders. While venomous, these desert creatures are generally shy and their bites rarely fatal. Chances are most park visitors will never see them.

## EATS & DRINKS

**Dinosaur Provincial Park** has a convenience store, open from mid-May to early September.

## Brooks Aqueduct

**Route:** From the tourist information building on the eastern outskirts of Brooks, drive 3 kilometres south of the Trans-Canada Highway on a dirt road to reach the aqueduct. **Note:** The site's interpretive centre is open daily 10:00 a.m. to 5:00 p.m. from mid-May to Labour Day. Admission charged. Phone 403-362-4451; www.history.alberta .ca/brooksaqueduct.

When it opened in 1915, the Brooks Aqueduct was the longest structure of its kind in the world. Today, this concrete skeleton is a national and provincial historic site and an elegant testimonial to a marvel of engineering.

In 1912, the challenge for the Canadian Pacific Railway was to build an aqueduct that would span a 3.2-kilometre valley and carry water from Lake Newell, a new reservoir, to the eastern lands of this irrigation district. The problem was complicated by the need to maximize the water flow without losing much elevation.

The Brooks Aqueduct is a National as well as Provincial Historic Site.

The engineering solution was to build a unique, dish-shaped concrete flume supported by more than 1,000 columns. In less than three years, a crew of 300 men had completed the aqueduct, using as much concrete as it would take to build basements for some 630 houses. It's now considered one of the 10 greatest engineering achievements in Alberta's history.

The aqueduct brought agricultural fertility to some 55,000 hectares of farmland for 65 years. But, as the years passed, the badly deteriorating concrete structure could no longer keep up with the rising demand for water. In 1979, it was replaced by an earth-fill canal capable of carrying nearly 50 percent more water. While utilitarian, the canal is visually insignificant next to the classical symmetry of the concrete dinosaur that stretches off into the prairie distance.

## Kinbrook Island Provincial Park

**Route:** From Brooks, drive 13 kilometres south on Secondary Highway 873 and 2 kilometres west to reach Kinbrook Island Provincial Park.
**Note:** For park information, phone 403-362-2962.

Kinbrook Island Provincial Park is a small "island," accessed by a causeway, that extends on a strip of land into the eastern waters of Lake Newell. The 38-hectare park features two campgrounds, picnic areas, a sandy beach, warm water swimming, a boat launch, and irrigated trees and shrubs that provide shade from the summer sun. It's also one of the best birdwatching areas in southeast Alberta.

Covering 7,100 hectares, Lake Newell is the largest artificial lake in Alberta. Fed by waters diverted from the Bow River at the Bassano Dam, the lake is an important storage reservoir for irrigating large tracts of otherwise arid grassland. It was created in 1914 by flooding a low-lying area within two large coulees and diking eastern runoff areas.

Dams have often been rightly criticized for destroying or significantly altering the surrounding habitat. But while irrigation has transformed the dry prairie landscape, Lake Newell and nearby irrigation

Sunbathers congregate on the shores of Lake Newell.

wetlands have created an oasis in southeast Alberta for more than 100 species of birds.

The lake is the summer home of Alberta's largest colony of double-crested cormorants and a sizable breeding population of American white pelicans. The white pelican, a threatened species in Alberta, nests on aptly named Pelican Island in the southwest corner of Lake Newell. With a weight of up to 8 kilograms and a wingspan of more than 2 metres, the pelican is one of the largest birds in the world. Rather gawky looking on land or water, it soars elegantly when airborne.

Boats aren't allowed within 1.6 kilometres of Pelican Island so as not to disturb these sensitive birds. But boaters can angle elsewhere in this deep lake for whitefish, northern pike, and rainbow trout. A commercial whitefish fishery has been in operation on Lake Newell since 1936.

Fish and birds aren't the only treasures of Lake Newell. Approximately a kilometre beneath the surface are pools of oil trapped in rock reservoirs that millions of years ago were sandy river islands and bars. These oil deposits are currently being tapped by wells drilled on an angle from the lakeshore.

Given the lake's size, it can be difficult to watch birds from shore. Fortunately, nature lovers can get much closer to a diversity of birds at Kinbrook Marsh, along the edge of Kinbrook Island Provincial Park. This former shallow bay was separated from Lake Newell by three dikes in 1988, creating a permanent marsh full of reeds, cattails, and willows. This is one of several wetland projects undertaken by the Eastern Irrigation District in partnership with Ducks Unlimited and Alberta Fish and Wildlife.

A 4.5-kilometre interpretive trail—with several viewpoints and an observation tower equipped with a powerful scope—has been developed around the marsh. A shorter morning or evening stroll along the edge of this rich habitat might reveal Canada geese, mallard ducks, shy American bitterns, great blue herons, pelicans, and even great horned owls. In the shallows might be lurking muskrat, beaver, or mink.

The marsh borders on another important ecosystem, the mixed-grass prairie. While irrigated agriculture has converted much of the native prairie in this region to cropland, large tracts of grazing land are still in a mostly natural state.

These hardy prairie grasses are well adapted to tolerate infrequent rainfall, extreme cold, drying winds, and drought. Their branched roots form dense tangles that absorb moisture and nutrients and hold the soil together. Narrow leaves and a thick protective layer also conserve water. Since the grasses grow from their base, they can be grazed, cut, trampled, or burned, and continue to grow. But ploughing kills them.

# West

LAKE LOUISE

FIELD

Bow River

Ghost River Valley

Big Hill Springs Provincial Park

Bow Valley Provincial Park

Yamnuska

22

BANFF

1A

COCHRANE

CANMORE

68

1

Spray Lakes Reservoir

40

Elbow River

66

22x

Smith-Dorrien Spray Trail

BRAGG CREEK

CALGAR

Kananaskis Country

Kananaskis Lakes

Highwood Pass

# WEST OF CALGARY

Veteran Calgary travellers might think they know all the attractions west of the city. After all, they may have journeyed dozens, if not hundreds, of times to the mountains.

But have they discovered the charms of Bow Valley Provincial Park, which contains one of the most diverse ecosystems in Alberta? Have they detoured off the Trans-Canada Highway to visit the Sibbald Creek area and its wealth of ancient history? Have they ventured into an old prisoner-of-war camp along the Kananaskis Highway? Have they walked above the hoodoos in Banff or wandered up the narrow valley of Heart Creek? Do they know that the first large-scale ranch in Alberta was located west of the city?

There is much to discover west of Calgary that isn't in the glossy mountain brochures. Even the drive west on the busy Trans-Canada Highway and the not-so-busy 1A Highway can reveal a great deal about the landscape and the area's history to those willing to look beyond the pavement and the beckoning peaks.

The Bow River Valley is the central corridor for trips in this section. The river arises from near the Wapta Icefield, north of Lake Louise, and follows a broad, glacially carved route through the mountains and onto the plains. This corridor contains the major highways, towns, and tourist attractions west of Calgary. The Bow Valley funnels the chinook winds that warm the winter valley and create unique ecosystems. It also contains the Canadian Pacific Railway, which, through an aggressive advertising campaign and the construction of two major hotels, unveiled the mountains as an international tourist destination in the late 19th century.

The other destinations in this section follow tributaries of the Bow River. One trip follows the Elbow River out of Calgary and into the low mountains west of Bragg Creek. Two others head south along the Kananaskis and Spray valleys, where visitors can engage in numerous recreational activities or simply marvel at the impressively folded mountains, formed tens of millions of years ago.

There are also trips into the tourist meccas of Banff and Lake Louise. With a little effort, it's possible to take short walks that quickly leave the camera-clicking and shopping bag–toting hordes behind. Even heavily visited Lake Louise still maintains a majestic splendour a century after it was unveiled to an awestruck world.

## COCHRANE AND GLENBOW RANCH PROVINCIAL PARK

**Route:** From the western terminus of Bow Trail, go north on 85th Street and then west on Old Banff Coach Road, soon angling right to stay on this road and following it as it crosses the Trans-Canada Highway. Turn west on a road that passes Springbank Airport en route to a junction with Highway 22, which is followed north to its intersection with Highway 1A. The Cochrane Ranche is on the right. Glenbow Ranch Provincial Park is 4 kilometres southeast of Cochrane on Glenbow Road, off Highway 1A.

**Driving Distance:** About 33 kilometres one way.

**Note:** The Cochrane Ranche visitor centre is open daily 9:00 a.m. to 5:00 p.m. from mid-May to Labour Day. The grounds can be visited any time of the year. Phone 403-932-2902; www.cochrane.ca. Phone 403-297-5293 for hours of Glenbow Ranch Provincial Park's visitor centre.

Cochrane is a booming bedroom community of Calgary, with sweeping views of the nearby foothills and mountains. It is also considered the birthplace of large-scale ranching in western Canada. This tour passes through modern farm country *en route* to Cochrane and its shrine to early ranching. On the return journey, it stops at Glenbow Ranch Provincial Park, a superb addition to the recreational park system in the Calgary area.

Old Banff Coach Road seems a misnomer for a narrow highway that soon peters out and has no history as a stagecoach route. Yet in the late 1800s, this was an alternative approach to the Morley Mission and the mountains beyond. Travellers would head west from Fort Calgary, following the open prairie along the Bow River, which was crossed at several places between Cochrane and Morley. The road was primarily used in winter, when the main route west (today's Highway 1A) was covered in snow.

In 1909, Norman Lougheed followed the Banff Coach Route in the first car trip from Calgary to Banff. He drove in two deep wagon ruts through Springbank, crossing the Bow on the Cochrane Ferry. Not far beyond Calgary's current city limits, he'd have passed the dairy farm of Ebenezer Healy, who built the area's first cheese factory in 1888.

Today, acreages increasingly cover Springbank, but there are still small farms where horses and cattle graze. This urban-rural mix continues on the north side of the Trans-Canada Highway as the road passes housing and a small equestrian centre. The Calgary area is Canada's horse capital, with many acreage owners keeping a horse or two for riding, adding to a population of diverse breeds raised for show or herding cattle. Not surprisingly, Canada's largest dude ranch, the 1,800-hectare Griffin Valley Ranch, is just northwest of Cochrane.

The road continues west through farmland and past the small but busy Springbank Airport. Just before the Highway 22 junction, the road climbs to a hilltop offering a magnificent panorama of mountains. From here, it's a short drive north to Cochrane. One of Canada's fastest-growing communities, Cochrane's population has soared to 18,000 people, with exploding development straining its small-town status.

Bronze statue at Cochrane Ranche.

On the town's northwest edge is Cochrane Ranche Provincial Historic Site, a monument to a grand failure in nineteenth-century ranching. In 1881, Quebec senator Matthew Cochrane obtained from the Canadian government the first of the 100,000-acre ranching leases in southern Alberta. For the annual sum of one cent per acre, these ranch owners could graze cattle on grasslands once roamed by bison.

In two great cattle drives, nearly 12,000 animals were herded from Montana to Cochrane's ranch. Alas, many animals were lost to harsh winters and poor management. By 1884, the Quebec businessman had moved his cattle south to a new lease near Cardston that eventually prospered. The Cochrane operation briefly experimented with sheep and then horse ranching, but much of the lease was soon relinquished to provide land for homesteaders.

Today at Cochrane Ranche, visitors can tour a 62-hectare historic site that once contained a manager's house, a bunkhouse, a blacksmith shop, and a stable. During the ranch's operation, well-heeled managers would arrive with pianos, polo ponies, and fine china, while hired hands lived in leaky barracks.

The visitor centre contains artifacts of this era and provides a brief history of area ranching, with interpretive programs in late spring and summer. Walk up the hill to the impressive bronze statue of a rancher on horseback, designed by local artist Malcolm MacKenzie. This perch overlooks Cochrane and mountains such as the prominent Devil's Head.

A highlight of any visit is strolling up Big Hill Creek Valley through a surprisingly diverse landscape of spruce, aspen, prairie grasses, sandstone outcrops, and wildflowers fed by springs seeping down the hillside. Beaver dams in the creek bottom have created a wetland that attracts several bird species.

The Big Hill Valley was carved into its U shape by melting waters from an early ice age. These meltwaters emptied into the nearby Glacial Lake Calgary, an ice-jammed lake that covered the Bow Valley from Calgary west to Morley. Today, Big Hill Creek winds through the ranch and Cochrane to the Bow River. Those with enough time can follow a nice creekside trail to the river.

Another worthwhile side trip is to drive 6.5 kilometres west of Cochrane on Highway 1A and then go north on Grand Valley Road. In early summer, it's a beautiful drive, with the deep valley flanked by rolling slopes of green. Return by taking Township Road 280 east for a short distance and then going south on Horse Creek Road to Cochrane's western outskirts.

From here, it's a short drive southeast on Highway 1A to Glenbow Ranch Provincial Park. Created in 2008, the 1,314-hectare park is situated on slopes above the Bow River, providing outstanding views of foothills and Front Range peaks to the west and, closer at hand, a diversity of bird life. More than 28 kilometres of paved and gravel walking and cycling paths lead steeply down into the river valley, allowing visitors to explore grasslands, wooded areas, and riverside habitats.

The park also has a rich human history, starting with Aboriginal hunters who corralled bison in coulees. The community of Glenbow sprang up in the valley flats in the late 1800s, first as a stop on the

Canadian Pacific Railway and later as the base for sandstone and brick quarries; sandstone blocks from here were used in the construction of Alberta's legislature building in Edmonton.

Originally part of the historic Cochrane Ranche, the site eventually became a private ranch under the Harvie family, who recently donated the lands to the province, allowing the park to be created. There are expansion plans that would create a park stretching from Calgary all the way to Cochrane along the river valley.

## EATS & DRINKS

Cochrane has long been famous for **MacKay's Ice Cream** (220–1st Street W), and it's becoming increasingly well known for its hot beverages. **Cochrane Coffee Traders** (114–2nd Avenue W) roasts its own beans and bakes delicious fruit and coffee cake muffins, while **Java Jamboree** (9, 312–5th Avenue W) features award-winning baristas working a Synesso espresso machine and a lunch menu of wraps, paninis, and quesadillas. Not to be outdone, **Tea . . . and Other Things** (110–2nd Avenue W) boasts 167 types of tea and related paraphernalia. Nearby, the cozy **Blue Dog Café** (110–3rd Avenue W) serves Creole-style lunches. Check out **Guy's Cafe & Bakery** (6, 2019 Grand Boulevard) for soup and a sandwich, or **Mehtab East Indian Cuisine** (2008, 120–5th Avenue W).

# BIG HILL SPRINGS PROVINCIAL PARK

**Route:** From the intersection of Crowchild Trail and Nose Hill Drive NW, drive 10.5 kilometres west on Highway 1A. Head north on Secondary 766 (Lochend Road) for 11 kilometres and west on Secondary 567 for 3.2 kilometres. A 2-kilometre access road leads south to Big Hill Springs Provincial Park. An alternative approach is to drive 8 kilometres north of Cochrane on Highway 22 and then 6.5 kilometres east on Secondary 567 to the park entrance road.
**Note:** The park is a day-use area, open 7:00 a.m. to 11:00 p.m. Phone 403-297-5293.

Big Hill Springs Provincial Park is a wooded gem just 20 minutes from the city limits. Jammed within its 31.5 hectares are spring-fed wetlands, cool forest, prairie grasslands, and a rich human history. Much of this diversity can be experienced on a short interpretive hike. Pack a picnic lunch or supper and you've got all the makings for a great escape from the city.

Be forewarned: Big Hill Springs is often crowded on warm spring and summer weekends. To quietly watch birds or hike in solitude, arrive early in the day. Take care also to preserve this tiny jewel. Stay on the main trails and don't pick the wildflowers or other native plants.

The park is located at the south end of the surprisingly deep Big Spring Coulee, where spring waters run down the hillside and into Big Hill Creek. The entire Big Hill Valley was carved during an early ice age by melting waters that emptied near Cochrane into the massive Glacial Lake Calgary. That lake is long gone, but beavers have built dams within the coulee along Big Hill Creek, creating a small lake and an extensive marsh.

Wetlands just north of Big Hill Springs Provincial Park.

On the interpretive trail through Big Hill Springs Provincial Park.

These watery spots near the park entrance and the adjacent woodlands provide prime habitat for migratory and breeding birds. The diversity of birds includes bald eagles, prairie falcons, northern saw-whet owls, rufous hummingbirds, great blue herons, and two rarities: the sharp-tailed sparrow and the yellow rail.

Prehistoric Aboriginal people were drawn to this area by the year-round supply of spring water and the shelter and wood provided by the valley forests. Discoveries of buffalo bones and ancient camps lead archaeologists to believe a nearby cliff was used as a buffalo jump.

At the turn of the century, local ranchers and even Calgarians would arrive in Big Hill Springs by horse and buggy for a leisurely day of picnicking. In 1891, D. M. Radcliff chose the coulee for Alberta's first commercial creamery, a water-powered operation later moved to Red Deer. Half a century later, the province built a trout hatchery along the spring. Its failure is commemorated by the remains of a concrete foundation.

The best way to see the heart of Big Hill Springs Provincial Park is to take a looping 1.6-kilometre interpretive walk that starts behind a stone fireplace. The trail immediately enters cool forest and follows the course of the descending spring waters, which run in braided streams through grasses. The grey formations along the way are tufa mounds, deposited by spring waters of sufficiently warm temperatures and low pressures. An exposed tufa ridge nearby was formed by a once-dammed and now-abandoned stream channel.

In late spring and early summer, the aspen woods are filled with western Canada violet, shooting stars, wild roses, and star-flowered Solomon's seal. The trail climbs to a viewpoint overlooking two narrow valleys carved by meltwaters from retreating glaciers and now adorned by prairie grasses and sandstone outcrops.

The proximity of the surrounding prairie is evident up here in the encroachment of crocuses, sage, and fescue grasses. A small stand of willows, marking the transition from prairie to forest, soon gives way to the dappled light of thicker aspen forest, home to a variety of songbirds. From the high side of the valley, the trail descends steadily through spruce trees and a dense ground cover of cow parsnip, indicative of water seeping underground.

# GHOST RIVER VALLEY

**Route:** From the Canada Olympic Park traffic lights, drive 18 kilometres west on the Trans-Canada Highway, 13 kilometres north on Highway 22 to Cochrane, and 13 kilometres west on Highway 1A. Go north on Forestry Trunk Road (Highway 40) for 24 kilometres and turn west onto a gated rough gravel road (just past Richards Road). Follow it for 16 kilometres to a hilltop parking area.

**Driving Distance:** About 85 kilometres one way.

**Note:** The hilltop overlooking the Ghost River Valley can be reached by car, but a high-clearance vehicle, preferably with four-wheel drive, is recommended for the steep hill and rocky riverbed crossings beyond. Otherwise, it's a 3.5-kilometre hike or mountain bike ride to the Black Rock trailhead (see description below).

Here's an opportunity to put that sport utility vehicle to its intended use. Panoramic views and steep walls of limestone that attract rock

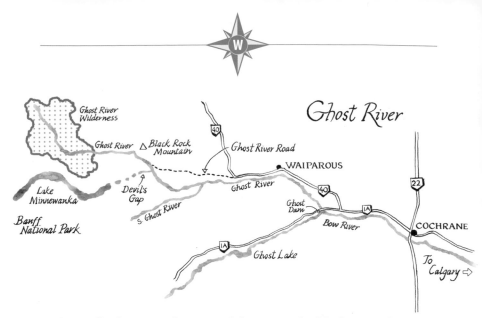

and ice climbers are the reward for a rough ride into and up the windswept Ghost River Valley. It's also a chance for ambitious hikers to scramble to the abandoned fire lookout at the summit of Black Rock Mountain and gaze over the Front Range peaks, forested foothills, and prairies.

Despite its proximity to the city, the Ghost River Valley is unknown to many Calgarians, though the black "thumb" of Devil's Head in its midst is a prominent peak west of the city. The lack of a four-lane access highway and glaciated majesty are more than offset by a sense of wildness and isolation that you won't find around Banff or Lake Louise.

But don't expect wilderness tranquility, either. This valley is a favourite destination for all-terrain vehicles, dirt bikes, and random camping in large trucks. The Ghost and, especially, the parallel Waiparous Valley to the north are also infamous for their long-weekend parties, though a new management plan for both areas should help reduce the impact of these thoughtless offenders. Still, the Ghost River Valley is often quiet, and considerable opportunities exist for rambles to places frequented by few people.

The approach to the Ghost River Valley is a lovely drive, particularly in the fall, when the yellow aspen make a lovely contrast with stands of dark green spruce and Douglas fir. From the 1A Highway turnoff, the paved forestry trunk road winds north through a wide valley of

Fall aspen in the Ghost River Valley.

grassy foothills and gradually thicker forest, passing by the tiny communities of Benchlands and Waiparous along the way. Once onto the bouncy Ghost River Road, it's worth stopping at 4 and 6 kilometres for splendid views up the valley to the peaks of the Palliser Range such as Mount Aylmer, which straddles the Banff National Park boundary.

The next viewpoint is the 16-kilometre hilltop parking area. Straight ahead are the steep yellow limestone walls of Phantom Crag, one of many rock- and ice-climbing cliffs in the Ghost. To the right, you can follow the gravelly main channel of the muted Ghost River upstream by off-road vehicle past Black Rock towards Devil's Head and then on foot all the way to its headwaters below Aylmer Pass, some 30 kilometres distant.

To the left, another valley leads through Devil's Gap to Lake Minnewanka; high-clearance vehicles can be driven for a couple of rough kilometres to the Banff park boundary. Early Aboriginal peoples used this route to reach the mountains. Later, 19th-century explorers, including Sir George Simpson, head of the Hudson's Bay Company, and James Hector of the Palliser Expedition, followed it. This route

was also the scene of battles between the Plains Blackfoot and the mountain Kootenai, and Aboriginal graves apparently line the riverbanks. According to native legend, ghosts wandered the riverbanks, picking up the skulls of those killed in battle, hence the name, though Palliser called it Dead Man River.

The modern-day river is a ghost of its former self, thanks to a 1942 diversion canal that channels much of its water through Devil's Gap into the dammed Lake Minnewanka in Banff National Park. (If you walk or drive through Devil's Gap, the diversion channel is mainly hidden behind a rock ridge.) Water from the Ghost thus helps generate power at both the Cascade station (beside the Trans-Canada Highway east of Banff townsite) and at Ghost Lake, where the river merges with the Bow River west of Cochrane along Highway 1A. Immediately downstream of the diversion canal, the Ghost River channel is dry most of the year, except when water is released into it during high stream flow. Farther downstream, groundwater and surface runoff cause the river to resume its flow.

While the Ghost Valley has been significantly impacted by water diversions, recent clear-cutting, and humans seeking recreational diversion, some 15,000 hectares of its upper watershed have long been protected within the Ghost River Wilderness. This area, which swings north along the Banff boundary to the Ghost River's source, can be explored on foot by backpackers prepared for some route-finding, bushwhacking, and perhaps encounters with grizzly bears. Much of the lower Ghost Valley, other than the valley floor, is now included in Don Getty Wildland Park and thus should be better protected from future impact.

### Black Rock Hiking Option

This 5-kilometre hike climbs 900 vertical metres to an abandoned fire lookout. It's a good trail that gets steeper and somewhat more exposed near the rocky summit of Black Rock Mountain. You need good boots, especially for the initial descent, of somewhat slippery rock, from the summit. To reach the trailhead from the hilltop parking area (about 3.5 kilometres by vehicle, bike, or foot), descend the steep hill, turn right on a gravel track that swings left to cross the rocky riverbed, and then turn right again (at a cairn) on a smaller side road. The trail starts in woods on the far side of another riverbed crossing.

The well-beaten trail soon bends left and begins climbing through stands of lodgepole pine and spruce to open slopes that provide glimpses east over the foothills. Above the treeline, the trail swings left onto a ridge, then back to the right through a gap in limestone cliffs to an open bench. A final push up the summit block's switchbacks leads to the windowless old lookout, now clad in cedar shake siding. This windswept, 2,460-metre perch offers tremendous views west to Devil's Head and the upper Ghost Valley, north to the Waiparous Valley and east across the prairies. On a clear day, you can see Calgary's downtown office towers.

The Black Rock Mountain Lookout was built in the late 1920s and early 1930s; the building's timber and later supplies were hauled up by pack horse. A telephone line was erected to provide communications with the nearest ranger station. Constructed on four cement blocks and heated only by a one-burner gas stove, the building was often cold and drafty; one attendant said he mostly stayed in his sleeping bag during bad weather. The lookout was closed in the early 1950s and replaced by the Mockingbird Fire Lookout to the northeast.

# 1A HIGHWAY TOUR

**Route:** From the junction of Crowchild Trail and Nose Hill Drive NW, follow the 1A Highway northwest through Cochrane and Exshaw to the Trans-Canada Highway overpass just east of Canmore.
**Driving Distance:** 94 kilometres one way.

For many years, the 1A Highway was the major transportation corridor between Calgary and Banff. In fact, parts of this route along the north side of the Bow River date back more than a century. Today, the 1A Highway provides a leisurely alternative approach to the moun-

tains as it winds along the north side of the Bow River. The unhurried pace also encourages travellers to pull over at the many points of historical and natural interest along the way.

Leaving Calgary, the trip initially traverses a high plateau overlooking a succession of plains, foothills, and mountains. James Hector, a member of the Palliser Expedition, travelled this way in 1858 and remarked upon the profusion of flowers and exhilarating view of distant, snowy peaks. On the right, the rolling hills that house the acreages of Bearspaw are excellent examples of knob-and-kettle topography, formed at the end of the last ice age by stagnating glaciers.

In 1875, Reverend John McDougall rode east along this route from his mission at Morleyville (west of today's Cochrane) to visit the new North West Mounted Police post at Fort Calgary. Known as the Morleyville Trail, this rutted track became an important link between the two settlements.

The plateau ends suddenly on the brow of Cochrane Hill, offering a stunning view of Cochrane, the Bow Valley, and the Rocky Mountain Front Ranges. The aforementioned Hector, who spent a night camped below, called this magical spot Dream Hill. The winding highway that once descended the long, steep incline was replaced in the late 1940s by a more direct plunge. A sharp turn at the bottom, resulting in numerous backyard crashes, was eliminated a decade later when the road was rerouted behind the town.

Cochrane is named for Senator Matthew Cochrane, who in 1881 established Western Canada's first big ranch, a 40,000-hectare spread based just west of the current town. The Cochrane Ranche briefly increased traffic along the Morleyville Trail. But harsh winters and poor management decimated the cattle herd, prompting Cochrane to move much of the operation south to near Cardston in 1884. For a more detailed description of Cochrane and its history, see pages 210–14.

The construction of the Canadian Pacific Railway through the Bow Valley in 1883 drained the route of most traffic until the arrival of the automobile two decades later. William Cochrane (no relation to

McDougall Memorial United Church, along the 1A highway.

the town) made the first recorded car trip through here, driving his vehicle perhaps as far as Morley. In 1909, Norman Lougheed made the first complete car trip from Calgary to Banff, a full day's excursion. Though several bridges and culverts had been added a year earlier, much of the route followed wagon ruts.

The road was gravelled in 1924–25, making motor travel much easier, at least when the surface was dry. It was now called the Blue Trail, its blue signposts corresponding with colour-coded maps published by Alberta's motor clubs. The road was paved in 1932 and renamed Highway 2, later changed to Highway 1. Rebuilt in 1947, the route saw its number changed again a decade later (to the current 1A) when the new Highway 1 (the Trans-Canada) opened south of the Bow River.

West of Cochrane, the highway soon passes Ghost Lake. The lake was formed in 1929 when Calgary Power built a hydroelectric dam on the Bow River. Ghost Lake is now a popular spot for sailing, windsurfing, and ice sailing, thanks to the strong winds that funnel through the Bow Valley.

Beyond Ghost Lake, the road traverses an open bench above the river. Soon visible on the left is the historic McDougall Memorial United Church. It's well worth stopping to walk around this splendid restored church, read the interpretive signage, and gaze across the broad Bow Valley to nearby foothills and Front Range mountains.

Here in 1873, George McDougall and his son John established Morleyville, a Methodist mission. It was one of southern Alberta's early settlements, other than fur-trading forts and whisky posts. In 1876, George McDougall died and was buried in the churchyard, after losing his way on the winter prairie to the east.

The Stoney were a Sioux tribe apparently pushed west in the early 1700s to the foothills and mountains of south-central Alberta. Their normal route west veered north of the current highway from Morley and followed the Ghost River to Devil's Lake (now Minnewanka) and past today's Banff. In the mid-1800s, missionaries and explorers followed this route into the mountains.

After signing Treaty No. 7 in 1877, the Stoney moved to their current reserve. Frustrated by what they saw as restrictive hunting and travel regulations, a breakaway group moved north in the mid-1890s to sacred ancestral grounds at Kootenay Plains, near Saskatchewan River Crossing. With the bison and other game animals largely decimated, the Stoney turned to farming. But their greatest resource has been the abundant supply of natural gas under the reserve.

At Stoney Indian Park, 12 kilometres west of Morley, the Stoney maintain a small herd of bison on grasslands above the Bow River. Here, where Old Fort Creek enters the river canyon, the Hudson's Bay Company in 1832 established Peigan Post, a short-lived trading post burned to the ground by the Blood First Nation soon after it was abandoned.

The Stoney are also venturing into tourism. The nearby Nakoda Lodge, built in 1981, is a handsome conference facility and guest lodge on the shores of Chief Hector Lake. The conference facility contains a learning centre, a small museum, and a gallery dedicated to Aboriginal art. The lodge also provides a fine view across the lake to Mount John Laurie, commonly known as Yamnuska (see pages 258–62).

Running along the base of Yamnuska's high cliffs is the McConnell Thrust, which separates the foothills here from the Front Range mountains. The fault marks the line along which a massive block of older limestone thrust up over a much younger layer of shale. The resistant limestone now forms Yamnuska's vertical grey cliffs, prized among rock climbers, while the shale has largely been eroded into the scree slopes below.

Near the town of Exshaw, mining has aided the process of erosion. Here, limestone is processed into cement and related products at two plants. A third plant processes magnesite, mined elsewhere, into magnesium oxide. From 1902 to 1930, the eastern park entrance to Banff National Park was at Exshaw. The boundary was then retracted to its current position to allow for commercial developments in the Canmore area.

Just beyond Exshaw is the Grotto Canyon parking lot, where visitors can take a fine 2.5-kilometre interpretive walk. The canyon was primarily carved over a few thousand years by the rush of glacial meltwaters. Today, the stream bed is nearly dry, allowing visitors to walk along the narrow canyon bottom for much of its length. High walls shelter the canyon, allowing unusual vegetation such as Douglas maple to grow here. Near the end of this hike, the canyon forks. A right branch climbs quickly to a small waterfall, while the left leads to a broader valley.

Grotto Canyon has long been a sacred place for Aboriginal people, who painted red figures on smooth panels of rock. These centuries-old paintings, called pictographs, are extremely fragile, so admire any you see at a distance. Climbers are also attracted to these short, steep walls. They've drilled bolts (fairly permanent pieces of shiny protection) into the rock to safeguard first and subsequent ascents.

Back in the car, you soon pass Gap Lake, a popular fishing spot for brown trout and mountain whitefish up to 2 kilograms in size. In 1800, explorer and map-maker David Thompson became the first

white person to enter this part of the Bow Valley, when he led a party on foot as far west as Gap Lake. The ascending road beyond the lake is a good place to see bighorn sheep and view the four summits of Mount Lougheed across the valley.

Not far from Canmore's outskirts is the Old Camp picnic area, site of a government relief camp during the 1930s. The Depression project gave work to about 80 men, who maintained and upgraded the 1A Highway for 20 cents a day plus room and board, clothing, and a tobacco ration.

**EATS & DRINKS**

See Cochrane stops on page 214.

# ELBOW RIVER TOUR

**Route:** From the traffic lights on Sarcee Trail just south of Richmond Road SW, follow Highway 8 west for 21 kilometres to a T-intersection. Go 10.5 kilometres south on Highway 22 to Bragg Creek and then 3 kilometres farther to another intersection. Follow Highway 66 west to its terminus at Little Elbow Campground.
**Driving Distance:** About 65 kilometres one way.

This trip traces the Elbow River upstream for much of its length, transporting visitors from high plains through forested foothills to low mountains. Along the way are opportunities to view riverine habitats, overlook a fine waterfall, and take an alpine hike. This is a good afternoon outing or evening picnic destination that can easily be extended to a full day. Be prepared, though, for throngs of motorists and cyclists on sunny weekends from late spring through early fall.

In 1814, explorer David Thompson mentioned an east-flowing river that turned sharply north at an "elbow." The river he described is the Elbow River, its abrupt turn occurring at what is now Glenmore Reservoir in southwest Calgary. Fed by this modest river, the reservoir collects sufficient water to meet nearly half the city's needs.

The Elbow River is thought to be millions of years old. During the formation of the Rocky Mountain Front Ranges, it continued its eastward journey, carving its way down through the gradual uplift of bedrock. Today, the Elbow still carves through the bedrock, exposing a timeline of rock layers that can be seen at such places as Elbow Falls.

The wider Elbow Valley was sculpted into a U shape thousands of years ago by glaciers advancing east out of the mountains. Parts of the upper valley, however, apparently escaped the brunt of the last ice age, creating an ice-free corridor for migrating animals and early native hunters. Near the Bragg Creek Valley, there was once a glacial lake—an arm of the larger Glacial Lake Calgary—fed by meltwaters from the Elbow River and Jumpingpound Creek.

In more recent times, the Elbow region was the overlapping hunting grounds of the Sarcee, Peigan, and Stoney people. The Stoney Trail, a major trading route along the foothills between Rocky Mountain House and Fort Macleod, passed through the Bragg Creek area.

The Sarcee, now known as the Tsuu T'ina, own lands south of Highway 8 and on both sides of Highway 22 leading to Bragg Creek. Their economic developments along the latter include the Redwood Meadows golf course and several hundred adjacent housing units bought by non-natives.

Early white visitors to the area included Father Constantine Scollen, who, in 1873, erected the first church in southern Alberta, the Mission of Our Lady of Peace. The mission was moved two years later to the fledgling Fort Calgary. A cairn marks the site of the original mission—a crude cabin 12 kilometres north of Bragg Creek near Highway 22. Sam Livingston, one of the first white settlers in the Calgary area, later built a trading post near the mission site.

In the 1890s, ranching and coal mining arrived in the Elbow Valley. Bragg Creek is named after Albert Bragg, who homesteaded here briefly as a teenager, accompanied by his younger brother. Because of earlier fires, the first settlers often didn't have to clear land to start their farms and ranches. Ironically, much of this open land is now covered in trees.

Crossing a branch of the Elbow River near Little Elbow Campground.

Today, Bragg Creek is a bustling community nestled in coniferous forest at the base of the foothills. On weekdays, acreage owners commute to Calgary. On weekends, city dwellers arrive en masse to visit the hamlet's shops, restaurants, and numerous galleries. An increasing number are now venturing beyond the retail centre to explore the natural beauty of the upper Elbow Valley.

By heading west on Highway 66, you can stop at numerous spots along the Elbow for picnics and riverside walks. A good interpretive walk, 8 kilometres west of the visitor centre, is Paddy's Flat. This 2.2-kilometre trail—accessible from several campground loop roads—follows an old river terrace through forest and then loops back along the edge of the Elbow River.

These terraces were formed during periods when a swollen river cut rapidly through glacial gravel deposits to form a new channel, leaving the previous one high and dry. Over thousands of years, a sequence of these steps formed, descending to the current riverbed. The old terraces now support a diversified forest, with fast-growing lodgepole pine and aspen on the sunny flats, and white spruce and poplars along the edges of a spring-fed stream.

The most popular stop along the river is at Elbow Falls, 5.4 kilometres beyond Paddy's Flat. A 400-metre paved path (wheelchair accessible) leads to a viewpoint overlooking the falls. Here, the river has been funnelled into a gap in the exposed bedrock, where it plunges over a rock step into a foaming pool. In a few centuries, however, the constant battering of water on rock will have reduced these falls to rapids.

The road beyond Elbow Falls is closed from December 1 to May 15. From late spring through fall, you can continue west as the highway climbs to Rainy Creek Summit and descends to Little Elbow Campground, where the Elbow and Little Elbow rivers join. En route are impressive views to the southwest of Mount Glasgow and Banded Peak. Along with Mount Cornwall, these peaks retain their snow cover through much of the year and are thus easily seen from Calgary.

If time and energy permit, the 3-kilometre hike up to Nihahi Ridge is well worth the considerable effort. You can reach the trail by proceeding to the far end of the campground, walking along an old fire road for about 500 metres, and then turning right and following the Nihahi Ridge signs. The trail climbs steeply through a thick stand of lodgepole pine, which shelters the white spruce that eventually will succeed it. South-facing clearings are ablaze with wildflowers such as Indian paintbrush and brown-eyed Susan.

---

## EATS & DRINKS

For a hamlet, Bragg Creek has a number of choices for the day tripper. For coffee and/or breakfast, there's the **Boardwalk Café & Wine Bar** or the **Cinnamon Spoon**, both in the central shopping centre. Good lunch stops include **Infusion Contemporary Cuisine** (23 Balsam Avenue), a blend of French and Asian influences, and the **Bavarian Inn Restaurant** (75 White Avenue); try the schnitzel sandwich or the elk burger. **Creekers** offers excellent meals throughout the day (20 White Avenue).

The trail swings left across a grassy bowl dotted with wind-stunted trees and climbs onto a ridge with stellar views of the Elbow Valley and peaks to the south and west. It's possible to continue ascending the ridge on a fainter, narrower, and more exposed trail, but the loftier views are perhaps not worth the additional exertion.

## ⬥ JUMPINGPOUND MOUNTAIN HIKE

**Route:** From the Sarcee Trail traffic light just south of Richmond Road SW, follow Highway 8 west for 21 kilometres and Highway 22 south, past Bragg Creek, for 14 kilometres. Head west on Highway 66 for nearly 28 kilometres and, just before the Little Elbow Campground, go north on the gravel Powderface Trail road for about 18 kilometres, parking on the left beside the unmarked Jumpingpound Summit trailhead. Return to Calgary by continuing north on Powderface Trail for 17 kilometres and then east and north on Highway 68 for 23 kilometres to the Trans-Canada Highway, 35 kilometres west of Calgary. This loop drive can also be done in reverse.
**Driving Distance:** About 160 kilometres return.
**Note:** Highway 66 west of Elbow Falls and the Powderface Trail are closed from December 1 to May 15. The hike to the top of Jumpingpound Mountain is about 3 kilometres one way, with an elevation gain of 400 metres. For current trail and road conditions and possible closures, phone 403-949-4261. While there are map signs at the trailhead and all major junctions, the Gem Trek *Bragg Creek and Sheep Valley* map provides a more detailed overview of the area.

From its rather lowly perch at the front edge of the Rocky Mountains, the 2,225-metre summit of Jumpingpound Mountain offers a surprisingly superb panorama of peaks, forested foothills, and distant prairies. Best of all, this bird's-eye view is earned in only about an hour of uphill walking, making it a fine half-day alpine outing for reasonably fit families. As a bonus, the Powderface Trail access road provides a pretty, winding valley drive between two ridges.

On a weekend, an early departure will ensure that you miss the throngs headed to Bragg Creek and the recreational attractions along

Looking south from Jumpingpound Mountain.

Highway 66 to the west (see the Elbow River Tour on pages 226–30). The crowds definitely thin, other than the odd cow and mountain biker, when you turn onto the Powderface Trail, usually a relatively good gravel road with the odd rough spot. The twisting road—flanked by Powderface Ridge to the east and the higher, rockier Nihahi Ridge to the west—initially climbs through open pine forest and bushy meadows before dropping steadily to the valley bottom. Just beyond a logged hillside and a crossing of stony Canyon Creek, you reach the Jumpingpound Summit trailhead.

After immediately crossing a bridged branch of Canyon Creek, the broad hiking trail begins a steady climb east through spruce and lodgepole pine forest sprinkled with bright, shade-loving wildflowers. Halfway up, there's an impressive stand of well-spaced, large pines with little understorey. A short side trail here leads to a bench, offering a glimpse of western peaks and serving as an appetizer for the panoramas beyond.

Soon enough, the trail levels off at a junction with a trail following the long, broad spine of Jumpingpound Ridge, a popular ride for mountain bikers. Go north for about five minutes on the Jumpingpound Ridge Trail and then take a side trail right to quickly leave the woods behind and easily reach the top of Jumpingpound Mountain, which except for a small outcrop of rocks looks more like a rounded hill than a peak.

But the views are impressive in all directions. To the near east is barren Moose Mountain, topped by a fire lookout and sitting on a large dome of sour natural gas and oil, which is steadily being tapped by nearby wells. The distinctive quartet of peaks bookended by Mount Glasgow and Banded Peak are on the southern horizon, while snow-capped Mount Bogart and the four summits of Mount Lougheed rise above lower, nearer ranges to the west. In the northern distance, foothills give way to the broad flats of the Bow Valley.

After soaking up these views, you can wander northeast to a lower summit that connects to the long north ridge of Moose Mountain. If you desire more exercise than a quick return the same way, you can hike either north or south along Jumpingpound Trail, both routes

Fall aspen along Jumpingpound Creek.

leading back to the road in about 6 kilometres. To save walking back down the road, leave a second car at either Canyon Creek, 3 kilometres to the south, or at Jumpingpound Creek, 6 kilometres to the north.

The return drive north follows the lovely meanders of Jumpingpound Creek, passing large willows and aspen interspersed with denser spruce and pine forest. In places, the lush vegetation nearly hems in the road. Not far beyond, the broad open meadow along Sibbald Creek signals the end of the winding Powderface Trail. Highway 68 leads through Sibbald Flats on gravel and undulating pavement back to the busy Trans-Canada Highway.

## EATS & DRINKS

See Bragg Creek (page 229).

# SIBBALD CREEK LOOP

**Route:** From the Canada Olympic Park traffic lights, drive 35 kilometres west on the Trans-Canada Highway. Take the Sibbald Creek Trail exit and follow Highway 68 south and then west for 37 kilometres to Highway 40, which is followed north to the Trans-Canada and back to Calgary.

**Driving Distance:** About 140 kilometres return.

This tour of the forested foothills 45 minutes west of Calgary has something for everyone: excellent birdwatching, trout fishing, camping, interpretive hiking, and native history. The only thing missing is wilderness. Logging, natural gas exploration, cattle grazing, and even target shooting are allowed in this eastern section of Kananaskis Country, aptly called a multiple-use area. Still, this is a fine foothills introduction, frequently bypassed by motorists heading for the mountains.

Serious birdwatchers often flock to the wetlands along Sibbald Creek Trail, where in spring and summer up to 50 species of birds

Looking west across expansive meadows from Sibbald Viewpoint.

may be spotted through binoculars. The birding begins in a small slough to the right of the Sibbald exit off the Trans-Canada Highway. In late March to early April, this pond is a good place to see migrating trumpeter swans and the occasional tundra swan. The trumpeter swan, named for its bugling call, has a wingspan of more than 2.5 metres. Considered threatened in Alberta, this elegant, long-necked bird makes a brief spring appearance en route to northern breeding grounds, primarily in the Grande Prairie area.

Heading south on Highway 68, the route soon passes a series of wetlands fed by runoff from surrounding hills. The sloughy waters, grasses, willows, and nearby tree cover provide excellent habitat for a diversity of birds. Patient and timely viewers might see red-winged blackbirds, lesser yellowlegs, common snipe, red-winged hawks, yellow warblers, and pine siskins, to name a few.

At 5 kilometres, the road rises to a hilltop with a commanding view of thickly forested foothills. The underlying bedrock of these foothills consists mainly of relatively young layers of sandstone and shale. These soft rocks have readily eroded into rounded hills covered with layers of till deposited by glaciers. The soils are primarily leafy humus over sandy clays, typical of a forest environment.

The forest here is mainly coniferous, with white spruce covering cooler, moister north-facing slopes and lodgepole pine and some aspen on drier south-facing slopes. Not surprisingly, such healthy stands have attracted logging since the turn of the century. In past years, even the local citizenry has come here to fell lodgepole pines for Christmas trees. The nearby Jumpingpound Demonstration Forest is well used as an outdoor classroom by visiting groups of Alberta school students.

Just beyond is Sibbald Viewpoint, a lofty spot overlooking an expansive meadow, with Front Range peaks in the near distance. These grassy flats are named after the area's first rancher, Frank Sibbald, who introduced longhorn steers to the grasslands in 1890, 15 years after his family settled here.

The human history of this area goes back to the end of the ice age, when the first inhabitants roamed the area in pursuit of bison, woolly mammoths, and even camels. Archaeologists have unearthed several nearby prehistoric campsites containing bison bones and stone tool fragments, some 10,000 to 11,000 years old.

The Stoney (which means the "people who cook with stones") still consider these foothills a spiritual area. For years, they've performed the Sun Dance, an annual summer ceremony banned under the Indian Act from 1885 to 1951. The weathered remains of sacred lodges—both small aspens arched into the rounded shape of a sun and larger structures decorated with colourful strips of cloth—can be seen in a meadow along the Sibbald Flat Trail, a 1-kilometre interpretive loop from Sibbald Lake.

Another worthwhile hike from Sibbald Lake is Ole Buck Loop. This 3.6-kilometre loop trail climbs to a high point offering views of the lake below and Moose Mountain on the horizon. But perhaps the highlight is a lovely, mature stand of poplar that shelters a dense growth of cow parsnip. From the viewpoint, the trail drops steadily to grassy slopes that overlook the willowy meadows and beaver ponds of Bateman Creek.

Just beyond Sibbald Lake, Sibbald Creek Trail passes the north end of Powderface Trail. This summer gravel road provides access to excellent ridge walks along its east side. When passable, it also leads to the Little Elbow Campground and Highway 66 to Bragg Creek.

Still heading west, the now-gravel Sibbald Creek Trail makes sweeping slalom turns as it winds through a narrower, more heavily forested valley (take care to obey the speed limits on the washboard corners). Industrious beavers have created a series of willowy ponds here along Sibbald Creek, attracting anglers casting for rainbow and brook trout. The fishing pressure is heavier at nearby Sibbald Meadows Pond, which has a parking lot and picnic tables.

A nicer, quieter picnic spot is located a couple of kilometres farther along the steadily descending road to Lusk Creek, fringed in early summer with fragrant wolf willow and yellow dryads. From Lusk Creek, it's a short drive to the junction with Highway 40.

## KANANASKIS VALLEY

**Route:** From the Canada Olympic Park traffic lights, drive 61 kilometres west on the Trans-Canada Highway and exit onto Highway 40; follow it south for 50 kilometres to its junction with the Kananaskis Lakes Trail. Stop at the Barrier Lake visitor centre, 7 kilometres south on Highway 40, for information and brochures. Phone 403-673-3985.

**Driving Distance:** About 120 kilometres one way.

In theory, this should be a short day trip. After all, it's little more than an hour of straight driving from the city limits to this tour's end point. Yet so much scenery, history, and recreational and educational opportunities are packed into this 50-kilometre stretch of the Kananaskis Valley that a full day scratches only the surface. Consider this description, then, as a menu for a brimming buffet table, from which visitors can pile their plates as they choose. Second, third, and fourth helpings are recommended, at suitable intervals.

# Kananaskis Country

Highway 40 initially crosses the windswept Morley Flats that were once the bottom of a glacial lake. This lake was formed when melting icewaters from high in the Kananaskis Valley were blocked by an arm of the large Bow Valley glacier. When the glaciers receded about 10,000 years ago, the lake was drained.

Not long after, the first recorded humans entered the valley. These ancient ancestors of the Kootenai often spent their summers around Boulton Creek, close to Kananaskis Lake. They followed bison and elk down-valley to the shelter of winter camps at nearby Wasootch Creek and the Bow River. By the mid-1700s, the Stoney had driven the Kootenai west across the mountains and claimed the valley for hunting and fishing.

But their tenure was short-lived. The arrival of white explorers in the mid-1800s, followed by prospectors, trappers, and the like, resulted in forest fires, overhunting of elk, and the near extermination of the bison. After the Stoney signed Treaty No. 7 in 1877, they moved to their Bow Valley reserve, part of which extends across the flats and into the forests along Highway 40. As part of a tourism initiative, the Stoney have opened a casino and hotel at the junction of Highway 40 and the Trans-Canada Highway.

In the 20th century, white development subdued the Kananaskis River through a series of hydroelectric dams. The river, once called Strong Current by native peoples, now flows mostly tranquilly alongside Highway 40. Two beneficiaries of this development are canoeists and kayakers, who take advantage of the daily release of water from the upstream Barrier Dam to practise their whitewater skills. You can often see them performing their manoeuvres by walking down to the river from the Canoe Meadows parking lot, 5.5 kilometres south of the Trans-Canada Highway.

A few kilometres farther along, Barrier Lake and Dam come into view. The dam opened in 1947, creating a reservoir with a capacity of 25 billion litres. For a commanding view of the lake and the Kananaskis Valley, drive another 2.3 kilometres to a picnic area, where a short interpretive trail climbs to a hilltop.

Much of the tree clearing and earth moving for the Barrier Dam was done by German prisoners of war held captive at a nearby camp during World War II. At first, the camp held male Germans living in Canada as well as German merchant seamen captured overseas at the outbreak of war. Later, captured German soldiers were brought here, including some who fought under Erwin Rommel's command

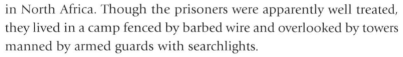

in North Africa. Though the prisoners were apparently well treated, they lived in a camp fenced by barbed wire and overlooked by towers manned by armed guards with searchlights.

In summer, visitors can tour one of the guard towers and the Colonel's Cabin—the former camp commandant's office and now a provincial historic site. To reach them, turn left at the Kananaskis Forest Experiment Station, 2.5 kilometres past the visitor centre.

Behind the cabin are two connected interpretive trails (2.3 kilometres in length) that explain the mixed forest ecology and forest management practices. One stop is at a small pit, where visitors can observe the four layers of soil that sustain this forest environment. For four decades, these lands were the site of a federal forest research station. The scattered survivors of one experiment—to plant non-native species such as Norway spruce and Jack pine—can be seen along the far loop. The forest research station has been replaced by the University of Calgary's Kananaskis Biogeoscience Institute.

The limestone cliffs along this section of the valley attract rock climbers. These athletes can often be seen from the road, scaling the

Fall cycling on paved pathway south of Ribbon Creek.

steep walls below Barrier Mountain. The slabs along nearby Wasootch Valley are one of the most popular training areas for climbers in the Canadian Rockies.

Just beyond Wasootch Creek are the Mount Lorette Ponds. A former bend in the Kananaskis River cut off by highway construction, these small ponds were dredged, stocked with rainbow trout, and ringed with paved trails. This popular family picnic and fishing spot is wheelchair accessible. There are also several nearby beaver ponds containing rainbow and brook trout.

Coming into view on the right is Mount Allan, the home of Nakiska Ski Resort and site of alpine skiing events at the 1988 Winter Olympics. Its selection over rival candidates in the valley to the west was controversial due to its proximity to wintering bighorn sheep and reliance on snow-making equipment. Mount Allan overlooks a cluster of other tourist and sporting developments near Ribbon Creek, including the three hotels of Kananaskis Village, a 36-hole championship golf course, and a deluxe RV park complete with satellite television hookups.

Visitors to the Ribbon Creek area can also hike or cross-country ski on a network of trails. This is the starting point for a lovely, paved cycling trail that winds south through forest along the highway for 7.3 kilometres to Wedge Pond.

The Ribbon Creek area is no stranger to development. The forests here were logged in the late 1930s and early '40s and the timber trucked out of the Kananaskis Valley via a forestry road completed in 1935. This was much easier than floating the logs to Calgary via the Kananaskis and Bow rivers, as was done from a logging camp to the south that opened in 1886. The lower slopes of Mount Allan were mined for coal from 1947 to 1952. Today, you can see remnants of these developments along a hiking trail up Ribbon Creek.

At 8.5 kilometres past the Ribbon Creek area, a side road climbs to the former Fortress Mountain ski resort, which closed in 2007 after surviving several financial crises and ownership changes. The road is now closed to vehicles, though intrepid cyclists or hikers can still

venture up its 8-kilometre length if they're intent on exploring old ski slopes ablaze with wildflowers in early summer. Just past the Fortress access road is the boundary to Peter Lougheed Provincial Park, which protects the finest mountain terrain in Kananaskis Country.

This trip ends at King Creek, just before the junction of Highway 40 with the Kananaskis Lakes Trail. It's well worth taking the level 800-metre walk up King Creek, shaded even in summer by its high walls. This narrow canyon was carved by glacial meltwaters, creating a passageway used today by bighorn sheep, elk, and deer as they move from high meadows to a salt lick on the west side of the highway. Interpretive signs along the way explain the ancient forces of mountain building here as well as such features as the lichen on the canyon walls.

---

### EATS & DRINKS

There are several restaurants and drinking spots at the hotels and golf course at Kananaskis Village. Snacks are available in the gas station at the Fortress Mountain turnoff.

---

## GOLDEN EAGLE MIGRATION

**Route:** From the Canada Olympic Park traffic lights, drive 61 kilometres west on the Trans-Canada Highway and exit onto Highway 40; follow it south for 23 kilometres. At the Kananaskis Village turnoff, head west for 1 kilometre and turn right onto the Stoney Trail road, which in about 100 metres reaches a parking area. On foot, walk north of the vehicle barrier and turn right on the Hay Meadow Trail. Follow it for less than a kilometre to a large clearing alongside the Kananaskis River (small buildings nearby).

**Driving Distance:** About 85 kilometres one way.

**Note:** Canmore (95 kilometres west of Calgary on the Trans-Canada Highway) hosts the Festival of Eagles in mid-October during the fall migration. Phone 403-678-1295 for information.

It's hard to believe that less than an hour's drive west of Calgary, a major migration of birds with 2-metre wingspans has been taking place for thousands of years—and no one knew about it. It wasn't until the early 1990s that ardent birdwatcher Peter Sherrington discovered that 6,000 to 8,000 golden eagles were flying twice a year over the Front Ranges of the Rocky Mountains between wintering grounds as far south as Mexico and breeding areas in Alaska and the Yukon.

That discovery has since spawned a weekend-long Golden Eagle Festival in mid-October in Canmore. There, visitors can scan the skies through spotting scopes, talk to avid birders, perhaps see a trained eagle up close, or take a guided hike up nearby Mount Lady Macdonald to view these magnificent birds riding thermal updrafts.

But if you want to see an average of 250 golden eagles in one day, head to the Kananaskis Valley during the peak spring and fall migrations in March and October. Pack a good pair of binoculars (or, better yet, a spotting scope; you won't see these high flyers except as a tiny dot with the naked eye), a picnic lunch, warm clothes, and a folding chair. Perhaps the best viewing site is Hay Meadow, beside the tranquil Kananaskis River, with panoramic views of the valley and peaks such as Lorette, Allan, Bogart, and Kidd. Your eyes, however, will mostly be trained east along the ridgeline of a peak, informally called Patrick, for the frequent passing of golden eagles.

The golden eagle is a majestic bird, with three times the visual acuity of humans. It's a fierce hunter, swooping down with powerful talons on snowshoe hares and, more rarely, young mountain goats or bighorn sheep. But an adult eagle doesn't usually eat during its long migration, which is a marvel of aerodynamics and energy efficiency.

Turning its wings 90 degrees into the wind, an eagle rises several hundred metres on an updraft, then glides on a descending angle of about one degree until it needs to climb again. Under good wind conditions, it can reach speeds of 120 kilometres per hour and probably cover up to 700 kilometres a day. During the peak of the migration, eagles are often in the air from 8 a.m. to 8 p.m., resting at night above

Scientist Peter Sherrington scans the skies above Patrick Peak in the Kananaskis Valley for migrating golden eagles.

the treeline or at an open expanse like the top of Plateau Mountain in southern Kananaskis Country.

Visitors to Hay Meadow can easily see several soaring golden eagles in a few minutes of spotting. But to get a true sense of this migration, be prepared to spend several hours in this magnificent spot. Consider that Sherrington and a handful of other unpaid volunteers have spent an average of 10 hours a day here seven months of the year since 1992, thus making a significant contribution to the understanding of these birds. By meticulously recording the passage of each eagle in the middle of this flyway, they can confirm, say, that breeding numbers are up in Alaska or that the mortality rate is high on southern wintering grounds, likely from hunters who prize their tail feathers.

Besides golden eagles, Sherrington and his fellow researchers have recorded some 225 bird species from Hay Meadow. Their sightings include many bald eagles; the occasional blue heron; large flocks of migrating ducks, geese, and loons; the strange spectacle of normally stream-hugging dippers flying high at dusk; the rarely seen gyrfalcon and turkey vulture; and the first Alberta sighting of white-throated

Majestic golden eagles make a major twice-yearly migration along the Front Ranges of the Rocky Mountains.

swifts. They've also seen plenty of deer, moose, and elk, plus the odd bear, lynx, or wolf. You, too, can see a lot of wildlife and the changing of the mountain seasons if, like Sherrington, you're willing to sit patiently and watch the natural world go by.

# STONEY TRAIL MOUNTAIN BIKE

**Route:** From the Canada Olympic Park traffic lights, drive 61 kilometres west on the Trans-Canada Highway and then go 9 kilometres south, turning right into the parking lot beside the Barrier Lake Dam.

**Driving Distance:** 70 kilometres one way.

**Cycling Distance:** About 14 kilometres, and 2 hours, one way, if a second vehicle is left at a parking area near Ribbon Creek. To do so, drive another 14 kilometres south on Highway 40, turn right at the Kananaskis Village turnoff, and right again after 1 kilometre.

**Note:** Trail maps and information on conditions can be obtained at the Barrier Lake Information Centre, about 2 kilometres north of the Barrier Dam parking lot. Phone 403-673-3985. A portion of the trail is closed from April 15 to June 15.

The Stoney Trail offers a pleasant, moderate mountain biking excursion along the far shores of Barrier Lake in the Kananaskis Valley. It's not a wilderness trip, as much of the undulating dirt and gravel route follows a power line right-of-way shared by equestrian riders. But there are plenty of early-season wildflowers, lakeshore birds, and mountain vistas, plus the opportunity for family exercise away from often-busy Highway 40.

From the parking lot, head west on the gravel path across Barrier Dam. Much of the tree clearing and earth moving for the dam was performed by World War II German prisoners held captive at a camp across the highway (see pages 238–39). The dam opened in 1947, creating a reservoir with a capacity of 25 billion litres and generating enough electricity for a town of 8,500 people. The TransAlta Utilities plant now operates by remote control. The lake is also used for boating and fishing, though most visitors are content to dabble their toes in the chilly mountain waters.

Once past the dam, follow the main, rocky trail up a steady incline, ignoring the first trail left and going left at the second junction (signed). Cruise southwest on a narrower trail through a lovely forest, which includes some large Douglas fir and an understorey of white geraniums, wood lilies, and Indian paintbrush. (Did you know that the brightly coloured "brush" is actually a leaf-like bract, enfolding the real, pale flower?)

The route soon follows the northwest shore of Barrier Lake, crossing the bridged Jewel Creek and passing a shoreline backcountry campground. Soon enough, you leave the forest behind to discover fine views over the lake of the surrounding mountains. Dominating the eastern skyline is Mount Baldy, which was known as Sleeping Buffalo Mountain to the Stoney people. The mountain's lower limestone cliffs, known as Barrier Bluffs, are popular among sport climbers, and its summit is an early-season destination for scramblers seeking exercise and a superb view of the Kananaskis Valley. During World War II, prisoners from the nearby internment camp were sometimes allowed to scale the peak unescorted.

The trail now heads south through open meadows lined with lodgepole pine and dotted with wildflowers. As the south end of the lake comes into view, watch for young families of Canada geese in early summer. The lake is fed by the Kananaskis River after it makes its final meander through a broad wetland.

Beyond the lake, the route swings southwest through meadows below Mount Lorette's long South Ridge, a popular route for rock climbers. You skirt a couple of beaver ponds before the final stretch south to the Stoney parking area near Ribbon Creek.

Those interested in a longer cycle or a smoother alternative can pedal along the paved Evan Thomas Bike Path. From Ribbon Creek, it heads south through open forest and past the Kananaskis Country Golf Course, crossing to the east side of Highway 40 just before reaching the Wedge Pond parking lot 8 kilometres distant.

# FALL LARCH HIKE

**Route:** From the Canada Olympic Park traffic lights, drive 61 kilometres west on the Trans-Canada Highway and then 68 kilometres south on Highway 40 to the Highwood Pass parking lot.

**Driving Distance:** 129 kilometres one way.

**Note:** The moderate hike into the upper headwaters of Pocaterra Creek rises about 100 metres over 2 kilometres.

Alberta lacks the fiery blaze of red and orange maples that marks fall in eastern Canada. Yet our southern mountains are blessed with the unique spectacle of a conifer that loses its needles each fall. In late September, an annual pilgrimage begins to see stands of alpine larch briefly turning a stunning yellowy-orange before shedding their needles. The short hike into upper Pocaterra Creek in the heart of Kananaskis Country is a lovely way for visitors of all ages to witness this rite of fall.

But don't expect solitude. Like the overrun Larch Valley near Lake Louise, the late September walk into Pocaterra Valley is rapidly gaining popularity, especially on sunny weekends, when young children and even small dogs join the hordes. The reason is easy access. Alpine larches grow near the treeline, generally at an elevation around 2,200 metres, meaning a fair climb on foot is usually needed to reach them. But thanks to the highest highway in Canada, visitors can see larch from the car as they reach Highwood Pass.

The finest larch stands in this area, however, are about a 45-minute walk away in a stunning alpine valley along Pocaterra Creek. From the parking lot, the route follows the Highwood Meadows interpretive trail for about 100 metres before angling left on a dirt track through a small grassy draw marked by a large depression. A well-beaten trail ascends left through often muddy woods and over a treed ridge. Emerging onto an avalanche slope, hikers can pause to look north along Pocaterra Creek to the jagged Elpoca Mountain on the horizon. The trail continues over a rock slide, then follows a small stream to a tiny pond ringed by larch. Ambitious hikers can

continue farther up the valley, turning left for Grizzly Col or right for Little Highwood Pass, though both involve much steeper climbs that soon leave the larch behind. Speaking of grizzlies, these bears often dig winter dens in larch stands in the Canadian Rockies.

Alpine larch are also commonly known as subalpine larch or as Lyall's larch, the latter for Scottish naturalist David Lyall, who first described these trees in 1858. They appear high in the mountains of the Pacific Northwest, southeast B.C., and the U.S. and Canadian Rockies. Within the latter, they're found as far north as Clearwater Pass, east of Bow Summit, beyond which the climate is apparently too cool to support them.

Alpine larch typically grow on moist, north-facing slopes near the treeline, where their only competition is subalpine fir and Engelmann spruce, which tend to be more stunted at this elevation. Larch are intolerant of shade, needing considerable light to develop their soft, translucent green needles each spring and summer. Occasionally, the larch will invade areas considered to be above the treeline, such as the alpine meadows around Healy Pass in Banff National Park. In parts of Banff's Bow Valley where fire has created sufficient openings (such as near Castle Junction), larch can be found as low as 1,900 metres. With their thin bark, alpine larch are themselves susceptible to fire, though major burns are uncommon near the treeline.

The alpine larch survives up here because of its hardiness—its ability to withstand cool summers and cold winters, high winds, avalanches, and snow patches that linger into July. But it's a tenuous existence. Larch don't germinate well at this elevation, and survivors grow very slowly during their first two decades; in one study, 10-year-old seedlings were only 4 centimetres high. During this time, however, they develop strong tap and lateral roots in the rocky soils. The annual loss of their needles also helps them withstand winter dehydration.

Once well established, alpine larch can live for centuries, with the older trees generally found at higher elevations. A dead, 838-year-old larch was found in Waterton Lakes National Park and a living 735-year-old specimen was discovered near Storm Mountain in

Fall larch hike along Pocaterra Creek.

Banff National Park. In Manning Provincial Park in southwest B.C.,
several alpine larch are believed to be nearly 2,000 years old, which
would make them Canada's oldest trees. Alpine larch are rarely
uprooted, though their knobby black limbs and trunk, weakened by
heart rot, may be toppled by high winds.

In well-sheltered, healthy stands like those at Panorama Ridge,
above Taylor Lake in Banff National Park, larch can grow to 20 metres
high. They're also seen in profusion in Banff's Bow Valley, along Highway 93 south of Castle Junction, and in many parts of Kananaskis
Country, especially at Little Elbow Pass. To find your own secluded
larch grove, gaze up to the treeline as you're driving through Banff or
Kananaskis in the fall and watch for dense patches of yellow.

# KANANASKIS COUNTRY LOOP

**Route:** From the Canada Olympic Park traffic lights, drive 61 kilometres west on
the Trans-Canada Highway to the Kananaskis Country exit. Go 50 kilometres south

on Highway 40 and turn right onto Kananaskis Lakes Trail, which provides access, in 12.5 kilometres, to the Canadian Mount Everest Expedition Trail. The return trip follows the Smith-Dorrien/Spray Trail north for 60 kilometres to Canmore and then back to Calgary on the Trans-Canada Highway. (Map on page 237.)

**Driving Distance:** About 285 kilometres return.

The Kananaskis Country Loop is a driving tour of sharp contrasts through the impressive Front Ranges of the Rocky Mountains. The first half is smooth sailing south on immaculate pavement past the numerous recreational developments of Highway 40. The return trip north is down a gravel highway that offers mountain scenery unencumbered by tourist hordes.

There's some method to this madness. For good or ill, recreational developments in Kananaskis Country, such as ski hills, golf courses, and hotels, have been concentrated along Highway 40 near Ribbon Creek. That leaves the Smith-Dorrien/Spray Valley in a fairly natural state, if you discount the Spray Lakes Reservoir, which preceded Kananaskis Country by nearly three decades. The creation of Spray Valley Provincial Park and Bow Valley Wildland Provincial Park in the early 2000s prevents further development there. The area's jewel, at the southern end of this loop, lies within Peter Lougheed Provincial Park and is similarly protected.

This is primarily a driving tour that circumnavigates the Kananaskis Range via broad, parallel valleys. But there are plenty of opportunities to stop en route, along with a magnificent short hike to a hilltop overlooking the Kananaskis Lakes. For a detailed description of the attractions along Highway 40, see the Kananaskis Valley trip on pages 236–41.

Kananaskis Country is named for an Aboriginal man who, according to legend, made a miraculous recovery from an axe blow to the head. As for the provincial park within Kananaskis Country, it is named after Peter Lougheed, the former Conservative premier. The provincial government created Kananaskis Country in 1977 as a 4,000-square-kilometre mountain playground and a nearby alternative to the crowded mountain national parks. Unlike those parks, it

The south face of Mount Kidd, along Highway 40, offers a classic example of rock folding.

was designated a multiple-use area that allowed some cattle grazing, logging, and natural gas extraction to continue, especially in its eastern and southern reaches.

While the Ribbon Creek area was once logged and mined for coal, this central section of Kananaskis Country is primarily devoted to recreational pursuits, most noticeably skiing, golfing, hiking, and camping. There are also opportunities to fish, kayak, ride horses, cycle, and even hunt for big game—at least outside Peter Lougheed Provincial Park.

Kananaskis Country also differs from the national parks in charging no entrance fees and allowing no towns. Nonetheless, hundreds of millions of dollars from oil royalties accumulated in the province's Heritage Fund were spent on roads and recreational facilities. Anyone who visits the 36-hole golf course, the RV park and campgrounds, or even the deluxe visitor centres will agree the province went first class.

Still the main attraction, I hope, is the mountain environment. The peaks along Highway 40 aren't only exquisite but also provide a graphic lesson in the forces of mountain building and erosion.

These mountains are made up of sediments deposited in inland seas several hundred million years ago and compressed into rocks such as limestones, dolomites, and sandstones. Between 80 million and 40 million years ago, colliding tectonic plates deep below the earth's surface unleashed great forces from the west, causing these horizontal layers to fold and fracture. Such folding is clearly evident in the south face of Mount Kidd. The fracturing created fault lines, along which older layers of rock were thrust up at a steep angle over younger rocks.

Today, the most visible layers in these peaks are the older, grey limestones, which now overlay brown sandstones and shales. Limestone is particularly resistant to erosion and thus forms many of the impressive faces of the Opal Range, on the east side of Highway 40 across from Kananaskis Lakes.

These mountain ranges also influence the climate. The east side of the Kananaskis Valley is somewhat drier than the west, where the higher peaks of the Kananaskis Range attract more precipitation. I've often hiked in sunshine on the east while the western peaks were shrouded in clouds.

The Kananaskis Range, in turn, gets considerably less precipitation than the peaks along the Continental Divide on the west side of the Smith-Dorrien/Spray Trail, one valley to the west. The divide, which marks much of the Alberta–B.C. boundary, is the height of land separating river systems that flow to opposite sides of the continent.

At a T-junction 50 kilometres south of the Trans-Canada Highway, turn right onto the Kananaskis Lakes Trail, which leads in 2 kilometres to the Smith-Dorrien/Spray Trail to the north. It's well worth detouring here to an interpretive trail, known as the ◢Canadian Mount Everest Expedition Trail, that honours the first Canadian ascent of the famous peak in 1982. To get there, continue on the Kananaskis Lakes Trail for another 10.5 kilometres to the White Spruce parking lot and the start of the trail.

This is a splendid 1.7-kilometre loop trail that climbs through a thick forest of spruce, pine, and Douglas fir to a high lookout between

Splendid hiking trail into Chester Lake off the Smith-Dorrien/Spray Trail.

the Upper and Lower Kananaskis lakes. The impressive view over an upper lake ringed with glacier-capped mountains was apparently even more spectacular before an earthen dam was built in the 1950s, drowning several forested islands and enlarging the lake.

The return drive along the Kananaskis Trail passes Boulton Creek, where archaeological digs have uncovered stone flakes and spear points used by Aboriginal peoples more than 8,000 years ago. Farther on, nestled in the lodgepole pine forest, is the Peter Lougheed Provincial Park visitor centre, which features several hands-on interpretive displays.

The Smith-Dorrien/Spray Trail crosses the muted Kananaskis River and swings past the Lower Kananaskis Lake on pavement that soon gives way to good gravel. In 1841, James Sinclair led a group of 200 Metis from Manitoba through this valley and over the nearby

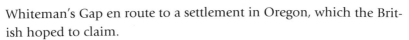

Whiteman's Gap en route to a settlement in Oregon, which the British hoped to claim.

A number of peaks along this valley—including Indefatigable, Invincible, Black Prince, Chester, and Sparrowhawk—are named after cruisers and destroyers involved, often disastrously, in the Battle of Jutland during World War I. Other mountains, on the left, honour commanding officers from the same war.

Past the Black Prince parking lot and hidden by a line of mountains to the west are the sizable Haig and Robertson glaciers. Farther on at Mud Lake, trails lead to Burstall Pass and Chester Lake, two of the more popular hiking and cross-country skiing destinations in Kananaskis Country. The ⚑Chester Lake route, in particular, is an excellent hike (4 kilometres one way, 300 metres of elevation gain) into an alpine meadow fringed in larch trees and backed by steep mountain walls.

The small earthen dam at Mud Lake marks a height of land from which creeks flow both north and south. This bump in elevation also helps account for a sudden and appreciable increase of snow depth along this stretch of road in winter.

Continuing north, the lengthy Spray Lakes Reservoir soon comes into view. The construction of Canyon Dam here in 1949 flooded smaller lakes and diverted much of the Spray River's flow from Banff to Canmore. The lake levels fluctuate significantly to meet electrical demands, preventing plants from growing along the shoreline. Once-plentiful native cutthroat have largely disappeared from the lake, replaced by stocked lake trout and whitefish that attract many anglers, particularly those who fish through the ice in winter.

Beyond the reservoir, the road narrows markedly and follows a winding course to Whiteman's Gap. A small pull-off provides a commanding view over the expanding town of Canmore and the surrounding Bow Corridor. This lofty perch is at the lip of a hanging valley, left dangling high above the Bow Valley after the latter was carved by advancing glaciers. The descent to Canmore on a bumpy gravel road is continuously steep, requiring steady braking.

```
═══════ EATS & DRINKS ═══════
See pages 241 and 266.
```

# ♨ BOW VALLEY PROVINCIAL PARK

**Route:** From the Canada Olympic Park traffic lights, drive 65 kilometres west on the Trans-Canada Highway. Take the Bow Valley Provincial Park exit and head north for 800 metres, turning left to reach most of the park trails.
**Driving Distance:** About 65 kilometres one way.
**Note:** This trip describes the section of Bow Valley Provincial Park north of the Trans-Canada Highway. Phone 403-673-3985.

On perhaps my 200th trip west to Banff's mountains, I finally pulled off the Trans-Canada Highway and discovered the jewel that is Bow Valley Provincial Park. There, within earshot of racing traffic, is an understated park with one of the richest ecosystems in Alberta. It's a meeting place of three zones—mountains, grasslands, and boreal forests—with two rivers and a spring-fed marsh adding to the biological diversity.

Consider that such disparate birds as bald eagles, rufous humming-birds, meadowlarks, ruffed grouse, and harlequin ducks can all be at home in the park. Or that this is the only place in the world where the tiger salamander of the prairies and the long-toed salamander of the mountains breed in the same location. During a leisurely hour's walk, you can spot dozens of wildflower species, including such show-stoppers as lady's slipper, western wood lily, and elephant's head.

The task, then, isn't finding points of interest but determining how to fit them all in. A good plan is to visit often and digest a bit at a time. At less than 45 minutes from Calgary, this is a perfect destination for a picnic supper and interpretive walk during the long evening hours of early summer. Indeed, the park is perhaps best seen in June and early July, when the flowers are at their peak.

Looking across a pond on Many Springs Trail in Bow Valley Provincial Park.

Between 1902 and 1930, this site was just inside the eastern boundary of an expanded Banff National Park. Once that protection was lost—to allow industrial development in the Canmore area—cattle grazing and rock quarrying ensued. Finally, in 1959, Bow Valley Provincial Park was established. Today it's bisected by the Trans-Canada Highway and bounded on two sides by the merging Bow and Kananaskis rivers. In the late 1990s, its southern boundary was expanded to include the Barrier Lake area.

The best way to explore the park area north of the Trans-Canada Highway is through its seven interpretive trails, each unveiling a different aspect of the park's treasures. You can reach all but one of these trails by following the signs along the lovely paved road that winds down through aspen stands to the broad Bow River. The riverside is a good place to picnic alongside grazing Canada geese and scan the far shores for nesting bald eagles.

The following is a sampling of the trails. But first, a plea to visitors: Do not pick the wildflowers! It's illegal to pick flowers in a provincial park and highly destructive to do so in an area that contains many rare species. I once saw a young woman happily displaying a bouquet of freshly picked wood lilies. When these beautiful orange flowers are picked, the plant dies.

## Many Springs Trail

This 1.6-kilometre trail, near the west end of the park, circles an unusual, spring-fed wetland that boasts abundant yellow lady's slippers in mid- to late June (please don't trample the underbrush to get close-up photos). Because the water temperature stays at a constant 6°C, a variety of animals and birds can be found here year-round. Elk and deer are also attracted by the minerals in the spring water. One interesting plant found along the water's edge is elephant's head, which on close inspection does resemble a column of purple elephant trunks. Another interesting inhabitant is a form of isopod, a tiny blind creature with a 400-million-year-old ancestry, which lives in underwater darkness.

## Montane Trail

This 1.5-kilometre walk from behind the park office explores the transition from prairie to forest. In the open meadows, ground-hugging

Yellow lady's slippers make their showy appearance along Many Springs Trail.

plants are well adapted to surviving the strong, drying chinook winds. The trail then follows a grassy esker—a serpentine ridge of gravel left by streams that once flowed under glacial ice. The homeward loop passes through a mature forest that includes a magnificent stand of Douglas fir. These ancient giants perhaps owe their longevity to their thick, fire-resistant bark.

### Flowing Water Trail

This trail, reached from the far end of the campground on the east side of Highway 1X, is a 1.4-kilometre tour of sharp contrasts. The trail begins in a cool, forested terrace intersected by iron-rich streams descending to the Kananaskis River. (While scenic, the river is largely barren, thanks to regular releases of water from an upstream dam that scour the river bottom.) It then climbs a grassy slope of wildflowers to an exposed hilltop, where strong winds have produced a dry climate and stunted trees. Farther along, nature's developer, the beaver, has fashioned dams, blocking the flow of small streams and creating an extensive marshland. Compare this to the nearby handiwork of human developers, who some decades ago built hydroelectric dams on the Kananaskis and Bow rivers.

> **≡ EATS & DRINKS ≡**
>
> A park campground store sells groceries and snacks.

## ♦ YAMNUSKA

**Route:** From the Canada Olympic Park traffic lights, drive 65 kilometres west on the Trans-Canada Highway, take the Seebe/Exshaw exit, and go 4 kilometres north on Highway 1X. Head 2.2 kilometres east on Highway 1A and turn left on a gravel road that soon leads to a parking lot.
**Driving Distance:** About 71 kilometres one way.

**Note:** The trail to Yamnuska's east ridge climbs 430 metres in elevation over 3.5 kilometres. Hikers should be in good physical condition and equipped with sturdy boots, especially for downhill sections.

With its impressive face of grey limestone, Yamnuska is a landmark peak guarding the entrance to the Rocky Mountains west of Calgary. It also overlooks an incredibly rich mixture of natural features and wildlife habitats, befitting a designated natural area. From late spring through fall, it's an excellent choice for a short, though steep, hike to its east ridge, with superb views over the Bow Valley.

The peak is officially known as Mount John Laurie, in honour of the man who devoted much of his life to helping Alberta's Aboriginal people. But most locals know it as Yamnuska, a Stoney term meaning either "wall of stone" or "flat mountain." It's affectionately called Yam by climbers, who have put more than 70 routes up its south face, making it the most important rock wall in the Canadian Rockies.

Yamnuska marks the transition from the foothills to the Rocky Mountain Front Ranges. As well, it often marks a rather abrupt change from clear eastern skies to cloudy mountain weather. On such days, the peak is often framed by striking bands of arching white clouds.

The base of Yamnuska's south face also clearly delineates a famous geological dividing line known as the McConnell Thrust Fault. Here, 525-million-year-old Eldon Formation limestone rocks have been thrust some 40 kilometres east, up and over top of 75-million-year-old mudstones and sandstones, disturbing the softer underlying rocks very little in the process. The McConnell Thrust—named for geologist R. G. McConnell, who helped map the area's rocks for the Geological Survey of Canada in the 1880s—is one of the world's major faults, extending some 400 kilometres. Along the fault line near Yamnuska, calcareous springs reach the surface and help feed a surprising number of small lakes and ponds.

Yamnuska's lower slopes and valley bottom are also a naturalist's delight, reflecting the merging here of mountain, foothills, and prairie ecosystems. More than 180 bird species have been recorded in the area, ranging from great grey and horned owls to ospreys and

Yamnuska marks the transition from foothills to the Front Ranges of the Rocky Mountains.

northern orioles. Wildflowers are abundant (more than 300 species identified), highlighted by brilliant spring displays of prairie crocus and yellow lady's slippers. The Yamnuska area is similarly rich in human history, yielding discoveries of prehistoric teepee rings, hearths, and stone tools.

More recent human usage, however, threatened to significantly impact Yamnuska's unique natural heritage. A sandstone quarry has long been in operation at the mountain's base, and random camping and off-road vehicle use were steadily increasing, as were the number of trails crisscrossing the lower mountain slopes. A plan for a recreational vehicle park below Yamnuska was the final impetus for the Alberta government to create Yamnuska Natural Area in 1997, encompassing 1,600 hectares below John Laurie and Goat mountains.

To minimize visitor impact, a new parking area was created at the east entrance of the natural area, and random camping and off-road vehicle use was eliminated. With the help of volunteers and some minimum-security prisoners, a single access trail was built to the base of the climbing cliffs, avoiding the quarry, which continues to be mined but within its current boundaries. More recently, Yamnuska Natural Area was added to Bow Valley Wildland Park, thus providing more enforcement for protecting the area.

From the parking lot, the trail to the East Ridge of Yamnuska climbs steadily through a lovely aspen forest to a junction. Straight ahead lies the climbers' access route, which switchbacks steeply up towards the east end of the south face. Instead, head right on the gentler hiking trail, which traverses east before ascending more steeply alongside a small, steep-sided valley. Notice the lush growth of tall spruce and aspen in the shaded valley and compare it to the stunted aspen and grasses of the exposed slope to the right. The thick forest soon gives way to more barren slopes with scattered trees and shale outcrops.

The steep limestone walls of Yamnuska's South Face are a magnet for rock climbers.

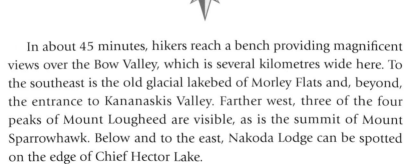

In about 45 minutes, hikers reach a bench providing magnificent views over the Bow Valley, which is several kilometres wide here. To the southeast is the old glacial lakebed of Morley Flats and, beyond, the entrance to Kananaskis Valley. Farther west, three of the four peaks of Mount Lougheed are visible, as is the summit of Mount Sparrowhawk. Below and to the east, Nakoda Lodge can be spotted on the edge of Chief Hector Lake.

Those with sufficient energy can climb another 130 vertical metres to the ridge crest (offering views into the next valley) and perhaps continue up to the east end of Yamnuska's main wall. A somewhat down-sloping trail traverses west under impressive vertical walls of yellow and grey limestone but is exposed to scree slopes below and rockfall hazard from climbers above. Numerous high-speed tracks head straight down the mostly soft scree to intercept the climber's trail, which is followed left to rejoin your ascent trail. Of course, the safest choice is to return the way you came up.

## ♦ HEART CREEK

**Route:** From the Canada Olympic Park traffic lights, drive 74 kilometres west on the Trans-Canada Highway. Take the Heart Creek/Lac Des Arcs exit and go south on the overpass to reach the parking lot and trailhead.

**Note:** Hiking distance is 3 kilometres one way. Allow at least two hours. Interpretive brochures for Heart Creek are available at the Barrier Lake Visitor Centre, 6.5 kilometres south of the Trans-Canada Highway on Highway 40.

This is a pleasant family stroll up the narrow and biologically diverse Heart Creek Valley. The trail is mainly flat, crisscrossing the creek seven times on wooden bridges. Visitors armed with interpretive brochures can learn about the creek ecology, while young children can float sticks and, despite parental warnings, hop on streamside rocks. For the intrepid, there's the option of a strenuous hike and scramble to the top of Heart Mountain.

From the parking lot, the trail initially parallels the highway as it crosses over a treed hump. Turn right at a junction (700 metres) to enter Heart Creek Valley, a defile between Mount McGillivray on the right and Heart Mountain on the left. Soon the gurgling waters and high walls swallow the highway's din.

Unlike the broad, glacially sculpted Bow Valley behind you, this is a narrow, V-shaped valley formed over thousands of years by Heart Creek. Although tiny today, the spring-fed creek was undoubtedly a torrent at the end of the last ice age, as melting waters hastened the process of carving a channel through the softer layers of sedimentary rock.

The tall cliffs shield the valley from the full brunt of the warm chinook winds that lash the Bow Valley in winter, often drying and damaging trees. As a result, Heart Creek has a cooler but more consistent climate that allows a diversity of plants to thrive. Mixed in with the usual low mountain aspen, pine, spruce, and occasional Douglas fir are paper birch and even some shrubby Douglas maple.

The rock walls lengthen into high cliffs halfway up the short valley. Large slabs of rock thrusting almost vertically upward along fault lines are clearly visible on the lower slopes of Heart Mountain, to the left. Look high on the right for small caves, scooped from the limestone walls by the forces of water, ice, and wind. On lower rocks, small spruce have anchored their roots in cracks formed by long cycles of freezing and thawing.

What the mountains give, they also take away. Several trees have been all but bowled over in one place, apparently by a slide from the slopes above.

The trail ends at an abrupt narrowing of the valley, where the creek spills in a small waterfall over a rock step. At low water, it's possible to edge around a tight, slippery corner to get a close look at the falls. In winter, climbers frequent this tongue of frozen water to practise their ice technique. From spring through early fall, you're likely to see sport climbers on many of the valley's lower walls, inching their way up the steep inclines.

High up on the ridge of Heart Mountain, with the Bow River Valley below.

## Heart Mountain Option

Accomplished hikers who don't mind a short piece of exposed scrambling can ascend the northwest ridge of Heart Mountain. It's named for the heart shape of its upper reaches, best seen from 1A Highway to the north. The distinctive formation is the result of a prominent downward fold, called a syncline, in the rock strata.

Be forewarned: the rocky ascent to the first summit is relentlessly steep, gaining nearly 900 metres of elevation in less than 3 kilometres. Sturdy hiking boots are recommended, especially for the descent. At one point, it's necessary to climb about 5 metres of rock on good holds to gain the upper ridge, to the left. Most other difficulties can be avoided by detouring left. If in doubt along the way, turn around and enjoy your lofty vantage point before descending.

The rewards of reaching the top are splendid views of the Bow Valley and peaks to the south. Those seeking further adventure can carry on to the true summit and descend on another northwest ridge to the east to make a complete circuit, returning to the parking lot via a wooded trail that parallels the Trans-Canada Highway. The rest of the trip is considerably easier than the ascent but adds a couple of hours to the outing.

## ◢ CANMORE

**Route:** From the Canada Olympic Park traffic lights, drive some 85 kilometres west on the Trans-Canada Highway. Take one of the four exits into Canmore.
**Driving Distance:** About 95 kilometres one way.

When Canmore's last coal mine closed in 1979, many residents worried about the long-term viability of this small mountain town. But after the 1988 Winter Olympics exposed Canmore's beauty to the world, the real estate and tourism markets exploded.

Today, Canmore is bursting at the seams, with a population of some 18,000 full- and part-time residents from around the world. With development and residency restrictions in nearby Banff, Canmore has become an attractive alternative, though the town's real estate prices are now among the highest in Alberta. Canmore has also become a magnet for a mix of artists, climbers, and young, transient workers, who join the few remaining former coal mine workers.

Having expanded its boundaries to Dead Man's Flats to the east, Canmore still has significant room for expansion of housing, hotels, and golf courses. Already, there are serious concerns that development in the narrow Bow Valley is gobbling up critical wildlife habitat and squeezing essential travel corridors for grizzly bears, wolves, and elk.

For visitors, Canmore offers many outdoor recreational opportunities, including nice cycling and walking paths and a variety of historical attractions from its coal-mining past. The vibrant downtown also offers lots of good restaurants, cafés, and drinking establishments, with a number of fine decks from which to soak in the summer mountain views.

## EATS & DRINKS

Canmore has more cafés and good restaurants per capita than any town or city in Alberta. The best coffee is found at **Communitea Café** (117, 1001–6th Avenue); also check out the infusion teas, seaweed salads, and rice bowls. The finest espresso is at **Mountain Mercato** (102, 817 Main Street). Other popular coffee hangouts include the **Rocky Mountain Bagel Company** (two locations: 830 Main Street and 1306 Bow Valley Trail), and **Beamer's Coffee Bar** (two locations: 737–7th Avenue and 1702 Bow Valley Trail; try the huge, healthy muffins). Good breakfasts range from the filling and informal at **Craig's Way Station** (1727 Mountain Avenue) and **Summit Café** (1001 Cougar Creek Drive) to the more upscale offerings of **Chez François** (1604–2nd Avenue).

Canmore is also unique for its wealth of takeout lunches. For a picnic or hike, pick up big, inexpensive sandwiches at **Bella Crusta** (702–6th Avenue) or **Valbella Gourmet Foods** (104 Elk Run Boulevard; featuring its famous smoked meats). For a sit-down lunch, try the fine soups and breads at **JK Bakery** (1514 Railway Avenue) or the excellent thin-crust pizzas from the wood-fired clay oven at **Rocky Mountain Flatbread Co.** (1, 838–10th Street).

On a hot summer's day, you can't beat burgers and beer at the **Drake Pub** (909 Railway Avenue) or the **Grizzly Paw Brewing Company** (622 Main Street; it brews its own beer). A growing list of top-end restaurants is led by **Crazyweed Kitchen** (1600 Railway Avenue), one of the best and most innovative eateries in Alberta. It's also worth visiting **Thai Pagoda** (1306 Bow Valley Trail), **La Belle Patate** (authentic poutine, 102 Boulder Crescent), and **3 Sisters Bistro** (104, 75 Dyrgas Gate); try its fabulous lemon pie.

### Canmore Historical Tour

**Route:** Take the second Canmore exit onto Highway 1A west, turning left at the traffic lights and left at the second set of lights onto 8th (Main) Street and into downtown Canmore. To reach the Canmore Nordic Centre, turn left at the west end of 8th Street and follow the signs for 4 kilometres.

**Note:** The Canmore Museum and Geoscience Centre (902B–7th Avenue) is open noon to 5:00 p.m. Mondays and Tuesdays and 11:00 a.m. to 5:00 p.m. the rest of the week from mid-May to early September, with slightly reduced hours the rest

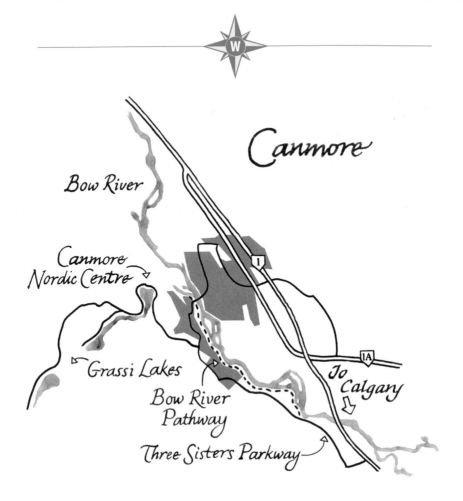

of the year. Admission charged. Phone 403-678-2462; www.cmags.org. • For information on summer and winter activities at the Canmore Nordic Centre, phone 403-678-2400.

In recent years, Canmore has become a modern boom town, attracting upscale tourism and residents seeking a mountain address. But the town was built on the booms and busts of a much sootier resource—coal. This trip is an excursion into that past, plus a brief introduction to Canmore's newer attractions.

Canmore, from a Gaelic word meaning "big head," originated in 1883 as a scattering of businesses that served the construction of the national railway as it moved west into the mountains. The new railway brought to Canmore a Canadian Pacific Railway divisional point and prospectors seeking coal to fuel the train engines.

In 1886, the Canmore Coal Company began tapping the rich coal seams beneath the mountains south of town. Soon, other coal mining communities—with names like Prospect, Georgetown, Mineside, Anthracite, and Bankhead—sprang up between Canmore and Banff. Most of these instant towns were short-lived, quickly becoming ghost towns.

To visit the grassy site of one of these former mining towns, drive up to the Canmore Nordic Centre, which sits on reclaimed coal-mining lands. The Nordic Centre was developed to host the cross-country skiing and biathlon events at the 1988 Winter Olympic Games and is now a provincial park. Today, the refurbished centre's maze of trails attracts competitive and recreational skiers in winter, and hikers and mountain bikers in summer. You can rent mountain bikes and cross-country skis at the site.

The Georgetown interpretive loop is a pleasant forest walk, reached by following the signs from behind the biathlon range (a summer trail brochure can be picked up at the day lodge). The trail descends through a mixed forest of pine, white spruce, and aspen, which is typical of the lower vegetation belt on mountains, known as montane forest. This bench above Canmore is sufficiently high and sheltered to retain much of the precipitation that falls on this dry east side of the mountains. Still, snow-making equipment is needed on some ski trails to make up for nature's shortcomings: a strong chinook wind can quickly melt any type of snow.

The trail leads to a clearing once occupied by Georgetown, a vibrant coal-mining community of Italians, Poles, and Germans. Although it contained fewer than 200 residents, Georgetown boasted cottages with electricity and running water, a company store, and a community hall where a local orchestra frequently played.

Yet Georgetown survived only from 1912 to 1915, falling victim to slumping coal prices and a lack of financing at the outbreak of World War I. When the mine closed, many of the buildings were skidded on logs down to Canmore, where some are still in use. Today, all that remains of Georgetown are the footings of these vanished buildings in a grassy clearing.

The road back into town passes Mineside, now a neighbourhood of west Canmore that contains the houses of many former miners. Above the Bow River nearby are several stately houses, dating back to the 1890s, that were built for mine officials. Mining continued above Mineside until 1979, when the last of Canmore's coal mines closed.

While residential and commercial development is now rampant throughout an expanding Canmore, there are still vivid examples of its early days. Heading back east along 8th Street (Main Street), visitors can stop in at the Canmore Hotel, built in 1890. Across from the hotel is the Canmore Museum and Geoscience Centre, which features historic mining memorabilia and hosts special exhibits throughout the year.

Farther east is the Ralph Connor Memorial United Church, in operation since it was built in 1890. Its first minister, Charles Gordon, was responsible for a district that encompassed towns, railway stations, and mining and lumber camps reaching to Field, B.C. Gordon later received international acclaim under his pen name, Ralph Connor, for novels such as *Black Rock* and *Sky Pilot*.

Nearby, on the banks of Policeman's Creek, is the town's original North West Mounted Police barracks. This mud-chinked log structure was erected in 1892 in response to complaints about an increasingly rowdy group of single men employed by the railway and mines, who constituted the bulk of the town's 500 citizens. Vacated by the police force in 1929, the barracks became a private residence for 40 years. It's now a provincial historic site operated by the Canmore Museum. Phone 403-678-1955 for visiting hours.

Just east of the barracks, you can finish the tour by taking a short stroll on the boardwalk that passes through marshy grasses near Policeman's Creek. The creek, controlled by an upstream sluice gate, is one of the braided channels of the Bow River meandering through central Canmore. The town's streams and backwaters, some fed by springs, provide important spawning habitat for trout and winter refuge for hundreds of mallard ducks.

### Bow River Pathway

**Route:** From downtown Canmore, drive west to the end of 8th (Main) Street. At the four-way stop, turn south on 8th Avenue, which bends into Rundle Drive. Cross the Bow River Bridge and park in the small lot on the left.
**Trail Distance:** The described route is about 12 kilometres return, though longer and shorter versions are options.

The cycling and walking trails along the Bow River in Canmore are arguably the most scenic urban pathways in Alberta. Visitors can cruise along spacious asphalt or hard-packed tracks beside the broad, braided Bow and past million-dollar homes—with a gorgeous backdrop of peaks including The Three Sisters to the south, Ha Ling and Rundle to the west, and Cascade to the more distant northwest.

The Canmore area has more than 200 kilometres of trails, offering a wide range of difficulty for hikers, joggers, equestrians, and, particularly, mountain bikers. This extensive trail network, combined with the explosive growth of Canmore's population and tourist industry, has resulted in the serious shrinking of habitat and travel corridors for bears, cougars, elk, and wolves in the relatively narrow Bow Valley. To protect this critical habitat, human use in the Benchlands area (on the northeast side of the Trans-Canada Highway) is largely restricted to designated trails, most of which are now in Bow Valley Wildland Provincial Park.

The well-used riverside trails through the more heavily developed centre of Canmore have, at least until now, posed fewer serious human-wildlife conflicts. The gently undulating paths are generally wide and very popular with everyone from families pushing strollers to ambling seniors.

There are trails of varying quality on both sides of the Bow River, including one extending a considerable way northwest below the Canmore Nordic Centre and eventually reaching Banff via a rough

Jogger passes Chinook sculpture on Bow River Pathway in Canmore.

track. The route described here starts at the west side of the Bow River vehicle bridge and follows the southeast shore below the lower Three Sisters development properties.

Near the bridge-side parking lot is a Trans Canada Trail kiosk recognizing those who have contributed to this mammoth dream of establishing a nationwide network of hiking, cycling, and winter recreational trails. While a few eastern provinces now have trails crossing their lands, Alberta has so far produced a disappointing patchwork. This is largely the result of spirited resistance from some rural landowners and municipalities, who don't want a recreational trail passing near their properties, even on abandoned rail lines.

Beyond the kiosk, the trail bisects a patch of fragrant wolf willow and then swings around tiny Canmore Creek, which is nonetheless an important spawning area for brook, brown, and native cutthroat trout. Native plants such as Indian paintbrush and cow parsnip line the path, as do plantings of trees and flowers and long stretches of yellow roadside weeds. Walkers and cyclists also pass by lovely gardens fronting stately homes.

At about 2 kilometres, the path passes below a couple of old and now closed mine shaft entrances, graced by old coal-hauling carts/wagons. These relics, along with visible coal seams, are the only reminders that for nearly a century coal was the bedrock of this community, until the last mine closed in 1979. Much of these old, coal-bearing lands have been transformed into much more lucrative housing developments and golf courses, which will eventually extend east to near Dead Man's Flats.

A little farther on, a lovely side trail goes left across a small bridge and passes through cool, mature forest along a quiet back channel of the Bow River. It soon climbs back to the main, paved path near a crossing of Three Sisters Parkway. The trail on the far side continues southeast for another couple of kilometres to a parking lot just past the Trans-Canada Highway access road closest to Dead Man's Flats.

For those seeking further adventure, it's also possible to continue east on a rougher track to the road below the Dead Man's Flats quarry. Beyond, the Bow Link, part of the Trans Canada Trail, carries on east for about 8 kilometres to the Heart Creek parking lot. This is a much rockier trail with numerous short, steep hills that might appeal to intermediate mountain bikers or hikers.

Most people will be content to return leisurely the way they came, unless they have left a second vehicle at the Heart Creek parking lot. Back at the initial trailhead parking lot, it's worth going a short distance farther northeast past the Rundle power plant (capable of producing electricity for a town of 35,000 people), crossing the old railway bridge, and then looping back along the other side of the river.

## Grassi Lakes

**Route:** From the west end of 8th (Main Street) in downtown Canmore, go south and follow the Canmore Nordic Centre signs for 4 kilometres. Continue past the centre's turnoff for another kilometre on Spray Lakes Road, turning left on a short access road to reach Grassi Lakes parking lot and trailhead.

**Trail Distance:** The hike is 2 kilometres one way, with a 250-metre elevation gain. Allow two hours or more return.

Grassi Lakes is one of the better short hikes in the Canadian Rockies and a fine family outing. It offers expansive views of the Bow Valley and, at trail's end, two exquisite ponds backed by a high rock wall. Long a spiritual place for Aboriginal peoples, Grassi Lakes is today a tranquil retreat less than an hour from the bustle of Canmore.

Once called Twin Lakes, these blue-green ponds were renamed in honour of Lawrence Grassi, an Italian woodcutter who came to Canmore in 1916 to work in the coal mines. Here, he and fellow miners took advantage of a strike in the 1920s to build the stone steps, bridges, and strategically placed benches on this well-graded trail. Many of these features have subsequently been replaced. An accomplished climber, Grassi was also renowned for the meticulous and sensitive trails he built around Lake O'Hara in Yoho National Park.

From the parking lot, the trail leads up through a mature forest of pine broken by aspen and underlain by low shrubs, early-season violets, Indian paintbrush, and wild strawberries. Higher, a scattering of moisture-loving birch foreshadows the emergence of a series of tiny streams seeping across the trail. Farther along, water and vegetation continue a fascinating interplay, evident in mosses growing from dripping rocks and algae waving from their underwater anchors.

The trail swings onto a hillside clearing that overlooks the reservoir and town of Canmore, providing views across the valley to the peaks of the Fairholme Range. Though the Bow Valley here is but 2 kilometres wide, it has been crammed over the years with human developments. Visible are two highways, a railway, coal-mining scars, and, most recently, housing and tourism complexes spreading up both sides of the valley.

Close at hand is a shiny steel penstock, which funnels dammed water from the hanging valley above to the reservoir below. It's part of the Spray Hydro System, in operation since 1951 and capable of meeting the electrical needs of 100,000 people. Aesthetically more pleasing is a large waterfall splashing down the rock face. In winter, it freezes into a swath of ice that attracts many climbers.

The blue-green waters of Grassi Lakes.

The trail climbs more steeply up rock steps, complete with a hand-rail, and then levels out as it crosses a rushing stream emptying out of the first lake. The blue-green waters here contrast with a deeper blue in the upper lake.

Despite the visual presence of nearby power lines and penstocks, this place still conveys the magical sense that it must have held for Aboriginal peoples who used this valley for 11,000 years. They carved their stories in the rocks and sought shelter in caves above the upper lake. The honeycombed cliffs are the 400-million-year-old remnants of a reef that developed in a shallow sea. Today, they're a popular attraction for sport climbers, who have built a short access trail from the small reservoir pond above the cliffs.

In the mid-1800s, the passage above these cliffs between Ha Ling Peak and Mount Rundle became a favoured access route for crossing the mountains into present-day British Columbia. One of the most remarkable treks through what was named Whiteman's Gap was undertaken by James Sinclair, who led 200 Metis settlers from Manitoba through the mountains to Oregon in 1841.

Return to the parking lot via an old fire road, which passes the remnants of a log cabin in the woods along the way.

#  BANFF

**Route:** See below.

There's more to the town of Banff and its environs than the Banff Springs Hotel and a strip of high-end shopping malls. A block or two removed from Banff Avenue, the din of cars and cash registers is replaced by the quiet and beauty of a small mountain town, albeit with a population of 8,500 people, some 7,500 of whom are permanent residents.

From the centre of Banff, those on foot can embark on lovely walks along the Bow River or amble around the spring-fed marshes below the historic Cave and Basin. Motorists can tour along Tunnel Mountain Drive or head to Lake Minnewanka, both of which offer ample viewpoints and opportunities for short walks. The three trips described below are just a sampling of Banff's natural and historic delights, which may surprise even frequent and/or jaded visitors to Alberta's most famous town.

## En Route to Banff

**Route:** From the traffic lights at Canada Olympic Park, drive 110 kilometres west on the Trans-Canada Highway to the eastern entrance to Banff.

Think of the Trans-Canada Highway west of Calgary not as four lanes of high-speed freeway between points A and B but as a means of being transported through a fascinating corridor of natural and human history. On aesthetic grounds alone, this is one of the finest entrances to a mountain range imaginable. Even frequent visitors to the mountains can admire vistas that change with the seasons, the weather, and subtle variations in lighting.

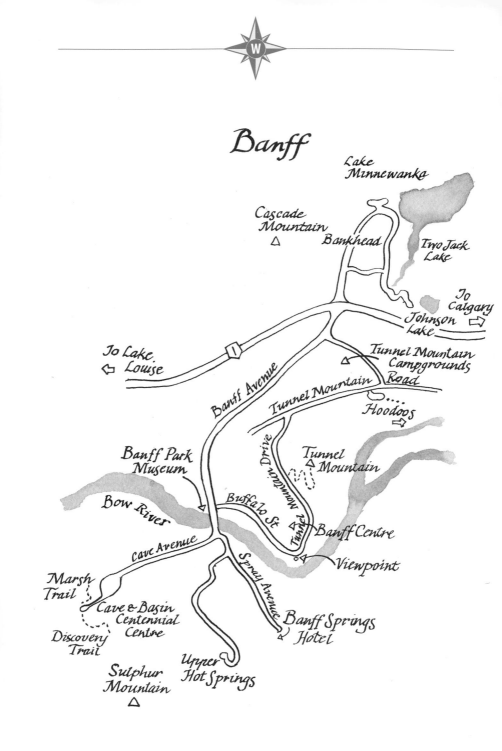

# Banff

Lake Minnewanka

Cascade Mountain △

Bankhead

Two Jack Lake

To Calgary

Johnson Lake

To Lake Louise

Banff Avenue

Tunnel Mountain Campgrounds Road

Tunnel Mountain

Hoodoos

Mountain Drive

Tunnel Mountain △

Banff Park Museum

Bow River

Buffalo St

Tunnel

Banff Centre

Cave Avenue

Spray Avenue

Viewpoint

Marsh Trail

Cave & Basin Centennial Centre

Discovery Trail

Upper Hot Springs

Banff Springs Hotel

Sulphur Mountain △

## EATS & DRINKS

It's easy to gorge oneself in 🔥 Banff. For coffee, tea, and snacks, try **Evelyn's Coffee Bar** (three locations: 119 and 201 Banff Avenue and 229 Bear Street), **Jump Start Coffee & Sandwich Place** (206 Buffalo Street), and **Banff Tea Company** (208 Caribou Street). Excellent breakfasts and lunches are available at **Coyotes Southwestern Grill** (206 Caribou Street), **Wild Flour Bakery** (211 Bear Street; try the sourdough breakfast sandwich), and **Sleeping Buffalo Restaurant & Lounge** at Buffalo Mountain Lodge (107 Tunnel Mountain Drive). Sample the pizza at the **Bear Street Tavern** (211 Bear Street) or have a drink and an appetizer at the fabulously restored **Juniper Hotel & Bistro** (base of Mount Norquay Road), with expansive patio views across the Bow Valley. **Barpa Bill's Souvlaki** (223 Bear Street) has good, inexpensive Greek takeout and excellent fries, while **Balkan the Greek Restaurant** (120 Banff Avenue) offers casual family fare. Pub food and drink is well represented by **Banff Avenue Brewing Co.** (110 Banff Avenue) and **St. James's Gate Olde Irish Pub** (207 Wolf Street). At the Banff Centre, the **Vistas Dining Room** offers excellent buffet-style meals alongside superb mountain views.

This route between Calgary and Banff was accidentally forged by a group of Irish-American gold seekers in 1864–65. Leaving the Banff area for the North Saskatchewan River to the north, they got lost and ended up following the Bow River to present-day Calgary.

For many years, the road west of Calgary followed the 1A Highway, now a quiet backwater on the north side of the Bow River (see the 1A Highway Tour on pages 221–26 for a complete description). Today's Trans-Canada Highway was built on the river's south side in the late 1950s and upgraded to a four-lane freeway a decade later.

The initial stretch of highway bisects rolling farmlands, where herds of cattle can often be spotted. The strong chinook winds that sweep the Bow Valley keep these fields clear of snow most of the winter, allowing cattle, deer, and even some non-migrating ducks to feed.

About 15 kilometres west of Canada Olympic Park, the highway climbs to a hilltop offering a panoramic view over plains, forested foothills, and the Rocky Mountains. Among the more prominent Front Range peaks are Mount Glasgow and Banded Peak to the southwest, which often retain their snow cover well into the summer.

The road soon dips to cross Jumpingpound Creek. Along the creek to the north is a cliff, over which Aboriginal people used to drive buffalo to their death, hence the name. The leisurely curious can take a pleasant detour here by following a gravel road north and west through the countryside, rejoining the Trans-Canada at the Sibbald Creek Trail exit.

Not far beyond, the road crosses the first of several low, parallel ridges that mark the start of the foothills. Resistant sandstones generally underlie the ridges, while the dips in between are of softer shale. Where the sandstone is exposed, the ridges are called hogbacks. The underlying bedrock in these foothills is a complex structure of thrust faults and folds, created by the same great forces that forged the mountains to the west.

In depressions along the highway are small, reedy sloughs, which provide important habitat for nesting and migratory birds. A pothole slough beside the Sibbald Creek Trail exit is often the best place in the Calgary area to see migrating trumpeter swans in the spring.

The road climbs to its highest point at Scott Lake Hill, where the elevation and sheltered slopes allow thick coniferous forests to grow. The views on the descent are superb, as the bending road unveils a continuously expanding sweep of peaks.

The ensuing stretch of the Morley Flats is largely barren and windswept. Its underground formations nonetheless contain large quantities of natural gas, enriching the coffers of the Stoney, whose reserve is situated here. The flats east of the Morley interchange feature impressive examples of drumlins. These are tapered hills of till, or gravel, shaped by glaciers that flowed eastward over them, leaving the blunt nose facing upstream and the pointed tail downstream.

Walking along the Bow River Pathway in Banff.

During the last ice age, glaciers advancing east from the Lake Louise area carved the U-shaped valley that's clearly visible along the Bow Corridor. An arm of this glacier blocked the Kananaskis Valley, creating a glacial lake fed by meltwaters from mountain glaciers to the south. The lake drained when the glaciers disappeared some 10,000 years ago, leaving behind this flat valley bottom. The glaciers also deposited in the Bow Valley large quantities of unsorted till. The sand and gravel deposits near Bow Valley Provincial Park, for example, are more than 80 metres deep.

To the north of the park is the impressive face of Yamnuska (officially known as Mount John Laurie), a popular rock-climbing spot. The McConnell Thrust at the base of Yamnuska's face marks the geological boundary between foothills and the Front Ranges of the Rockies. The abrupt change in elevation here is due largely to the limestone mountain faces, which are much more resistant to erosion than the softer shales and sandstones of the foothills.

The highway soon takes a sweeping bend around Lac Des Arcs, a shallow lake fed by the Bow River and often buffeted by strong winds. In spring and fall, a diversity of ducks, geese, and swans stop here during their migration and can be observed from a new lakeshore interpretive trail, as can nesting great blue herons.

William Van Horne, the president of the Canadian Pacific Railway, wanted to build a resort along Lac Des Arcs after passing through the area in the late 19th century. Those plans were quickly scuttled when a subsequent visit revealed a much lower, muddier lake.

The area has, however, long attracted development, as the cement plant across the lake indicates. Indeed, limestone rock from Exshaw Mountain has been feeding plants here since 1906. At the nearby Grotto Mountain, which harbours an extensive network of caves, lime was first commercially extracted in 1884 by a man named McCan-leish. After he mysteriously disappeared on a trip to Calgary, an employee, Edwin Loder, assumed the operation.

A more vivid incident is commemorated at Dead Man's Flats. Here, in 1904, a French immigrant farmer, Jean Marret, was killed by his axe-wielding brother, François, who had complained of strange noises in his head. Found guilty and insane, François was dispatched to an asylum in Ponoka, south of Edmonton.

The boundaries of Canmore now stretch east to Dead Man's Flats and encompass a steadily increasing amount of tourism and housing development in the narrow valley. For the first three decades of the 20th century, this area was located within Rocky Mountains National Park. The boundaries of the park, renamed Banff National Park, were retracted westward in 1930 to allow for industrial development in the Canmore area.

Beyond Canmore, motorists are accompanied into Banff by the long flank of Mount Rundle. It's actually a massif, or a series of individual peaks. The northeast face displays high cliffs of limestone and dolomite at the base and summit and scree slopes of shale in

Overlooking Vermilion Lakes and Mount Rundle (rear) from west of Banff.

between. The mountain is named after Robert Rundle, a Methodist missionary who travelled among the area's native tribes in the early 1840s. Straight ahead is the impressively folded Cascade Mountain, named for the waterfall that splits its face and attracts winter ice climbers.

A road from Calgary reached the Banff park gates in 1906, but automobiles were officially banned from the park until 1915. Once the gates opened, there was no turning back. Today, several million people pass through the gates by car every year. Just before Banff townsite, the road passes the Cascade Power Plant, its hydroelectric generator fed by waters from Lake Minnewanka. Across the highway from the power plant is the grassy site of Anthracite, a coal-mining town that existed from 1886 to 1904.

### Banff Historical Tour

**Route:** From the south side of the Bow River Bridge in Banff, drive 1.3 kilometres west to the Cave and Basin parking lot. The Banff Park Museum is located on the north side of the bridge.
**Note:** The Cave and Basin National Historic Site is open daily 9:00 a.m. to 6:00 p.m. from mid-May through September, with site tours three times a day. Hours are reduced in winter. Admission charged. Phone 403-762-1566. • Banff Park Museum National Historic Site is open daily 10:00 a.m. to 6:00 p.m. from mid-May through September (daily tours at 3:00 p.m.), with reduced winter hours. Admission charged. Phone 403-762-1558.

### Cave and Basin National Historic Site

The cradle of Canada's national park system is a steamy hole in the ground with an acrid stench. In 1883, William McCardell shimmied through the hole and down a crude ladder into a cavern filled with hot sulphurous waters. McCardell and his two companions, railway surveyors in search of gold, laid claim to these hot pools. But it was a federal government eager to promote tourism that in 1885 set aside 26 square kilometres of land, later expanded to become Canada's first national park.

Log bathhouses were soon erected, attracting tourists and those seeking cures for everything from syphilis to gunshot wounds. For a time, the mineral waters were bottled and sold as an aid to digestion, the liver, and the kidneys. By the 1920s, the Cave and Basin was a comfortable spa with a swimming pool.

Today, tired tourists revive themselves not at these bathhouses but in the nearby Upper Sulphur Hot Springs, where the water temperature often reaches 40°C. The rest of the Cave and Basin National Historic Site has been restored to appear much as it did a century ago. Visitors can still follow the low entranceway to the dimly lit cave the surveyors discovered, dip a finger into the slightly warmer waters of the old basin, and watch a video in the Bathhouse Theatre.

Cave and Basin National Historic Site.

There's also much to see outside the buildings. The 400-metre Discovery Trail follows the trickling streams of warm water up the hill to where they emerge from the mountainside. These hot springs begin as rainwater and melting snow that filter more than 2 kilometres down through the ground on the other side of the mountain. Warmed by heat radiating from the earth's molten interior, the now mineralized and pressurized water flows back to the surface along the Sulphur Mountain fault line.

The emerging hot springs deposit calcium carbonate, dissolved from the limestone bedrock during the water's underground migration. These deposits form soft, porous rock known as tufa, which over thousands of years has accumulated here to a depth of 7 metres.

The hot mineral waters, with their distinctive odour, flow down the hillside, feeding the Cave and Basin and the Vermilion wetlands below. You can visit this unique habitat by following the looping 500-metre Marsh Trail on a boardwalk below the Cave and Basin. The constant supply of warm water allows watercress to grow year-round and inspires robins, killdeer, and mallard ducks to forgo their usual migrations. From spring through fall, a large variety of other water birds can be spotted on the marsh from a wooden blind.

This warm wetland was also the home of the Banff longnose dace, a minnow unique to the area. Unfortunately, the introduction of competing tropical fish in the 1960s may well have precipitated the dace's demise. It was declared extinct in 1991.

### Banff Park Museum National Historic Site

Western Canada's oldest natural history museum is well worth visiting for its unusual architecture and impressive wildlife collection. It also serves as a reminder of how park values have changed over the decades.

The Banff Park Museum was built in 1903, replacing a smaller museum erected across the river in 1895. The building—the oldest park facility in the national park system—represents a so-called railroad pagoda style of architecture, featuring cross-log construction, a lantern skylight, and interior panelling of Douglas fir.

The museum was originally intended to attract wealthy tourists and introduce them to wild creatures that were safely dead and stuffed. Students of natural history were also attracted to this "University of the Hills."

The museum's earliest specimen is an 1860 merganser duck. Most of the other wildlife was collected early last century from various parts of the world, including the park. Though the hunting of game animals such as elk and bighorn sheep was banned within the park in 1890, a predator control program continued for some decades, claiming the lives of wolves, coyotes, eagles, and owls, some of which ended up in the museum. Other specimens were once residents of a zoo and aviary that operated on the museum grounds from 1904 to 1937 and contained such exotic species as a polar bear and turkey vulture.

Times have changed, and the emphasis is now on viewing animals and birds in their natural surroundings. The collection, however, has more recently benefited from the considerable roadkill on the park's highways.

Perhaps the recently renovated museum's most compelling exhibit is a huge grizzly skin. It comes from a garbage-addicted bear that in 1980 killed one person and mauled three others on the town's doorstep before being snared and shot. The bullet hole is clearly visible between the bear's eyes.

## Tunnel Mountain Drive

**Route:** From the intersection of Buffalo Street and Banff Avenue (just north of the Bow River Bridge) in Banff, follow Buffalo Street east as it angles right to become Tunnel Mountain Drive. At 4 kilometres, turn right on Tunnel Mountain Road, which passes the Hoodoos en route to its junction with Banff Avenue at Rocky Mountain Resort.
**Driving Distance:** 10 kilometres one way.

Tunnel Mountain Drive is perhaps the finest short drive near Banff townsite. It climbs along the side of Tunnel Mountain, passing numerous pull-offs that offer superb views up and down the Bow Valley. Along the way are an optional hike to Tunnel's summit and a short walk overlooking the Hoodoos.

The construction of Tunnel Mountain Drive began in the late 1880s as a continuation of Buffalo Street. Trees were cleared and rock was dynamited to create a roadway for horse-drawn tallyhos up the hillside above the Bow River. One tightly winding section had to be removed following the official introduction of cars to the park in the mid-1910s.

The road initially climbs to a viewpoint overlooking Bow Falls and the Banff Springs Hotel. The falls have cut into the intersection of two geological formations. The rocks along the Bow River's north banks are some 75 million years older than the Sulphur Mountain siltstones on the south. Smooth-plated siltstones from this formation were used in the construction of the Banff Springs Hotel and the nearby park administration building.

Mount Rundle, from Hoodoos Trail.

From a parking lot at 1.2 kilometres, a 4.8-kilometre trail descends to follow the Bow River to the hoodoos. You can reach the river, where the Spray River enters, more directly on a steep, slippery trail from the same parking lot, if you like adventure. Looking across the swiftly flowing Bow, you can see the golf course fairways, a favoured dining spot for elk. Nearby, on this side of the river, is a magnificent stand of ancient Douglas fir, their massive, furrowed trunks decorated with mosses.

Back on the road, you soon pass the Banff Centre campus. Its roots go back to 1933 when my great-uncle, E. A. Corbett, started a summer theatre school here. Under the guidance of his successor, Donald Cameron, it became the world-renowned Banff School of Fine Arts. Today the Banff Centre also boasts a school of management, a summer-long arts festival, an international television festival, and a mountain film festival.

At 2.5 kilometres, the road crosses the Tunnel Mountain Trail. From this junction, it's a 1.5-kilometre hike up through lodgepole pine and Douglas fir to the summit, once topped by a fire lookout. Though the climb is steady, the view east down the Bow Valley and over the Fairholme Range is ample reward.

Mount Rundle, to the southeast, was attached to Tunnel Mountain until glaciers cut a notch, subsequently deepened by the Bow River into a valley, between the two. The Bow is thought to have previously detoured around the north side of Tunnel Mountain, following the Cascade River and Minnewanka Lake valleys before rejoining the current channel on the plains. Some 10,000 years ago, receding glaciers deposited moraines that blocked that channel and created a lake to the west. The lake's accumulating meltwaters eventually spilled through the notch between Rundle and Tunnel to form the new channel.

Tunnel Mountain seems a misnomer on two counts. A planned tunnel through the mountain was scrapped in 1883 when the Canadian Pacific Railway line was detoured north. But the name stuck. At a mere 1,690 metres, Tunnel also scarcely qualifies as a real mountain in the Canadian Rockies, though the tall cliffs on the south and east faces are certainly impressive and attract climbers.

Farther along Tunnel Mountain Drive are pull-offs with less lofty but still inspiring views west along the Bow Valley and north to Cascade Mountain and the ski slopes of Mount Norquay. At a cluster of condominiums, the road turns right and follows a dry, open terrace dotted with trees. It's a typical montane forest environment, attracting grazing elk and mule deer.

For 2 kilometres, the road passes the Tunnel Mountain Campground, the largest such facility in the mountain national parks, with more than 1,150 sites. When the campground was first moved here from the golf course area in the 1930s, some citizens complained it was too far removed from the town's businesses. Townsfolk are no doubt glad of its distance today, given its size and reputation for late-night revelry.

The road soon reaches the Hoodoos. A 500-metre asphalt trail (wheelchair accessible) follows the northeast bank of the Bow River and leads to viewpoints overlooking the hoodoos. Hoodoo is a variation of the word *voodoo*, reflecting the often fantastic shapes they assume. Interpretive signs explain how running water has washed away the hard slopes of glacially deposited till, leaving behind these isolated pillars. But their once-protective caps have disappeared, exposing them, too, to the relentless forces of erosion.

### Lake Minnewanka Loop

**Route:** From the Trans-Canada Highway interchange at the east entrance to Banff townsite, drive north past Bankhead to Lake Minnewanka. From the lake, continue the loop to Two Jack Lake and back to the highway.
**Driving Distance:** 16 kilometres return.

Lake Minnewanka, the largest lake in Banff National Park, is one of the area's most popular destinations. Its charms can be discovered in an hour or so, a trip extended by visiting an abandoned coal-mining community, walking up a narrow canyon, or having a picnic. The lake can also be toured by boat and its depths plumbed by hook for lake trout.

From the Trans-Canada Highway, the road passes beneath the impressive folds of Cascade Mountain, named for the waterfall that splits its face. The coal seams at the mountain's base were first mined at the beginning of the century to help power the Canadian Pacific Railway's engines. The resulting mining town of Bankhead prospered, supporting a population of 1,000 at its peak. But by 1922, the mine had closed, the victim of difficult mining conditions, poor markets, and labour unrest.

Many of Bankhead's buildings were demolished or moved to Banff or Canmore. But the mining site can still be toured on a short interpretive trail leading down from the Lower Bankhead parking lot. Just up the road, the Upper Bankhead parking lot provides access to further remains of concrete foundations.

Beyond Bankhead, the road soon leads to Lake Minnewanka. The Minnewanka Valley likely once cradled a stretch of the Bow River as it surged out of the mountains. The channel was abandoned some 10,000 years ago, when an overflowing glacial lake to the west carved a new course between Mount Rundle and Tunnel Mountain.

The valley has also long been a major transportation corridor. The Stoney first used it as an entry to the mountains, a route followed in the mid-1800s by explorers, missionaries, and even settlers bound for Oregon. In the late 1880s, a road built from Banff to Lake Minnewanka ushered in an era of tourism that remains unabated.

Early on, the small resort community of Minnewanka Landing was built along the near shore, and tour boat operations were launched. A hydroelectric dam built at the lake's outlet in 1912 and expanded in 1941, however, raised the water levels by nearly 25 metres and extended the lake's length by 8 kilometres. The resort was abandoned, its foundations today visited only by fish and scuba divers.

But tourism is resilient. Visitors still flock here to walk the shores or take a boat cruise to Devil's Gap at the east end of the lake. Anglers in small boats troll for sizable lake trout, though the catches are considerably fewer than a century ago.

North of the parking lot is a concession, and a picnic area frequented by bighorn sheep. Just beyond, a trail along Lake Minnewanka's northwest shore leads through pine and fir forest to soon cross Stewart Canyon on a large wooden-truss bridge. A short side trail leads up this impressive limestone gorge, where the Cascade River enters the lake.

In 1841, George Simpson, governor of the Hudson's Bay Company, called it Peechee Lake after his native guide who lived along the shore. A more enduring name was Devil's Lake, used by both native inhabitants and early white visitors. In 1916, it was renamed Minnewanka, meaning "lake of the water spirit."

From the Lake Minnewanka parking lot, the road continues across an earth-filled dam to a viewpoint overlooking the lake before dropping past Two Jack Lake. At a junction, a spur road leads left to

Johnson Lake, crossing en route a canal carrying water from Lake Minnewanka down to the Cascade power plant on the Trans-Canada Highway. Johnson Lake, ringed by a trail, is a tranquil spot for a picnic and birdwatching. Return to the junction and turn left to regain the Lake Minnewanka Road, which leads back to Banff.

## LAKE LOUISE

**Route:** From the Canada Olympic Park traffic lights, drive 170 kilometres west on the Trans-Canada Highway to the Lake Louise exit. Lake Louise is reached by a 4-kilometre paved road, which also provides access, via a 12-kilometre spur road, to Moraine Lake.
**Driving Distance:** About 190 kilometres one way.

Lake Louise probably boasts more tourists per scenic square metre than any place in the Canadian Rockies. Yet the splendour of this mountain setting remains largely undiminished. It's even possible, with a little effort, to escape the hordes that troop to this alpine mecca.

This trip visits the two "must-do" highlights, Lake Louise and Moraine Lake, and offers a couple of short walks to complete a most pleasant day. If you want to see the sights in relative quiet, it's best either to get under way very early or arrive in the late afternoon. Incidentally, the hamlet of Lake Louise, at 1,539 metres, is the highest permanent settlement in Canada.

The Stoney called Lake Louise the "Lake of Little Fishes." It was briefly named Emerald Lake by its first white visitor, Canadian Pacific Railway surveyor Tom Wilson, led here by Stoney guide Edwin Hunter in 1882.

Keen to attract rail-travelling tourists to the mountains, the Canadian Pacific Railway erected the Lake Louise Chalet at this exquisite location in 1890. When this small structure burned down three years later, it was quickly replaced by a second chalet. Several wings were added over the next 20 years to accommodate a steady increase in summer visitors, who were now arriving by road in horse-drawn

Looking towards Lake Louise from below Mount Victoria.

carriages and, later, by a tramline ascending from the Laggan train station. A second fire destroyed much of the building in 1924, but a new wing was built within a year. Subsequent additions and renovations have made Chateau Lake Louise into a major mountain hotel and convention centre.

Beyond the lake's far shore shines Mount Victoria. Its long snowy ridge is a classic alpine climb, usually tackled from a high stone hut named after Philip Abbott, the first climber killed in the Rockies. His death on nearby Mount Lefroy in 1896 prompted the CPR to import Swiss guides to safely lead wealthy foreign climbers up the area's peaks.

To escape the throngs that gather along the lake's shores, take the 1-kilometre hike from behind the boathouse to Fairview Lookout. Soon you'll be enveloped in the silence of a mossy forest of spruce and fir. The steepness of the slope and its northern aspect shield the forest from sun and wind and thus allow it to retain moisture. As you ascend this Cadillac trail, consider the plight of early explorers bushwhacking over the deadfall and hummocky ground.

Moraine Lake and the Valley of Ten Peaks. (Susanne Swibold photograph)

A signed trail to the right rises to a small lookout high above Lake Louise and the chateau. Far below, tiny tourists trek along the lake-shore, many bound for an alpine tea house. The lake's colour turns in spring from a bluish hue to milky green. The milky colour is the result of rock flour—rocks ground by glaciers into a fine dust—deposited by meltwater in the lake, where it reflects every colour but the emerald you see. The small glacier at the head of nearby Moraine Lake isn't actively feeding the lake, so it retains a more consistent blue throughout the year.

If time and energy permit, it's well worth hiking 3 kilometres steadily up the main trail to the Saddleback, which is ringed with larch and offers a fine view of the North Face of Mount Temple. A further strenuous 45 minutes to an hour up the scree switchbacks leads to the summit of Mount Fairview, the effort rewarded by a superb panorama of peaks, principally of Mount Victoria.

Back at the parking lot, it's a short drive to Moraine Lake. The lake's blue waters reflect a wall of glaciated peaks that constitute one end of the Valley of Ten Peaks. In 1894, American climber Samuel Allen named these peaks after Stoney numerals 1 to 10. Today, only the ninth and tenth peaks, Neptuak and Wenkchemna, retain those Stoney names. If you look closely at the cliffs across the lake, you can make out the horizontal layers of limestone on top of shale on top of sandstone.

The near end of the lake is dammed by a jumble of boulders, deposited either by a rock slide or an ancient glacier. A short interpretive trail leads to the top of this rock pile, from which point the picture that graces Canada's old 20-dollar bill was taken. Along the way, you can learn about ripple marks and trilobite tracks in rocks that trace their origins to sands and muds transported from as far away as Manitoba and deposited in a 500-million-year-old inland sea.

Moraine Lake is thronged with tourists throughout the summer. In late September, scores of hikers make the 3-kilometre pilgrimage up to Larch Valley to see the deciduous subalpine larch needles that have turned to orange. A fine, shorter, and much more level hike is to Consolation Lakes.

Be forewarned that the area's trails, because of bear activity, often carry a restriction that hikers must travel in tight groups of four or more (smaller groups can often hook up with others at the trailhead). Check at the Parks Canada Visitor Centre at the entrance to the shopping mall in the hamlet of Lake Louise for any such restrictions.

On the way back to Calgary, a much quieter alternative to the busy Trans-Canada Highway is the parallel Bow Valley Parkway (Highway 1A), which runs from Lake Louise to just before Banff. (Note: Travellers are asked to avoid this route between 6:00 p.m. and 9:00 a.m. from March 1 to June 25 to help protect wildlife.) En route, Highway 1A passes Johnston Canyon, justly famous for its dramatic paved walk (2.7 kilometres one way) along a canyon wall and past two waterfalls.

# BURGESS SHALE HIKE

**Route:** From the Canada Olympic Park traffic lights, drive 193 kilometres west on the Trans-Canada Highway to the Yoho Valley Road and follow it 15 kilometres north to the Takakkaw Falls parking lot.

**Driving Distance:** 208 kilometres one way.

**Note:** The Burgess Shale and Mount Stephen fossil beds are closed to visitors except those on a Yoho-Burgess Shale Foundation guided hike, offered from early July to mid-September. The 10-hour Burgess Shale guided hike, offered Friday to Monday, is 20 kilometres return and gains 750 metres in elevation ($120 for adults, $65 for students, and $25 for children under 12). The 8-hour Mount Stephen hike, Saturday and Sunday, is 6 kilometres return and has a 780-metre elevation gain ($90 for adults, $65 for students, and $25 for children under 12). Participants should be reasonably fit. Phone 1-800-343-3006 for reservations and information or check www.burgess-shale.bc.ca.

The Burgess Shale, a UNESCO World Heritage Site, is arguably the most important fossil discovery in the world. It exquisitely preserves an abundance and diversity of 500-million-year-old marine organisms and provides unique insight into how animal life appeared on earth.

The only way to legally see these fossils up close is on a guided hike, either a full day trip to the Burgess Shale high on Mount Field (the trip described here) or a shorter excursion to the nearby trilobite beds on Mount Stephen, above the town of Field, B.C. It's a terrific opportunity to learn in detail about this fossil record from a paleontologist or geologist, perhaps spot researchers at work, and enjoy the alpine splendour of Yoho National Park along the way. The Burgess Shale Foundation now also offers guided hikes that examine the effects of climate change on area glaciers.

Burgess Shale hikers convene across from Takakkaw Falls ("magnificent" in Cree), Canada's third-highest waterfall, which funnels meltwaters from the Daly Glacier into a thunderous free fall of 254 metres. From its start near the youth hostel, the century-old trail climbs steeply through heavy timber and then levels out shortly before reaching tiny Yoho Lake, overshadowed by the impressive north face of Wapta Mountain.

Just beyond, the trail swings south at the forested Yoho Pass and traverses beneath Wapta's steep limestone cliffs, offering stellar views over the Emerald Valley to Michael Peak, Mount Carnarvon, and Noseeum Falls. An airy trailside luncheon spot looks nearly 900 metres down to vibrant Emerald Lake and its upscale lodge. Not far from Burgess Pass, only guided hikers are allowed to turn east off the main trail for a final steep climb to the Walcott Quarry, just below the north ridge of Mount Field (video cameras are apparently used to detect unauthorized visitors).

The quarry is named for Charles Walcott, head of the Smithsonian Institution when he stumbled on these rich fossil beds in 1909. (The Mount Stephen beds, across the highway, were investigated by R. G. McConnell of the Geological Survey of Canada in 1886 after railway workers discovered an abundance of trilobite fossils.) Walcott and family members spent the next decade excavating the quarry and hauling some 65,000 fossils away to Washington, D.C. The good news is that this and surrounding quarries have produced about 200,000 fossils to date, with many more to be uncovered by ongoing

Guided hikers inspect the Burgess Shale's Walcott Quarry.

scientific research. The continued excavation of fossils in a national park, researchers argue, is justified by its considerable contribution to scientific knowledge.

This abundance of fossils in such a confined area is a miracle of evolutionary and geological forces. The Burgess Shale animals lived more than 500 million years ago on a large carbonate reef, called the Cathedral Escarpment, at the edge of the ancient North American continent in a warm, shallow sea. Occasional mudslides would sweep over the escarpment, burying and instantly killing organisms and allowing their preservation to begin immediately. Over the next 250 million years, these fossils became buried under about 10 kilometres of accumulated sediments, which hardened into rocks that were eventually thrust up into today's mountains. Despite incredible pressures, heat, and erosion over this time, these fossils somehow survived, encased in shale.

Most animal fossils found elsewhere retain hard bits such as shells and skeletons. The Burgess Shale is unique in its beautiful preservation of soft body parts such as feathery gills, muscle bands, and even guts. It also harbours more than 120 fossilized marine animal species, several of which had never been seen before. These range from the numerous and striking trilobites and marellas, or lace crabs, to the five-eyed opabinia, the flower-like dinomischus, and the worm-like pikaia, which with its primitive spinal cord is our oldest known ancestor.

Because of this well-preserved diversity of fossils, the Burgess Shale has helped shape scientific understanding of how life has evolved. In particular, it provides the most complete fossilized record of the so-called Cambrian explosion more than 500 million years ago, when many complex animal forms—including those with segmented bodies, jointed limbs, and spinal cords—appeared over a relatively short 10–20 million years. The Burgess Shale thus provides a snapshot of an evolutionary outburst that dominated the world's oceans over the next 300 million years.

Although truckloads of Burgess Shale and Mount Stephen fossils have been shipped to far-flung museums over the years, there are plans to repatriate some of those fossils and keep new discoveries in a facility

Mountain goats above Walcott Quarry.

in nearby Field. Monies from the guided hikes and other fundraising initiatives are being collected to build a learning centre/museum to accommodate various educational groups as well as researchers.

While in the small mountain community of Field (population 300), it's worth staying at a bed and breakfast or inn. Established in 1885 during construction of the Canadian Pacific Railway, Field remains a division point for the railway and is the headquarters for Yoho National Park.

## EATS & DRINKS

The delightfully named **Truffle Pigs Bistro and Lounge** (up the hill in Field) offers good meals in the **Kicking Horse Lodge**, while the nearby **Siding General Store** features backed goods and soups. It's also well worth a visit to the nearby, elegantly rustic **Emerald Lake Lodge** for a drink or lunch; try the Rocky Mountain game platter.

# ◐ HOT PICKS

*Listed roughly in order of my personal preference.*

## Most Scenic Drives/Loops

## Best Short Drives

## Best Viewpoints

## Prettiest Towns

## Nicest Downtown Historic Renovations

## Nicest Urban River Parks and Pathways

## Best Interpretive and Short Walks

## Best Longer Hikes

## Best Birdwatching Spots

## Best Wildflowers

## Best Picnic Spots

## Best Museums

189  Blackfoot Crossing Historical Park
48  Head-Smashed-In Buffalo Jump
171  Royal Tyrrell Museum
89  Remington Carriage Museum
65  Frank Slide Interpretive Centre
139  Reynolds-Alberta Museum

## Best Small Museums

33  Nanton Lancaster Society Air Museum
58  Kootenai Brown Pioneer Village
187  Hanna Museum and Pioneer Village
98  Roulston Museum
80  Sir Alexander Galt Museum
110  Torrington Gopher Hole Museum

## Best Historic Sites

180  Atlas Coal Mine National Historic Site
284  Banff Park Museum National Historic Site
126  Historic Markerville Creamery Museum and Stephansson House
282  Cave and Basin National Historic Site
23  Bar U Ranch National Historic Site
103  Rocky Mountain House National Historic Site
13  Big Rock
84  Village of Stirling National Historic Site

## Best Private Attractions

134  Ellis Bird Farm
150  Stettler Steam Train
81  Alberta Birds of Prey Centre
107  Custom Woolen Mills
109  PaSu Farm

## Best Eats per Capita

## Best Coffee

## Best Mascots

# INDEX

# ACKNOWLEDGEMENTS

Researching and writing a wide-ranging book such as this wouldn't have been possible without the assistance of many people. Although I travelled all the routes described in this book, it was sometimes in the company of others, who patiently put up with all the stops and detours along the way. Others suggested excellent trips that would otherwise have been bypassed. I'm especially indebted to the expertise of geologists, geographers, historians, and naturalists who answered my queries and proofread parts of the text.

These contributors include Kelly Adams, Leslie Bell, Jane Bilsland, Don Cockerton, Dale Cole, Helen Corbett, Mary Corbett, Norma Corbett, Graeme Dales, Dorothy Dickson, Anne Elton, Jacquie Gilson, Betty Anne Graves, Rosa Gross, Nancy Hansen, Carrie Harbin, Gary Harbin, Chris Harvie, Sheila Jacobson, Fareen Jadavji Jessa, Colin Jones, Peter Jones, Ed Jurewicz, Forbes and Di Macdonald, David May, Paul McNeil, Teresa Michalak, Lisa Patel, Anne Pope, Jim Robertson, Fenn Roessingh, Marg Saul, Bob Sharpe, Peter Sherrington, Leslie Shillington, Nancy and Dennis Stefani, Stacey Steil, Ken Stengler, Seana Strain, Susanne Swibold, Lawrence Tanner, Cliff Wallis, Cleve Wershler, and Brendan Wilson, and my editors over several editions—Linda Ostrowalker, Elaine Jones, Ben D'Andrea, Robin Rivers, AnnMarie MacKinnon, and Taryn Boyd. I'd also like to thank the staff of Kananaskis Country, the Parks Canada Agency, and the numerous people working in the small museums and information centres of southern and central Alberta who provided information and documents.

# ABOUT THE AUTHOR

Bill Corbett is a Calgary writer with interests in the outdoors, history, and the environment. He is the author of *Best of Alberta: Outdoor Activities in Alberta's Heartland* and *The 11,000ers of the Canadian Rockies* (winner of the Canadian Rockies Award at the 2005 Banff Mountain Book Festival). His articles have been published in such magazines as *Canadian Geographic, Explore, Western Living, Canadian Business,* and *Maclean's.* An avid mountaineer and backcountry skier, he can often be found exploring the diverse landscapes of his native Alberta.